intermediate

real life

C000154097

Make your mark!

SARAH CUNNINGHAM   PETER MOOR

1 learning style

Grammar	Present tenses
	State and activity verbs
Vocabulary	Education and work
	Learning and the mind
Phrases	Having a conversation

Vocabulary & Reading

Education

1 Look at the photos of two unusual schools. What do you think is happening in the photos?

2 **Words 2 know** (1.2) Check the words in blue. Read about the two schools. Answer as many of the questions as you can for each school.

Secondary schools

1 Is the school:
– a private school or a state school?
– a single-sex school or a mixed school?

2 Does it specialise in any subjects?

3 Which subjects are compulsory? Which are optional?

4 How many pupils are there in the school?

5 Do pupils wear a uniform or their own clothes?

6 Who makes the rules: the head teacher, the staff or the pupils?

7 Is there a lot of discipline?

8 Do any pupils have special responsibilities?

3 SPEAKING Discuss the questions in pairs.
- Which information in the text surprises you?
- What are the good and bad things about each school in your opinion?

I don't think it's good that there are only forty pupils at Sands.

4 Write some notes about your school, using the questions in exercise 2 to help you.

I go to ... school in ... It's a state secondary school and it specialises in languages.

5 In pairs, A and B, roleplay a conversation. Answer the questions in exercise 2. A: answer about your school. B: answer as if you are Ashley or Laura.

A: Do you go to a private school or a state school?

B: (Laura) It's a private day school. How about you?

A: My school is a mixed state school.

MINI WORKBOOK exercises 6–7 page 101

A different way to learn

(1.4)

A **The Brit School** is the only state school for performing arts in Britain. It prepares students aged 14–19 for careers in theatre, music and film. Students study compulsory subjects like Maths and English every week but they also choose special options like acting, dance and singing. Former students include the singers Amy Winehouse and Leona Lewis.

Ashley, 17, is in Year 12:

My main subject is Theatre. The course lasts two years and this week we're working on a political drama that we're writing ourselves. My friends are practising right now. Next week we're producing a musical. I'm getting fantastic experience – my skills are really improving. Brit students sometimes get professional work, too. For example, this term I'm acting in a TV medical drama and next summer I'm appearing in a musical in London.

B **Sands** is a private day school with about forty pupils, girls and boys aged 11–17. It's a democratic school: there is no head teacher, **pupils don't wear uniform** and they always call their teachers by their first names. Lessons are optional, even Maths and English. **Every week the school has a meeting** and teachers and students vote about the rules together.

Laura, 15, is a pupil:

'Before Sands, I went to the local secondary school but for me there was too much discipline. At Sands, teachers talk to you as an individual and we all work together. For example, we voted to learn Spanish, so two of **our teachers are learning Spanish online** with us. **Next term we're going on a school trip to Spain.** Pupils also have responsibilities: at the moment, **some students are cooking lunch** and some are sweeping the classrooms. I feel that **I'm becoming more confident at Sands.**'

Grammar **Focus**

Present simple and continuous

6 Read what Ashley and Laura said about their schools again and answer the questions.

- What do students do every week?
- What particular things are they doing at the moment?

7 Read *Grammar2know*. Find another example in bold in text B of rules a–f.

MINI WORKBOOK exercises 1–3 page 100

Grammar **2know**

Present simple

Use the present simple:

a to describe things that are generally true:
*The school **prepares** students aged 14 –19.*

b to talk about regular actions:
*Students **study** Maths and English every week.*

Time expressions: *every week, once a month, usually, always, never*

Present continuous

Use the present continuous:

c to talk about actions in progress at the moment of speaking:
*My friends **are practising** right now.*

d to talk about actions happening in the present period but not at the moment of speaking:
*This week, we**'re working** on a political drama.*

e to talk about gradual changes in the present period:
*My skills **are improving**.*

Time expressions: *at the moment, (right) now, these days*

f to talk about definite arrangements for the future:
*Next week, **we're producing** a musical.*

Time expressions: *tomorrow, next week/month/Tuesday*

8 Put the verbs in the correct tense, to show that the situation is changing.

1 British schools (change) *are changing*!
2 More pupils (stay) at school until they are eighteen.
3 Subjects like Film Studies (become) more popular.
4 Exam results (improve) but some people say that exams (get) easier.

9 **a** Put the verbs in the correct tense.

Like most teenagers, Ellie Morton ¹ *goes* (go) to school five days a week but she ² _____ (not catch) a bus to school like her friends. After breakfast, she ³ _____ (go) upstairs to her study to meet her teacher, her father Andrew.

'Educating children at home ⁴ _____ (become) more popular nowadays,' says Andrew. 'Children ⁵ _____ (not always get) individual attention in classes of thirty. I ⁶ _____ (teach) all Ellie's subjects and we ⁷ _____ (learn) together. Right now, she ⁸ _____ (prepare) for her A-levels. She ⁹ _____ (take) the exams this June, a year early. This week, we ¹⁰ _____ (study) European history and we ¹¹ _____ (also work) on Ellie's art project. Next weekend, we ¹² _____ (visit) the National Gallery. We always ¹³ _____ (work) on a variety of topics, so that Ellie ¹⁴ _____ (not get) bored.'

b (1.3) Listen and check. Would you like to study in the same way as Ellie? Why? Why not?

Vocabulary & Listening
Education and work

1 In pairs, think of one positive achievement and one negative thing that might happen:
- in your school career

    + you pass all your exams

    − you fail an exam
- in your working life.

2 **a** Words **2 know** (1.5) Check the words in blue. Which did you think of in exercise 1? Which words can you see in the picture?
- getting a **pay rise**
- **failing an exam** because you didn't **revise**
- getting **promotion**
- getting good **qualifications**
- **earning** a high **salary**
- getting an **apprenticeship** with a good company
- getting **the sack**
- getting good **marks** in your **coursework**
- (not) finding **job satisfaction**
- being **unemployed**.

b Put the words in exercise 2a in the correct column in the table.

Education	Work
	getting a pay rise

3 **a** Read the statements and <u>underline</u> the option that you think is true.
1 *Boys/Girls* revise more and get better marks in exams.
2 *Boys/Girls* do better in Maths and Science.
3 More *boys/girls* go to university.
4 More *boys/girls* do apprenticeships.
5 *Boys/Girls* get better marks in coursework.
6 *Boys/Girls* prefer three-hour exams.
7 *Men/Women* need better qualifications to get the same job.
8 *Men/Women* earn higher salaries on average.
9 *Men/Women* focus more on promotion and pay rises.
10 *Men/Women* focus more on job satisfaction.

b (1.6) Now listen to a radio programme about gender in education and work. Circle the answers the experts gave. Were they the same as yours?

4 (1.6) Listen again and answer the questions.
1 Why are girls doing better at school, according to Kevin Dryden?
2 Why is working life more difficult for women than men, according to Kate Hume?

5 Discuss the questions with the class.
- Do you like exams or would you like to do more coursework?
- Which will be most important in your career, money or job satisfaction?
- Are the ideas in the programme about men and women true in your country?

   " *I don't think Kevin Dryden's ideas are true in this country because ...*

MINI WORKBOOK exercise 8 page 101

Grammar Focus
State and activity verbs

6 Read the online comments A–D about the radio programme.

1 Match the people to the comments.

☐ a parent   ☐ a student

☐ a teacher   ☐ an older man

2 Who agrees with Kevin Dryden? What examples do they give?

3 What explanation did Richard's pupil give for the differences between boys and girls?

4 What is the problem according to Alan?

(1.7) **BOYS AND GIRLS IN EDUCATION** *have your say!*

A I'm in Year 11 and I'm doing my GCSEs this year. I agree with Kevin Dryden – most boys think revising is 'uncool'. Most girls in my class want to get good marks but the guys just want to look good in front of their mates.

Natasha, Manchester

B I recently asked my teenage class why they think girls do better than boys in exams. One boy explained, 'Girls have a lot more time for studying than boys. Boys are too busy with other things like sport and computer games.'

Richard, Cardiff

C I think the problem is the schools, not the boys. When I was young, many years ago, schools were competitive – we tried to do better than other boys, in sport and in class. I don't think boys today are very different – they like competition, they want to be the best. But in schools these days, competition seems to be a bad word. Schools need to be more 'boy-friendly'.

Alan, Essex

D I **have** a fifteen-year-old son and he's taking exams at the moment. I'm having big problems with him – he can't concentrate. He**'s sitting** in the living room now 'revising'. He studies in there so that I can watch him, but when I go in, he's on the internet, or he's looking out of the window. If I ask why, he says, 'I'm tired right now, Mum … I need a rest. I'm just having a little break,' or 'I'm thinking, Mum, leave me alone!'

Sue, Yorkshire

---

7 **a** Which verb in bold in text D describes an activity and which describes a state?

b Read *Grammar2know* and check. <u>Underline</u> three more sentences with state verbs in A, B and C.

Grammar **2 know**

State and activity verbs

Use the present simple or present continuous to talk about activities:

> He usually **studies** in the living room.
> But today he**'s studying** in the bedroom.

Use <u>only</u> the present simple to describe states:

> I'm tired right now, Mum … I **need** a rest.

Verbs that describe states

- **be:**   I**'m** tired right now.
- **have:**   I **have** a fifteen-year-old son.
- **need:**   I **need** a rest.
- **liking/feeling**: *want, like, love, hate, prefer, care, don't mind*
  Boys **like** competition.
- **thought/opinion**: *think, know, understand, believe, remember, forget, agree*
  I **don't think** boys today are very different.
- **appearance/the senses**: *seem, look, sound, smell, taste*
  Competition **seems** to be a bad word.

Some state verbs also have an 'active' meaning:

> I **have** a fifteen-year-old son. ('possession' – a state)
> I**'m having** a break. (an activity)
> Some boys **think** revision is 'uncool'. (their opinion – a state)
> He's looking out of the window, he's **thinking**. (a mental activity)

8 Put the verbs in brackets in the correct tense.

1 I (be) really hot. I (need) a drink.

2 (you want) coffee? I (prefer) tea, I (have) a bad stomach.

3 Karina (act) strangely today, she (seem) a bit upset.

4 What (you read)? It's a detective novel but I (not like) it.

9 Decide if the *have* phrase in brackets describes an activity or a state. Put the verb in the correct tense.

1 It's very noisy because the neighbours (have a party).

2 Laura (not have any brothers or sisters).

3 Katie (have a new hairstyle) – it's really nice.

4 Anna can't come to the phone – she (have a bath).

5 Where's Steve? He (have lunch).

10 In pairs, ask and answer the questions using state verbs.

1 Do you think boys care more than girls about 'looking cool in front of their mates'?

2 Do you believe that girls have more time to study than boys?

3 Do you agree or disagree with Alan, that schools need to be more 'boy-friendly'?

MINI WORKBOOK exercises 4–5 pages 100–101

learning style

Reading & Vocabulary

1 a SCANNING What can you see in the picture? Guess the connection between goldfish and computers. Tick (✓) the best summary.

1 ☐ Goldfish become more intelligent when they live near computers.

2 ☐ People concentrate better when they have a pet goldfish next to their computer.

3 ☐ Computers are making people's concentration similar to goldfish's.

b Read the introduction and check your ideas.

2 Check the words in blue. Mark the activities. + (useful), – (unhelpful) and +/– (not sure). In pairs, compare answers.

Words 2 know (1.8)

☐ improve your **concentration**

☐ read things that are **not worth reading**

☐ **make sense of** what you are reading

☐ **learn** important **skills**

☐ learn **useless information**

☐ **set** yourself **goals**

☐ **make quick decisions**

☐ **ignore distractions**

☐ **solve problems**

3 Read section A of the text. Tick (✓) true and cross (✗) false.

1 ☐ People generally stay on websites for very short periods of time.

2 ☐ Email and instant messaging are good for people's concentration.

3 ☐ Julia Wood says her pupils get a lot of information online but don't think about it.

4 ☐ Anne Savan is a Music teacher who thinks that Science is good for her pupils' concentration.

5 ☐ The experiment with Nintendo Games in Scottish schools failed.

6 ☐ Ray Cole believes that people learn useful skills surfing the internet.

4 Discuss the questions in groups.

• Do you spend your time usefully online or not?

❝ I often read things that are not worth reading.

• Who do you agree with, Julia Wood or Ray Cole?

❝ I don't agree with Julia, I think you learn important skills on the internet.

(1.9)

Are you becoming a . . . digital goldfish?

Goldfish have pretty boring lives, so maybe it's a good thing they can only concentrate for nine seconds! But according to new research, humans are becoming like goldfish. Our attention span (the amount of time we concentrate on one thing) is getting shorter . . . and it's all because of technology.

A 'We move quickly from one site to another on the web,' says Doctor Ted Selker, a computer scientist from Massachusetts, 'and we are losing the ability to concentrate.' With millions of websites to choose from, the attention span of the average internet user is just seconds. There are other digital distractions too: email, instant messaging and quickie movies on websites like shortspan.com.

Some people are worried about the effect on young people. 'You need time to understand and think about what you read,' says secondary school teacher, Julia Wood, from London. 'Young people move from one website to another all the time and their brains become full of useless information but there is no time to make sense of it. I am trying to persuade my pupils to read more books, so that they concentrate on one subject for longer.'

Other teachers are trying more unusual methods to improve students' concentration. Welsh secondary school teacher Anne Savan was so worried about one class of fifteen-year-old boys that she started playing Mozart during her Science lessons. She says that it had an amazing effect: 'The music made them calmer, and their concentration was much better.'

In some Scottish schools, they have a technological solution to the problem. Pupils start their school day with brain-training games, using Nintendo games consoles. Again, teachers say that there is a big improvement in pupils' concentration.

But not everyone believes that there is a problem. Professor Ray Cole, an educational psychologist says: 'On the web, young people learn to make quick decisions about what is and isn't worth reading. They might look at five unhelpful websites very quickly, before stopping and reading a sixth useful website more carefully. In a world with so much information available, this is an important skill.'

5 a Is your concentration good? In pairs, do the quiz in section B to find out.

b Read the key on page 124 and find your score. Is the conclusion true?

6 a Read the tips in section C and choose the best ones to help your partner concentrate better.

b Which other tips do you find useful?

7 a Read *Active Study*. <u>Underline</u> examples of other suffixes in the text.

ACTIVE STUDY

Notice the endings of nouns (suffixes)

Suffixes can tell you if a word is a noun, adjective or adverb. Here are some common noun suffixes:

a nouns for people: *teacher doctor scientist*

b other nouns: *attention information persuasion experiment technology*

b Can you remember the noun form of these verbs? Read the text again and check.

verb	noun
1 concentrate	*concentration*
2 improve	_____
3 solve	_____
4 decide	_____
5 distract	_____

MINI WORKBOOK exercise 9 page 101

B How good is your concentration?

ZINE

Mark the statements T (true), PT (partly true) or NT (not true).

1 ☐ I have a special place for studying. I close my door and tell people not to disturb me.

do not disturb

2 ☐ I often text, email or watch TV when I'm studying.

3 ☐ I often get up from my desk for snacks or to find things.

4 ☐ When I start work, I plan what I'm going to do before my next break.

5 ☐ I can concentrate for an hour and a half, then I need a break.

6 ☐ When I sit down at my desk, I start thinking about other things that I need to do.

7 ☐ I often reread the same page again and again.

8 ☐ If other people are doing things near my desk, I can usually ignore it.

1.10

C For those with the attention span of a goldfish, here are some tips!

☐ Create the right work space. Remove distractions – turn off your phone and messaging alert.

☐ Get everything you need (pens, books) before you start.

☐ Set yourself a goal and a time limit. For strong concentration, work for about ninety minutes, then take a break.

☐ Perhaps you are worrying about other things instead of work? Write them on a 'to do' list, then forget them.

☐ Improve your concentration using the 'five more' rule. Say to yourself, 'I am going to read five more pages before I stop,' or 'I am going to answer five more questions.'

learning style

REAL TIME

HAVING A CONVERSATION

1 Look at the photo and answer the questions. Read the caption and check.

- What are Lori and Greg doing at the moment?
- What do you think their relationship is?
- What do you think will happen next?

2 (1.11) Listen to Greg and Lori's conversation and choose the correct answers.

1 What do Greg and Lori have in common?
   a They are both listening to Leona Lewis.
   b They both went to the same concert.
   c They both like Leona Lewis.

2 Why does Greg tell Lori that he met Leona Lewis?
   a He wants to take her to a Leona Lewis concert.
   b He wants to impress her.
   c He wants her to play in his band.

3 How does Lori feel about Greg by the end of the conversation?
   a She's becoming more friendly.
   b She doesn't like him.
   c She wants to end the conversation.

3 (1.11) Complete the conversation with the correct *Phrases2know*. Then listen again and check.

Phrases 2 know

Having a conversation

Attracting attention
Excuse me …/Hello!
I see you like music.

Greetings and introducing yourself
My name's …/I'm …
Nice to meet you.

Showing interest
Really?/Seriously?
That's amazing!
Wow!/Cool!

Asking for repetition and clarification
Sorry?
What was that?
What do you mean?

---

4 (1.12) Listen and practise saying the *Phrases2know*.

LORI has arrived in Edinburgh from London. At the station she meets a young man called Greg.

Greg: ¹ *Excuse me!* Hello!

Lori: Sorry? ² _____ ?

Greg: Hi … Is this your phone? I think you dropped it.

Lori: Oh yes, thank you.

Greg: No problem. I see you like music, what are you listening to?

Lori: Oh, it's Leona Lewis.

Greg: ³ _____ ? She's cool. I like her. As a person, I mean.

Lori: As a person? Do you know her? ⁴ _____ ?

Greg: Well, I met her in Edinburgh once – I live here.
⁵ _____ Greg, by the way.

Lori: ⁶ _____ Greg. I'm Lori. So you actually met Leona Lewis!
⁷ _____ ! She's my favourite singer in the whole world!

Greg: Yeah, I was at her concert here in Edinburgh, and someone invited me to her after-show party.

Lori: ⁸ _____ ! So did you actually speak to her?

Greg: Um, yeah, well, sort of …

Lori: ⁹ _____ ? What did she say to you?

Greg: Well, she, um – where are you going?

Lori: To my accommodation, it's near the University.

Greg: Cool! I'm going in that direction!

5 Imagine that you meet an interesting stranger at a bus stop. Act out the conversation using the prompts below and *Phrases2know* on page 10. You can invent information.

- Find a reason to start a conversation.
- Introduce yourself.
- Find out where the other person is from.
- Find a topic you're both interested in.
- Find out as much as you can about each other.

6 (1.13) Listen to Greg and Lori's conversation. Tick (✓) true and cross (✗) false. Then correct the false statements.

1 ☐ Greg lives in London.
2 ☐ Lori is in Edinburgh to start a course in Music.
3 ☐ Lori is learning to play three different instruments.
4 ☐ Greg is a musician.
5 ☐ Lori already knows a lot of people in Edinburgh.
6 ☐ Greg offers to show Lori around the city.
7 ☐ Lori gives Greg her mobile number.

> Greg and Lori are getting to know each other.

A FORMAL LETTER OF APPLICATION

7 Read Lori's letter and answer the questions.

1 Does Lori know the person she's writing to?
2 How does Lori start and end her letter?
3 In which section do you find:
  a ☐ information about Lori's background?
  b ☐ the greeting?
  c ☐ the conclusion?
  d ☐ information about Lori's ambitions and her reasons for applying to E.C.P.A?
  e ☐ Lori's reason for writing?
  f ☑ Lori's home address?
  g ☐ school address?

8 a Think of a university course you would like to do. Make notes under these headings:

- why you want to study there
- why you're writing the letter
- where you live now and who with
- your studies, interests and current activities
- your ambitions.

1 49 River Street
Bosley
BS14 7TH
23 April 2010

2 Edinburgh College of Performing Arts
4 North Bridge
Edinburgh
EH2 2TR

3 Dear Sir/Madam,

4 I am writing to apply to study Music at the Edinburgh College of Performing Arts.

5 My full name is Laura Jane Ash. I am eighteen years old and I live in Bosley, a small village in England, with my parents and my two brothers. I am attending Bosley High School and my subjects are English, Music, Art History and Spanish. I play the guitar and keyboards in a band. At the moment, I am learning to play the bass guitar. I love all kinds of music but my band plays mainly 'Indie' music. I also enjoy travelling and meeting people – especially if they like music!

6 My dream is to be a musician and I want to study at E.C.P.A. because it has a very good reputation as a centre for the performing arts.

7 I hope to hear from you soon.
Yours faithfully,

Laura Ash

Phrases 2 know

Greeting
Dear Sir/Madam
Dear Mr/Mrs/Miss/Ms …

Giving your reasons for writing
I am writing to apply …

Describing yourself and your background
My full name is …
I am … years old and I live in …

Describing your studies and interests
I am attending … school
My subjects are …
I also enjoy …
At the moment I'm learning to …

Describing your ambitions
My dream is to …

Ending
I hope to hear from you soon.
I look forward to your reply.

Signing off
Yours faithfully,
Yours sincerely,

b Organise your notes into paragraphs and write your letter. Use the *Phrases2know* and Lori's letter to help you. Write 120–150 words.

Grammar	Defining relative clauses
	Present perfect and past sim
Vocabulary	Sporting activites
	Likes and dislikes
Phrases	Asking for information

Vocabulary & Speaking

Sporting activities

1 Discuss the questions in groups.
- Do you do a lot of sport?
- What do you do to keep fit?
- Do you enjoy watching sport on TV?

2 Check the *Words2know*.

Words 2 know (1.14)

A
to win (x2)   to go   to lose (x2)   to get (x2)
to support   to join   to score   to enter
to beat   to do

B
a gym   fit   a match   a goal
the other team   a race   your best   injured
running   a competition   a (football) team

3 In pairs, do the quiz below. Check your scores on page 124. Do you agree?

4 a Read *Active Study*.

> **Notice verb collocations**
> Collocations are words that we use together often.
>
> verb + noun   *score a goal*
> verb + -*ing* form   *go running*
> verb + adjective   *get fit*

ACTIVE STUDY

b Match the words from A and B in exercise 2 to make collocations. Check them in the quiz.

to win a match

5 Test your partner on the collocations by reading out the verbs in box A.

A: to join ...   B: ... a gym

6 In pairs, think of a sport and give four clues, using the *Words2know* and other ideas. Can your partner guess the sport?

" *You don't score goals but you can enter competitions ...*

MINI WORKBOOK exercise 6 page 103

Are you into sport?

1 Your friend asks you to play in his ice hockey team. Before the match, you hope that
a ... you will score a fantastic goal.
b ... your team will beat the other team.
c ... you don't get injured.

2 You need to get fit, so you decide to
a ... go running every morning before school.
b ... join a gym.
c ... walk to the bus stop instead of going in the car.

3 Everyone has to enter the school swimming competition. You aim to
a ... win your race.
b ... do your best.
c ... persuade your PE teacher that you are sick.

4 Your local football team are playing a big match and it's on TV. You
a ... support the team one hundred per cent. You are really nervous that they might lose the match.
b ... hope they win and watch with interest.
c ... decide it's a good day to go shopping.

Grammar Focus

Defining relative clauses

7 **a** In pairs, read the Sporting Definitions quiz. Choose the correct answer.

b (1.15) Listen and check.

8 **a** Find four relative pronouns in bold in the quiz and complete *Grammar2know*.

b Find another relative clause in the quiz where we omit the relative pronoun.

Grammar **2** know

Defining relative clauses

Relative clauses give information using a relative pronoun:

*A scoreboard is a large electronic sign **which** gives information about the match.*

*The person **who** blows his whistle during a football match is the referee.*

Relative pronouns

To refer to things: ___*that*___ or _____
To refer to people: ___*that*___ or _____
To refer to places: _____
To refer to possession: _____

Omitting the relative pronoun

We can omit *who/which/that* when they are followed by a pronoun or a noun.

A bat is a thing (~~which~~) you use to hit the ball.

9 **a** Complete the sentences with *who, which, where* or *whose*.

1 Basketball is a game ___*which*___ requires a very high level of speed and fitness.
2 I have a brother _____ supports Manchester United.
3 The place _____ I go swimming is called The Jungle Gym.
4 The team _____ we played in the semi-final were much better than us.
5 The sportsman _____ I admire most is Jenson Button.
6 I have a friend _____ mother is a yoga teacher.
7 *SportsInfo* is a website _____ gives you all the latest sports news.

b Which sentences can omit the relative pronoun?

Sporting Definitions

1 The person **who** blows his whistle during a football match is the *manager/referee*.

2 The large electronic sign **which** gives information about the match is the *notice board/scoreboard*.

3 The place **where** the players get changed before a match is the *dressing room/waiting room*.

4 A footballer **whose** job is to score goals is a *defender/striker*.

5 The thing you use to hit the ball in table tennis is a table tennis *bat/stick*.

6 The 'seat' **that** goes on a horse's back is called a *saddle/sofa*.

7 The person you are playing against is your *opponent/opposite*.

10 In pairs, give definitions for the words in A using the phrases in B and C and a relative pronoun if necessary.

" *A stadium is a place where people watch sporting events.*

A
a stadium is …
a defender is …
the coach is …
goggles are …
a racquet is …
a stopwatch is …

B
a device …
the person …
a player …
a place …
the thing …
things …

C
… job is to stop the other team scoring goals.
… people watch sporting events.
… you wear when you are swimming or skiing.
… chooses the team.
… counts time very accurately.
… you use to hit the ball in tennis.

MINI WORKBOOK exercises 1–2 page 102

into sport

13

Grammar Focus

Present perfect and past simple

1 Look at the photos and answer the questions.

- What activities are Luke and Lisa passionate about?
- Are these activities popular in your country?
- What interests are you passionate about?

2 Read about Luke and Lisa. What do they think are the special things about their sports?

3 **a** Read two sentences from the text. What tense is the verb in bold?

1 I **started** Taekwondo when I was eight.

2 I**'ve** already **won** two international competitions.

b Do we know when each action happened? Read *Grammar2know* and check.

Grammar 2 know

Present perfect

a Use the present perfect to talk about actions that happened in the past, but are still important now:
I**'ve been** to some fantastic places.
I **haven't found** the perfect wave yet.
Have you ever **tried** a sport that's a bit different?

Time expressions: *already, yet, just, never, ever, recently*

Past simple

b Use the past simple for events that happened at a definite time in the past:
My parents **gave** me my first surfboard **when I was nine.**

c With a definite time, don't use the present perfect:
NOT: *I've met some cool people **last summer.***

Time expressions: *yesterday, last week at 10.00, in 2007, when I was eleven, three years ago, when?, what time?*

Passionate about...

Have you found the perfect sport for you? (1.18)
Have you ever tried a sport that's a bit different?

... surfing

'My parents gave me my first surfboard when I was nine. I was so happy I cried! In Bondi, everyone is into surfing – kids get up at six o'clock in the morning to go surfing before school. Businessmen surf before work – they take their business suits to the beach in their bags!

For me, the best thing is being outside in the sun with my friends and family. I spend every summer travelling up and down the coast, camping and surfing with my mates. I've been to some fantastic places and I've met some of the coolest people in the world. My girlfriend's Japanese and she's just started surfing too, which is really cool! I love searching for the truly perfect wave ... but I haven't found it yet!'

Luke

... Taekwondo

'Taekwondo is my life ... if you're not passionate about what you do, then why do it? When I was little, I found sport a bit boring. Then I started Taekwondo when I was about eight. Now I'm a black belt*– I'm really proud because I've already won two international competitions – not bad for a seventeen-year-old! Taekwondo is becoming very popular and I've recently met lots of people who are into Taekwondo ... people from all over the world.

Lisa

Some people call it a sport, but really it's much more than that ... our instructors teach us the physical movements, like the kicks, but I've also learned a lot about discipline and respect for other people, I think that's what makes it so cool. I can't imagine my life without Taekwondo!'

*someone at the highest level in martial arts

4 Read about Rebecca. <u>Underline</u> the correct words.

... sailing

When I ¹*have been / was* a little child, I ²*have loved / loved* being on the water, so it's not really surprising that I'm into sailing now. I ³*have joined / joined* my local sailing club two years ago and ⁴*I've already learned / I already learned* a lot. A lot of my friends from school ⁵*have started / started* sailing, too. Our team ⁶*have entered / entered* several sailing competitions but we ⁷*didn't win / haven't won* anything yet. My dream is to win a medal at the Olympics … our team ⁸*came / have come* fourth in the last Olympics!

Rebecca

5 **a** Use the prompts to make questions in the present perfect or past simple.

1 you like sport when you/be a small child? Which sports/play?

Did you like sport when …?

2 start/any new sports recently? When/start?

3 you/ever go sailing? When/go?

4 Which other water sports/you try? When and where/do them?

5 you/ever try any martial arts like Taekwando? you/enjoy it?

6 you/ever entered any sporting competitions? you/win?

b In pairs, ask and answer the questions.

MINI WORKBOOK exercises 3–4 page 102 and exercise 5 page 103

Vocabulary & Speaking

Likes and dislikes

6 **a** Make two lists of sports.

Sports I enjoy	Sports I find boring
volleyball	

b Compare your answers in pairs.

We both like volleyball.
We both hate golf.

7 **a** (1.16) Listen to four people talking about sporting activities. Mark them ✓✓ (loves), ✓ (likes), – (okay), ✗ (doesn't like), ✗✗ (hates)

Katie: – most sports ☐ running
Hassan: ☐ watching sport on TV ☐ tennis
Brendan: ☐ motor racing
Lily: ☐ swimming in the sea

b (1.16) Listen again and match the speakers (K), (H), (B), and (L) to the statements in *Words2know*.

Words 2 know (1.17)

1 ☐ I'm really **passionate about** (motor racing).
2 ☐ I **love** (swimming).
3 ☐ I'm **really into** (sport).
4 ☐ I **quite enjoy** (watching sport on TV).
5 ☐ I **don't mind** (most sports).
6 ☐ I **find** (tennis) a bit **boring**.
7 ☐ I **can't see the point of** (surfing).
8 ☐ I'm **not really into** (sport).
9 ☐ I **can't stand** (running).

8 Read the *Words2know*. Think of two alternatives to the words in brackets.

I don't mind *playing sport*.

9 Tell your partner how you feel about the activities in exercise 7, using the *Words2know*.

I can't stand running!
Really? I quite enjoy it.

10 WRITING Write a short paragraph about a sport or other interest that you are passionate about. Include information about:

- when you started
- who you do it with
- why you like it
- what you have done (clubs you have joined, competitions you have entered, etc).

MINI WORKBOOK exercise 7 page 103

15

Reading & Vocabulary

1 Describe the pictures in the text. Which sports are they playing?

2 Read the text. Match the headings a–f to the paragraphs 1–6.

  a ☐ How football went around the world

  b ☐ A brighter future for British sport?

  c ☑ Britain: the home of sport?

  d ☐ How a schoolboy changed the game of football

  e ☐ The origins of modern football

  f ☐ How tennis developed

3 Read the text again. Tick (✓) true, cross (✗) false and write (?) if there is no information.

  1 ☒ *Calcio storico* is the oldest form of football that we know about.

  2 ☐ Sheffield Football Club has existed for more than 150 years.

  3 ☐ Englishmen helped football become more popular in other countries.

  4 ☐ William Webb Ellis wrote down the rules of rugby.

  5 ☐ England has never won the Rugby World Cup.

  6 ☐ The French invented a game similar to tennis in the 1870s.

  7 ☐ No English person has won a Wimbledon title for more than thirty years.

4 a **Words 2 know** Find words or phrases in the text which mean:

  1 The person or team that wins a competition (paragraph 1): _____

  2 They say what is allowed or not allowed in a sport or game (paragraph 2): _____

  3 To become known about by more people and in more places (paragraph 4): _____

  4 To organise an event or meeting in a particular place (paragraph 5): _____

  5 The best achievement so far in a sport etc. (paragraph 6): _____

b (1.19) Listen and check.

5 Discuss the questions in groups.

  • Which sports is your country good at?

  • Who are the biggest sports stars in your country?

  • Did any sport begin in your country?

  • Do you think your country has a bright future in sport? Why? Why not?

How the English invented sports

… then the rest of the world beat them at their own game! (1.23)

1 Maybe the English are not world champions any more but they can say they invented some of the world's most popular sports. The modern games of football, tennis and rugby all started in England. Then others learned to play – and beat – the English at their own game …

2 A form of football was played in China more than 2,500 years ago; and people in Florence have played a variation of football known as *calcio storico* since the sixteenth century. Three hundred years later, in 1848, two football players from Cambridge University first wrote down the rules of football. The first organised football club was Sheffield F.C. – it started in 1857 and is still in action today.

3 British sailors took football with them to the ports of Italy, Brazil and Argentina where the game quickly found new fans. A number of famous clubs in Spain, Italy and Argentina were founded by Englishmen. But while the rest of the world developed its football skills, England didn't even play in the first three World Cups. When they finally entered for the first time in 1950, they lost their most important match – to the United States!

4 Like football, the game of rugby developed in England. According to legend, the game started when William Webb Ellis, a schoolboy at Rugby school, picked the ball up and ran with it. Again, it wasn't long before the game spread abroad … and again, England started losing. New Zealand, South Africa and Australia have won the Rugby World Cup five times between them … England has won it just once!

5 A game called *jeu de paume* was played in France nearly 800 years ago. It was similar to tennis but players used their hands instead of a tennis racquet and the ball was made of leather. It was so hard that it could cause injury, or even death! Then in the 1870s, an English army officer developed the rules for modern lawn tennis. The game was played with racquets, and a lighter ball, made of rubber. Wimbledon Tennis Club held the first lawn tennis championship in 1877, and the first seven champions were all English. Then the good news ended for English tennis. The last English tennis player to win Wimbledon was Virginia Wade … in 1977!

6 But perhaps things are changing. Many people believe that Andy Murray could win Wimbledon one day, although Murray always points out that he is Scottish, not English. And the British team won forty-seven medals at the Beijing Olympics in 2008 – a record for the Great Britain and Northern Ireland team. The 2012 Olympics are taking place in London, so hopes for the future are high!

Listening & Speaking

6 Read about Tom Daley. Why is he unusual?

Olympic Gold Medal Hopeful

Tom Daley seems like any other teenager. He lives with his parents in Plymouth and shares a bedroom with his younger brother. In his spare time he watches DVDs and goes on Facebook. But there's one thing that's different about Tom – at just fifteen, he is World Diving Champion, and an Olympic Gold Medal hopeful.

7 (1.20) Listen to six extracts from a radio interview with Tom. Match each extract to a question below (there is one extra question).

1 ☐ When did you first start diving?
2 ☑ Why did diving appeal to you?
3 ☐ When did you start taking it seriously?
4 ☐ What's your daily routine?
5 ☐ What trophies and competitions have you won?
6 ☐ What are your ambitions for the future?
7 ☐ How do you spend your free time?

8 (1.21) Listen to the full interview and make notes about Tom's answers. Compare answers in groups.

Tom first started diving when he was …

9 (1.22) Put the *Phrases2know* in the correct tense. Listen and check.

Phrases 2 know

Asking for information

When you (start) playing tennis?
How you (become) interested in it?
What (be) your daily training routine?
You ever (win) any competitions or medals?
You ever (break) any records?
You ever (have) any injuries?
What (be) your hopes for the future?

10 a You are going to act out an interview, imagining that you are a sports person. Choose one of the options below.

CAN YOU DO IT IN ENGLISH?

1 Think of a sporting hope from your country.

2 Look at the fact file about British Tennis player Andy Murray on page 124.

b Prepare your answers for the questions in *Phrases2know*.

c Act out the interview in pairs. Take turns to be the interviewer and the sports person.

MINI WORKBOOK exercise 8 page 103

into sport

activestudy1

Vocabulary

1 Complete the sentences with the verbs below in the correct form.

[apply   earn   score   set   special ✓   win]

1 Our school _specialises_ in Maths and Science.
2 Shelly _____ a good salary in her new job.
3 I'm going to _____ for a job before I finish university.
4 Kevin _____ a fantastic goal yesterday.
5 Amy is very hardworking and she _____ herself clear goals.
6 Did you know that Joe and Carol have _____ a sailing race?

ACTIVE STUDY **Learn collocations**

2 Complete the phrases with *get, have* or *do* to make collocations.

1 _get_ good marks
2 _____ well in exams
3 _____ injured
4 _____ responsibilities
5 _____ a successful career
6 _____ a pay rise
7 _____ the sack
8 _____ your best
9 _____ promotion

ACTIVE STUDY **Word formation**

3 Complete the text with the correct form of the word in brackets.

Helping yourself

Have you got problems with [1] _____ (concentrate)? Do you find it hard to focus on your homework and ignore [2] _____ (distract)? Don't worry. Many people have had similar problems. Some famous [3] _____ (science) did badly at school.
Make a [4] _____ (decide) to improve step by step. One [5] _____ (solve) is to plan what you want to do and divide it into short sections you can manage. If you don't succeed at once, don't worry and don't compare yourself with others: this is not a [6] _____ (compete). Soon, you'll be amazed at your own [7] _____ (improve).

ACTIVE STUDY **Notice word stress**

4 PRONUNCIATION (1.24) Listen to the words from exercise 3 and put them in the right column according to their stress pattern.

▪▫▫	▪▪▫▫	▫▫▪▫
distractions		

Grammar

5 Choose the correct verb form to complete the text.

A different kind of education

My little sister, Millie, [1] _____ to a Waldorf-Steiner school. She doesn't have to wear a uniform. She [2] _____ boring exercises. In lessons, the children sing, dance, play instruments and make things with their hands. They [3] _____ a lot of stories and poems. My sister [4] _____ to play African drums and to make bread. This week they [5] _____ a project on autumn festivals in different countries. Last month they [6] _____ for a concert.
Some people [7] _____ this is not real education but Steiner students do well in exams. [8] _____ impossible? They [9] _____ excellent language skills and are good at working independently. It [10] _____ you don't need to do hundreds of exam papers to pass exams. Alternative schools [11] _____ more popular but there isn't a Waldorf-Steiner secondary school in my town. What a pity!

1 a go   ⓑ goes   c is going
2 a don't do   b isn't doing   c doesn't do
3 a read   b reads   c are reading
4 a has already   b have already   c already
     learned   learned   learned
5 a do   b are doing   c have done
6 a have prepared b has prepared   c prepared
7 a think   b are thinking   c have thought
8 a Is that sounding b Did that sound c Does that
                                          sound
9 a have   b are having   c had
10 a seem   b is seeming   c seems
11 a become   b are becoming   c became

6 Complete the sentences with *who, which/that, whose, where* <u>only if necessary</u>. If no pronoun is necessary, write –.

1 The sports _____–_____ I enjoy most are swimming and diving.
2 The place _____ I feel happiest is the swimming pool.
3 My swimming coach is the person _____ taught me to be passionate about sport.
4 She encouraged me to take part in a competition _____ took place in our town last month.
5 I'm also grateful to the friends _____ support helped me win.

The Class of 2005 (1.26)

Five years ago my classmates and I finished secondary school and went our different ways. On the last day, we promised to meet again exactly five years later and see how everyone is doing. This week we kept that promise. So what's become of my class?

Matthew's a musician. No surprises there – that's what he's always wanted to do. Back at school, he was completely focused on his music and his only dream was to become a concert pianist. He finished music college a year ago and right now he's preparing for a series of concerts in the USA.

I remember Krishni as a very hard-working student who always got good marks and set herself clear goals. She's going to be a dentist in six months' time – she's just finishing her degree. I'm going to see her and ask her to check my teeth!

Danny was another good student. He works for a big company now, earns a good salary, and he's just got promotion … but he seems a bit bored. He didn't tell us much about his work.

Dean has always liked football more than studying. Some teachers made comments such as 'Kicking a ball round is not a career, young man.' Well, guess what? He's running a local football club for children. He's a great coach, the kids love him and he's making quite a lot of money!

Rachel says she's still thinking about what she wants to do in life. She travels a lot. She's already been to India, Iran, South Africa, Iceland and about a million other places. She's had several jobs. Right now she's preparing for a trip to Nepal. She's the one who's really enjoying life. And what about me? I'm studying to be a journalist. I've just applied for a job with one of the national newspapers; until I hear from them, I'm still writing for *The Campus Courier*.

The Campus Courier

Reading Skills

ACTIVE STUDY | **Read for specific information**

7 Read the article and the statements below. Tick (✓) true and cross (✗) false. Write (?) if there's no information.

1. ☐ Matthew has been successful in his most important ambition.
2. ☐ Krishni wanted to be a dentist while she was at school.
3. ☐ Danny seems to enjoy his job.
4. ☐ Dean did badly at school.
5. ☐ Rachel is worried about her future.
6. ☐ The writer works for a national newspaper.

Listening Skills

ACTIVE STUDY | **Listen for gist**

8 (1.25) Listen to four people giving their opinions on education today. Match the statements A–E to the speakers 1–4. There is one extra statement.

A. ☐ In general, education today is better than it was in the past.
B. ☐ There's not enough discipline.
C. ☐ Children take too many exams.
D. ☐ Lessons are not fun.
E. ☐ Young people leave school too early.

Speaking Skills

9 **a** Look at the photos of students doing sports at school. Choose one of the photos and describe it.

In Photo A, I can see …

b Compare the photos.

Photo A is different because … but they are similar because …

c Discuss the following in pairs.

1. Talk about the sports you like and don't like doing at school.
2. Do you think girls and boys should do sports together at school?

SKILLS STRATEGIES back cover

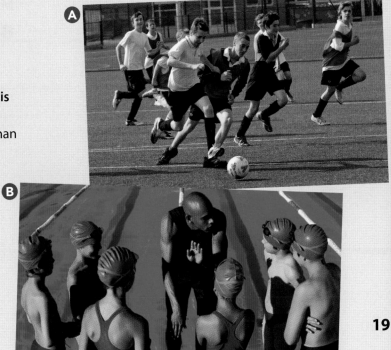

Ⓐ

Ⓑ

Grammar:	Comparisons
	Asking for descriptions
Vocabulary:	Physical description
	Describing people
Phrases:	Suggestions
	Describing someone you ac

Vocabulary & Listening

Physical description

1 Look at the photos and discuss the questions.

- Do you recognise the celebrities? Why are they famous?
- How old do you think their children are?
- Would you like to have famous parents? Why? Why not?

2 a (1.27) Listen to a TV show about celebrity news. Make notes about Georgia, Lourdes and Ray, using these headings.

1 Age: *Georgia – 17*

2 Why their parents are famous:

   Father Mick Jagger – Rolling Stones

3 Other information about the family:

b In what ways are their families unusual?

3 Words **2** know (1.28) Check the words in blue. Find a person in the photos who:

1 has **dark wavy** hair.   *Lizzy Jagger*
2 is going **bald**.
3 has **medium-length blonde** hair.
4 has a **round** face.
5 is in her **teens**.
6 is in his **seventies**.
7 is slightly **plump**.
8 is quite **scruffy**.
9 has **straight hair**.
10 is very **glamorous**.
11 is **middle-aged**.
12 is tall and **elegant**.

4 a Add the words from exercise 3 to the correct section in the word map.

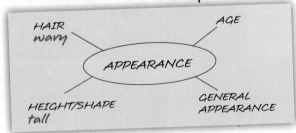

b Think of at least two more words to add to each section. Use the photos to help you.

Georgia Jagger (left) with sister, Lizzy, and mother, Jerry Hall

5 a Think of a famous person. Write sentences about his/her appearance using words from exercise 4.

b SPEAKING Tell the class about the person, adding details about why he/she is famous but don't say the name. The class must guess who it is.

> *She's quite small and very glamorous. She has dark, wavy hair and she's in her thirties. She is Spanish and is a famous film actress. Who is it?*

MINI WORKBOOK exercises 5–6 page 105

Grammar Focus

Making comparisons

6 a Which people in the photos do these sentences describe?

1 She isn't **as tall as** her mother.
2 She's **a little taller than** her mother.
3 He's **much younger than** his father.
4 Her hair is **similar to** her mother's but it's a different colour.
5 Her nose is **the same as** her mother's.
6 Her face **is completely different from** her mother's.
7 She's **less famous than** her mother.
8 He's **one of the most** famous actors in the world.
9 She's **by far the most** successful female singer ever.
10 She's **the shortest** woman **in the** family.

Ray with his father, Jack Nicholson

Lourdes with mother, Madonna

b Complete *Grammar2know* using the sentences in exercise 6a to help you.

Grammar 2 know

Making comparisons

He's **taller/more successful/better looking** _than_ his father.

She's the **tallest/most successful/best looking** one _____ the family.

Other comparative forms

He isn't as dark _____ his father.

She's less glamorous _____ her mother.

Describing small differences

She's a _____ short**er than** her daughter.

Describing big differences

Jack is _____ old**er than** Ray's mother.

Jerry was _____ _____ **the most famous** models _____ the world.

Jack is _____ _____ **the oldest** person in the photos.

Other useful phrases for comparing

She looks completely **different** _____ her mother.

Her clothes are **similar** _____ her mother's.

Her mouth's **the same** _____ her father's.

7 a Elsa is talking about herself and her brother. Complete the text with the words in the box.

> as   far   from   in   little ✓   much
> one   same   smallest   to

'This is my brother, Will, … he's a
¹ _little_ older than me – about a
year – but people often don't believe
we're brother and sister because he
looks completely different
² _____ me. To begin with he's so
³ _____ taller – I'm only 1.50 m
and Will's nearly 2 m tall! In fact he's
⁴ _____ of the tallest people
⁵ _____ his year at school. I'm the
⁶ _____ in the family. But that
doesn't matter – I'm by ⁷ _____
the nicest, and Will definitely isn't as
intelligent ⁸ _____ me! Physically,
I think he's very similar ⁹ _____ our
father but he's got the ¹⁰ _____
eyes as our mother – bright blue. '

b ⟨1.29⟩ **Listen and check.**

8 a Make six sentences about you and your family with the adjectives in the box. Describe big or small differences.

> tall/short   tidy/untidy   quiet/talkative
> confident/shy   similar/different
> dark/fair   old/young   plump/slim

I'm a little taller than my mother.
My uncle is by far the tallest person in our family.
My sister is similar to my mum.
I'm completely different from my sister because she's really talkative – I'm much quieter.

b Work in pairs and tell your partner about the differences between you and your family.

9 Discuss the questions in pairs.

• Would you like to have famous parents or not?

• What are the advantages and disadvantages, do you think?

MINI WORKBOOK exercises 1–2 page 104

Reading & Vocabulary

1 **Look at the photo and discuss the questions.**

1 The four girls in the photo are identical quadruplets. What do you think this means?

2 Do you come from a large family or not?

3 Which of these statements do you think is true?

> Having lots of brothers and sisters is fun because there is always someone to talk to, and you never feel lonely.

> In large families you don't have any privacy, you have to share everything and you don't get enough individual attention from your parents.

2 **SKIMMING Read the text quickly and answer the questions.**

1 Why are the Durst girls rare?

2 What has happened to them because of this?

3 Do the girls ever have problems knowing who is who?

4 Do they have similar interests?

5 Are they similar in personality?

6 How do the girls get on with the other students at school?

3 **Check the *Words2know*. Who in the text do they describe: M (Megan), K (Kendra), C (Calli), S (Sarah) or A (all)?**

Words 2 know (1.30)

argumentative	☐
dominant	☐
popular	☐
sensitive	☐
shy	☐
beautiful	☐
sociable	☐
150 cm tall	☐
light brown hair	☐
freckles	☐
a strong personality	☐

Quads! (1.31)

The Durst girls – Kendra, Megan, Calli and Sarah – from Buffalo, Minnesota, are extremely rare: they are identical quadruplets. There are only sixty sets of identical quads in the world, and the girls have been celebrities in the US since they were born, in February 1993. They have appeared on the *Oprah Winfrey Show*, and many other TV shows.

The girls look exactly the same – even they get confused and call each other the wrong name sometimes. All four have light brown hair and 'thousands' of freckles, and they are each about 150 cm tall. According to their English teacher, Alisa Ireland, 'They are all beautiful. How is their mother going to cope … with four beautiful teenage daughters?'

The girls also have similar sporting interests. All four play soccer, and Kendra, Megan and Sarah enjoy gymnastics, although Calli prefers basketball.

4 **a Divide the *Words2know* into two categories:**

• To describe appearance: *light brown hair*

• To describe personality:

b Do the phrases go with *be* or *have*? Read and check.

5 **Think of people you know who fit the *Words2know* and write sentences about them.**

My friend Laura is very argumentative.

MINI WORKBOOK exercise 7 page 105

The girls all have very strong personalities and their teacher says they are very dominant at school. 'The quads are really popular, everyone wants to be their friend,' says Alisa. 'They've become real leaders in their class … but they're all so different!'

According to friends and family, these days they don't agree about anything. Calli, the tomboy* of the family, is the most argumentative, apparently. Kendra is very 'girly', her sisters say, she always wants things to be clean and nice, and Megan is the most sociable – she loves make-up, clothes, going out and shopping. Sarah is the shyest and most sensitive of the four and she is also the nicest, according to her sisters.

'We don't think of ourselves as quadruplets,' says Megan. 'We think of ourselves as four sisters who were born on the same day.'

* A girl who likes traditionally 'boyish' activities, like climbing trees.

Grammar Focus

Questions with *look like, be like, like*

6 Match questions a–c to the correct answers. Read *Grammar2know* and check your answers.

a What does she look like?
b What is she like?
c What does she like?

1 Soccer and gymnastics.
2 She's got light brown hair and freckles.
3 She's got a strong personality and she's quite argumentative.

7 **a** Make questions for the answers with the person or name in brackets.

1 (*your best friend*) He's very tall with long dark hair and brown eyes.
   What does your best friend look like?

2 (*your neighbour*) He's really nice but he's very quiet.

3 (*your cousin*) He's not very tall, and he's got blonde hair and an earring.

4 (*David*) Football, heavy metal music and horror films.

5 (*Your grandparents*) They were really strict but they were very kind.

6 (*Hannah*) She's very similar to her sister – tall and blonde.

7 (*Your new Maths teacher*) She seems very nice and she's really young.

b In pairs, ask and answer the questions.

8 **a** Work in pairs. Write down the names of three people you know (friends or family).

Marta   Alex   my cousin Carlos

b Show the names to your partner. Take turns to ask and answer about the three people, using the questions in *Grammar2know*.

" *What does Marta look like?*
She's about 160 cm tall, and she's got short blond hair.
What's Alex like?
He's really friendly and funny.
What does your cousin Carlos like?
He likes playing the guitar and reading.

MINI WORKBOOK exercises 3–4 pages 104–105

Reading & Vocabulary

1 **What is your position in your family?**

a first-born   a middle child

a last-born   an only child

2 **Check the *Words2know*. Match the characteristics in the box to the definitions below.**

Words 2 know (1.32)

ambitious   bossy   easy-going   conscientious
indecisive   dynamic   organised ✓   punctual
self-centred   sensitive

This person …

1 ☐ does things in a careful, well-planned way.   *organised*

2 ☐ always thinks about him/herself.

3 ☐ always tells other people what to do.

4 ☐ often arrives on time.

5 ☐ is easily upset.

6 ☐ always does a job well.

7 ☐ wants to be successful.

8 ☐ can't decide about things.

9 ☐ is very calm.

10 ☐ is full of energy and ideas.

3 **Read the text and mark the characteristics in exercise 2: OC (only child), FB (first-born), MC (middle child) or LB (last-born).**

4 **Read the text again and match the descriptions 1–8 to the correct section in the text. <u>Underline</u> the information in the text that gives you the answer.**

1 This person thinks they know everything.

    eldest child

2 This person sometimes has difficulty concentrating.

3 This person is bad at making decisions.

4 This is probably the best person in the family to go to with a problem.

5 This person is happy to take control of situations.

6 This person often helps to solve problems between members of the family.

7 This person grows up quickly.

8 This person is probably the most fun to be with.

How birth order affects your personality (1.34)

Where are you in your family? Are you a big brother or sister, the baby or somewhere in the middle? Or maybe you're an only child? Wherever you are, psychologists believe your position in the family has an important effect on your personality. Selina Miley finds out more.

Only children

Only children are people who are pro-active: they mature early, they are dynamic, organised and conscientious, and they love facts and details. On the other hand, they hate criticism and they can seem far too sensitive to other people. As only children, they are often the centre of attention, so they can become angry if they don't get their own way … famous only children include golfer, TigerWoods, and pop stars John Lennon and Elton John.

Eldest child

Are you an eldest child? If so, you could be a natural leader … eldest children are often ambitious, punctual and hard-working, and regularly score higher marks on achievement tests. On the negative side, eldest children often feel jealous of their younger siblings, who often seem to get better treatment from their parents. First-borns can appear to be 'know-it-alls' who frighten other people with their bossy, insensitive attitude. So, maybe it's not surprising that more than half of US presidents have been first-borns!

5 Read *Active Study*. <u>Underline</u> examples of other prefixes and suffixes in the text.

Notice the suffixes and prefixes of adjectives

Adjectives often end like this:

jeal**ous**   ambi**tious**
organi**sed**   hardwork**ing**
sensi**tive**   punctu**al**

Some adjectives use prefixes to give the opposite:
unambitious   **in**sensitive   **dis**organised

MINI WORKBOOK exercise 8 page 105

Middle children

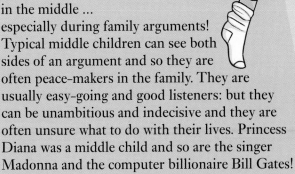

Middle children often seem to get the least attention from their parents and complain that they are always stuck in the middle ... especially during family arguments! Typical middle children can see both sides of an argument and so they are often peace-makers in the family. They are usually easy-going and good listeners: but they can be unambitious and indecisive and they are often unsure what to do with their lives. Princess Diana was a middle child and so are the singer Madonna and the computer billionaire Bill Gates!

Last-borns

Last-borns are often their parents' favourite, and their personality reflects this. Parents are often less strict with the youngest child, which can cause resentment from older children. They also have the least responsibility. On the positive side, last-borns have good people skills: they are sociable and love entertaining others. Many famous actors and comedians – Jim Carrey and Cameron Diaz for example – are youngest children. On the other hand, youngest children often have a short attention span and can be self-centred.

Listening & Speaking

6 (1.33) Listen to what Stefan, Melanie and Oliver say about the ideas in the text and answer the questions.

- What position is each one in the family?
- What brothers and sisters do they have?

7 (1.33) Listen again. Tick (✓) true and cross (✗) false. Give reasons for your answer.

1 ☐ Stefan's younger sister is very sociable and likes talking.
2 ☐ Stefan is more ambitious and dynamic than his elder brother.
3 ☐ Melanie thinks the article is true for her family.
4 ☐ She isn't as easy-going as her brother.
5 ☐ Her brother is the bossiest member of the family.
6 ☐ Oliver has brothers and sisters.
7 ☐ He doesn't think he's a natural leader.
8 ☐ He is easy-going and a good listener.

8 Make notes on these questions, then discuss in groups.

- Are the ideas in the text true for your family? Why? Why not.
- Is it true that middle children get the least attention from their parents?
- Do you think last-born children are their parents' favourite?
- Which do you think is the best/worst position in the family? Why?

LORI is talking to Kate, one of her new classmates. A young man, Nick, is also there.

MAKING AND RESPONDING TO SUGGESTIONS

1 Look at the photo, read the caption and answer the questions.

- Where is Lori? Who is she talking to?
- What is Nick doing?
- Do you think Lori has noticed Nick?

2 (1.35) Listen to the conversation. Choose the correct answer.

1 *Lori/Kate* has met Nick before.
2 Nick is writing *some music/some words* for a song.
3 *Kate/Nick* suggests that they form a band.
4 The title of Nick's song is *Girl With Long Brown Hair/Girl With Blue Eyes*.

3 (1.36) Complete the conversation with the *Phrases2know*. Then listen and check.

Two weeks later, Lori, Nick and Kate decide to form a band. They need a bass guitarist, a drummer – and a name.

4 (1.37) Listen and practise saying the *Phrases2know*.

Phrases **2know**

Making suggestions
What/How about …?
What do you think of these trousers?
Disagreeing with suggestions
I'm not sure about that.
I like the idea but …
It's not bad but …
Agreeing with suggestions
I think it's a good idea.
That's it! I love it!
I suppose so.
Well, all right, that will be fine.
Making an alternative suggestion
Here's another idea …
I've got a better idea.
Asking for agreement
Do we all agree?

Lori: We need a really original name for the band, something that's going to attract people's attention, so I've written down some ideas … [1] _____ 'The Chameleons'?

Kate: I think it's a good name, it's really original.

Nick: Hmm, [2] _____ , I think there's already a band called 'The Chameleons' …

Lori: Okay, [3] _____ . What do you think of 'E5'?

Nick: 'E5'?

Lori: E for Edinburgh and 5 because there are five of us.

Nick: Lori, [4] _____ there are only three of us!

Kate: Well yes, at the moment, but there will be five, when we get a drummer and a bass guitarist.

Nick: Listen, [5] _____ . What about 'BlueSky'?

Kate: That's it, that's the name, I love it!

Lori: Well, I suppose so – it's not bad.

Nick: So, [6] _____ ? The name of the band is 'BlueSky'.

Lori: Well, all right, but I still think 'The Chameleons' is better!

5 a In pairs, find a name for the students' café in your school. Follow the prompts and use the *Phrases2know* on page 26 to help you.

b Swap roles and decide on a name for an online school magazine. Act out your conversation for the class.

A Make a suggestion for the name.

B Disagree with the suggestion. Give a reason.

A Make an alternative suggestion.

B Disagree with the suggestion. Make your own suggestion.

A Agree to B's suggestion.

A DESCRIPTION OF SOMEONE YOU ADMIRE

6 Read Lori's essay and match the information a–e to the paragraphs 1–5.

a ☐ information about his/her early life

b ☐ examples of his/her achievements

c ☐ introduction/who you chose and why

d ☐ conclusion/reasons for admiring this person

e ☐ what you admire about his/her personality

7 You are going to write a description of someone you admire.

a Choose a person who inspires you:

- someone you know, e.g. a teacher, a neighbour, a relative OR
- your favourite musician, sportsperson, writer or TV personality.

b Make some notes about:

- why you chose this person
- his/her early life
- his/her main achievements
- other reasons for admiring him/her.

my musical inspiration

1 My musical inspiration is the English singer, Leona Lewis. One reason I admire her is because she's got a great voice. She also inspires me because she's so determined and ambitious.

2 Leona was born in London. She dreamed of a career in music from an early age. She wrote her first song at the age of twelve and made her first recording when she was only fifteen years old. In 2006, she became the first female winner of the British talent show, *The X-Factor* and she made her first album, *Spirit*.

3 Probably her greatest achievement was when she sang at the Olympics closing ceremony in Beijing in 2008 in front of a TV audience of three billion people.

4 Another reason I admire her is because she is not only a talented and successful singer, she is also a very brave person. She always speaks her mind on important issues such as cancer awareness and vegetarianism.

5 To sum up, Leona Lewis is my musical inspiration and an inspiration to all young people because she has already achieved so many great things in her career. She has sold millions of albums, she has won many music awards and she has appeared with artists like Take That and Mariah Carey … and she's only in her early twenties!

Phrases 2 know

Giving reasons

My inspiration is …

One/Another reason I admire him is because he …

He also inspires me because …

Describing biographical details

She was born/grew up in London.

She sang from an early age.

She started playing at the age of six.

Describing personality

She's in her early/late twenties/thirties.

She is a very determined/brave/talented person.

Describing achievements

In his career/life up to now he has …

Probably his greatest achievement was when …

Conclusion

To sum up, I admire Leona Lewis because …

In conclusion, I admire my father because …

8 Now write your description. Write 200–250 words. Use your notes from exercise 7b and the *Phrases2know* to help you. Remember to include an introduction and conclusion.

Grammar:	Obligation *make* and *let*
Vocabulary:	Describing jobs Working conditions
Phrases:	Discussing your opinions

Vocabulary & Listening

Work and young people

1 Look at the pictures and discuss the questions.

- Which pictures show life:
  – one/two hundred years ago? – now?
- How old are the people in each picture?

2 Words **2** know (2.1) PREDICTION Check the words in blue and read the sentences. Which sentences do you think are true and which are false?

100–200 years ago

1 Most poor people couldn't **educate** their children and **child labour** was common.

2 The **working conditions** for these children were very good – they were **well-paid** and **well-treated**.

3 Most young people from **wealthy** families needed to **earn their living**.

4 Young women generally had a lot of **career opportunities**.

These days

5 In many developed countries, like the UK, young people don't start **full-time work** until their early to mid-twenties.

6 In some countries, children still work because their parents need their **wages**.

7 They don't **work long hours** and get lots of breaks.

3 a (2.2) Listen to part 1 of a TV programme about child labour, and check your predictions about sentences 1–5 in exercise 2.

b (2.3) Listen to part 2 and check your predictions about sentences 6–7.

4 (2.4) Listen to the whole programme again and choose the correct facts and figures.

1 A hundred years ago, the normal age to start work was
  a four to five. **b** fourteen to **c** sixteen to
    fifteen.   seventeen.

2 200 years ago, young children sometimes worked in the coal mine for _____ a day.
  a ten hours **b** four hours **c** thirteen hours

3 In the world today, _____ children are working.
  a one in four **b** one in ten **c** one in 140

4 Many children in African mines are younger than
  a ten.   **b** twelve.   **c** twenty.

5 These children earn _____ a day.
  a $10   **b** $12   **c** 20 US cents

5 Do you find any of this information shocking? Is working life easier for young people today?

I think it's shocking that…

MINI WORKBOOK exercise 6 page 107

Grammar Focus

Obligation

6 **a** Read the sentences from the TV programme. Who do *they* or *them* refer to in each sentence?

> Modern graduates   Young ladies in the past
> Children 200 hundred years ago
> Companies who use child labour
> Wealthy young people in the past
> Children in parts of Africa today

1 They have to work ten or twelve hours a day.

2 They had to earn a living in coalmines and factories.

3 They weren't allowed to work – people thought it was wrong.

4 You must write to them and tell them how you feel.

5 We mustn't give them our money.

6 They didn't have to work at all.

7 They aren't allowed to take breaks.

8 They don't have to start work until they are twenty-three.

b Read *Grammar2know* and match the sentences 1–8 to the rules a–h.

Grammar **2** know

have to and must

Use *have to* and *must* to say that something is necessary.

a Use *have to* to describe rules and laws:

 They have to work ...

b Use *must* to show what the speaker thinks is necessary, strong advice or recommendations:

_____

c The past form of both verbs is *had to*:

_____

don't have to

d Use *don't have to* to say that something is not necessary:

_____

e The past form is *didn't have to*:

_____

not allowed to and mustn't

Use *not allowed to* and *mustn't* to say that something is not permitted.

f *Not allowed to* often describes rules:

_____

g The past form is *wasn't/weren't allowed to*:

_____

h *Mustn't* is often used for strong advice or recommendations:

_____

7 **a** Complete these sentences about the law in your country, using *(don't) have to* and *(not) allowed to*. If you are not sure, guess!

1 Ten-year-olds _____ have a job.

2 Fifteen-year-olds _____ have a part-time job.

3 Young men _____ join the army.

4 Foreign workers _____ have a work permit.

5 Employers _____ pay workers if they are sick.

6 Employers _____ pay workers a 'minimum wage'.

b Compare answers in pairs. If you are not sure, use *I think* or *I guess*.

“ *Employers have to pay workers if they are sick, I guess.*

8 (2.5) Read the article about powder monkeys and <u>underline</u> the correct words. Listen and check.

Powder monkeys

200 years ago, most poor children [1]*had to/were allowed to* start work when they were about 12. Many boys joined the navy. They [2]*had to/didn't have to* fight but they [3]*had to/were allowed to* work very hard, as servants for the adult sailors. They [4]*had to/were allowed to* climb ropes and carry gunpowder for the sailors: that's why they got the name 'powder monkeys'. Life was very hard and they [5]*were allowed to/weren't allowed to* leave the navy even if they wanted to. They [6]*often had to/were often allowed to* eat disgusting food but they [7]*had to/were allowed to* drink plenty of rum and beer. When they were eighteen, they [8]*had to/were allowed to* become real sailors, but only if they already had six years' experience at sea! Many stayed in the navy because it was a well-paid job in those days.

9 Your friend is going for a job interview. Use the prompts to give him/her some strong advice.

– look smart   *You must look smart!*

– wear old jeans and trainers

– answer all the questions fully

– appear interested in the job

– arrive late for the interview

– refuse to work at the weekend

MINI WORKBOOK exercises 1–4 pages 106– 107

working life

29

Vocabulary & Reading

Jobs

1 a Make a list of three jobs you'd like and three jobs you wouldn't like. Don't write them in order.

actor, nurse

b Show your list to your partner. Can he/she guess which jobs you'd like to do and which jobs you'd hate to do?

2 Check the *Words2know* and discuss the questions.

> **Words 2 know** (2.6)
>
> an advertising executive
> a call-centre worker
> a servant
> a farm labourer
> a fisherman
> a governess
> a miner
> a systems analyst
> a social worker
> a PR (public relations) consultant

- What were more common jobs in the past?
- Which are 'modern' jobs?
- Which jobs do you think are the most difficult?
- Which are the easiest?

❝ *I think being a social worker is a difficult job.*

3 PREDICTING You are going to read about two of the jobs in exercise 2. Look at the photos. Which jobs are they?

4 a **Words 2 know** (2.7) Check the words in blue. Which job do you think each description relates to: C (call centre worker), G (governess), or B (both)?

1 ☐ It is/was **respectable**.
2 ☐ It isn't/wasn't very **challenging**.
3 ☐ It is/was **badly paid**.
4 ☐ It is/was **fun** sometimes.
5 ☐ It is/was boring and **repetitive**.
6 ☐ It is/was very **stressful**.
7 ☐ **Employers** and **supervisors** are/were very **strict**.

b Read the text and check your answers.

A (2.8)

A job no one did twenty years ago

Today there are nearly a million call-centre workers in the UK but twenty years ago the job didn't exist.

What's it like to work in a call centre? Nicki Mathews, 18, says she's typical. 'It's a job for people like me, who don't know what they want to do! You have to answer calls all day so it's very repetitive. It's stressful, the callers shout at you but you aren't allowed be rude. It's really strict – the supervisors make you follow a script and they listen to your calls to check.

'They don't let you take breaks between calls. In some call centres, they don't let you go to the loo! It's not so bad where I work. If a caller upsets us, they let us have a break until we feel better. And they let us chat between calls – in some call centres, that's not allowed! We have a laugh, and you meet lots of people, because no one stays long!'

5 Discuss the questions about the text.
- What did/do the governess and the call-centre worker have to do?
- What would you enjoy or hate about these jobs?

6 SPEAKING Discuss the questions in pairs.
- Do you have a career in mind?
- Which things in exercise 4a will you look for in your job? What other things are important to you?

❝ *I don't want a job that's stressful ...*
I'd like to be a PR consultant ...

MINI WORKBOOK exercises 7–8 page 107

B

A job no one does now

150 years ago, it was the only job that a 'lady' could do.

Thousands of governesses in Britain lived in wealthy families, teaching their children. Young ladies became governesses because their own families had no money so they had to earn a living. The heroine of *Jane Eyre*, by Charlotte Brontë, was a governess. Jane was lucky and married her employer. But what was life like for real governesses?

The governess gave lessons, and in return, the employers let her live in their home and paid her only pocket money. But they often treated her badly: they made her eat her meals alone, and sometimes she had to share a bedroom with the children. Often, they didn't let the governess leave the house and she wasn't allowed to meet young men. In real life, it was very difficult for governesses to marry … and escape!

Grammar Focus

make and *let*

7 **a** Read sentences 1–4 from text A again and match the words in bold to explanations a–d.

1 **They make us** follow a script.

2 **They don't let us** take breaks.

3 **They let us** chat between calls.

4 **They don't make us** answer another call until we feel better.

a We don't have to

b We have to

c We're allowed to

d We aren't allowed to

b Check your answers in *Grammar2know*. Read text B again and find three examples of *make* and *let* in the past tense.

Grammar **2 know**

make and *let*

Use *make* + object + infinitive without *to* to force someone to do something:
*The supervisors **make us follow** a script.* (= we have to)
*They **don't make us answer** another call.* (= we don't have to)
*They **made her eat** her meals alone.*

Use *let* + object + infinitive without *to* to allow someone to do something:
*They **let us go** to the toilet.* (= we are allowed to)
*They **don't let us chat**.* (= we aren't allowed to)
*They **didn't let her leave** the house.*

8 Rewrite the sentences using *(not) make* and *(not) let*.

Call-centre workers:

1 The supervisors don't allow workers to argue with customers.

The supervisors don't let workers argue with the customers.

2 Some employers force employees to work long hours.

3 They don't allow workers to chat to customers.

4 They don't force employees to work at night.

Governesses:

5 Many families didn't allow the governess to go on holiday.

6 Sometimes they forced the governess to share a bedroom with their pupils.

7 Kind families allowed the governess to eat with them.

8 They didn't force the governess to do housework.

9 Use the ideas below to make six sentences about your school, using *make* and *let*.

Our Art teacher lets us listen to mp3 players during lessons.

> chat during lessons   wear earrings
> listen to MP3 players during lessons
> wear uniform   do a lot of tests
> eat and drink during lessons   study hard
> carry mobile phones   dye our hair

10 Think about your week. Are your parents strict or not? Explain why or why not, using *make* and *let*.

" *My mum's quite strict. She makes me …*
My dad's not very strict, he lets me …

MINI WORKBOOK exercise 5 page 107

Reading & Speaking

1 Match the jobs to the photos.

☐ a model ☐ a human statue

☐ a placard carrier ☐ a game tester

2 PREDICTION Discuss the questions.

- What do you think each person does in their job?
- What do you think are the positive and negative aspects of each job?

3 **a** Which of the jobs in exercise 1 do you think these sentences describe?

1 You have to be punctual and reliable.

2 It's tiring physically.

3 It's very rewarding.

4 You have to be very patient.

5 It's very repetitive.

6 You need to have a nice smile.

7 You have plenty of time to think.

8 It's a good way of getting experience for a future career.

b Read the text and check your answer.

4 Read the text again. Tick (✓) true and cross (✗) false.

1 ☑ Nick's friends think he earns more than he really does.

2 ☐ Placard carriers have to work even when the weather is bad.

3 ☐ Andrea doesn't like anything about her job.

4 ☐ Teresa Parks also has a job in the theatre.

5 ☐ She says she sometimes has problems with children.

6 ☐ Paula Hancock wants all her models to look like supermodels.

5 **a** Put the jobs from the text in order from 1 (easiest) to 4 (most difficult). Explain your order to a partner.

b Would you like to do any of these jobs? Why? Why not?

A

B

(2.10)

Easy money?

We all know that the key to success is hard work but some jobs appear less difficult than others. We look at four easy ways to make money. Or are they?

How about making money out of your favourite pastime? Many fans of computer games dream of making their fortune by playing their favourite games: as a game tester. Student Nick Chen was one of them. 'I'm mad about video games and my dream is to design games one day, so this is a great way to get experience,' says Nick. 'But it isn't as easy as my friends think. You play the games before the graphics are really developed, so they aren't so much fun. And you have to do the same level of the game again, and again and again, to find any possible problems ... the hours are actually really long, and the money isn't great ... about $10 an hour. Some of my friends think I'm earning thousands but that's only the top guys in video gaming ... not the little guys like me!'

Or perhaps you are more of an 'outdoor' type? So how about becoming a placard carrier? All you have to do is to hold an advertising placard for people to look at. For hours, in all weathers ... and the placard is very heavy.

'Sometimes, I think I'm wasting my life,' says Andrea, a young placard carrier living in London, 'and the pay isn't good. But I can read my book and sometimes people stop for a chat.'

C

D

If you like the idea of an outdoor job but prefer something a little more artistic, perhaps you could earn your living as a human statue? Just put on a shiny costume and then stand completely still, until someone gives you some money. 'It's not easy to stay still hour after hour, especially when a mosquito lands on your nose,' says Teresa Parks, an unemployed actress who has worked as a human statue in New York for nearly two years. 'But the reactions you get – especially from kids – can be really rewarding … and I get plenty of time to plan my acting career!'

But perhaps you're looking for something really glamorous? Why not become a model – you can travel the world and go to photo shoots in exotic places! According to Paula Hancock, who runs an agency for teenage models, the reality isn't quite so exciting.

'Many people have the wrong idea about modelling. Yes, you may get the chance to travel (though not always to exotic places!) and it can be well-paid, but most models aren't supermodels. There is far more work modelling for clothes catalogues, for example,' says Paula. 'In that kind of publication, people want to see normal-looking people wearing normal clothes. To be a successful model, you have to be punctual, reliable and have a great smile. You also have to be patient, as you spend a lot of time waiting for things to happen!'

6 Read the job advertisements and answer the questions.

- What is the job in each case?
- What kind of person does each employer want?

1

> ### Wanted: Waiting Staff
> ### For City-Centre Restaurant
> Thursday–Sunday Evenings 6–12 p.m.
> Applicants must be friendly and hardworking
> Experience useful but not essential

2

> ### SATURDAY ASSISTANT
> required for busy clothes shop.
> -
> Must be smart, polite and reliable.
> No experience necessary.

7 **a** Read about three candidates, Florence, Yara and Jack, on page 124. Decide which candidate is best for each job in exercise 6 and why.

b In pairs, discuss and decide the best candidate for each job. Use the *Phrases2know*.

CAN YOU DO IT IN ENGLISH?

Phrases 2 know 2.9

Discussing opinions

To me … is the best candidate, because he's got experience.

How about …? He's very polite.

Yes, but he hasn't got any experience.

Personally, I don't think … is suitable because she wants more hours.

Presenting your opinion

We think …

We've decided that … is best because …

We don't think … is suitable because …

8 WRITING Write about who you chose for each job in exercise 7 and why you didn't choose the other candidates.

We chose Florence to work for the restaurant because …

Yara isn't suitable for this job because …

activestudy2 (EXAMS)

Vocabulary

ACTIVE STUDY Learn words in groups

1 Put the words below into the categories in the table. Add two more words in each category.

> advertising executive ✓   bald   bossy
> self-centred   servant   conscientious
> indecisive   miner   plump   social worker
> scruffy

Appearance	Personality	Jobs
		advertising executive

2 Complete each sentence with one word.

1 He's a young graduate looking for his first f*ull-time* job.
2 My uncle works really long h_____ , from eight a.m. till six p.m.
3 Using child l_____ is illegal in Europe.
4 The working c_____ in this factory are very bad.
5 There were no c_____ opportunities in this town.
6 I can't travel around the world; I have to e_____ a living!

ACTIVE STUDY Notice silent letters

3 PRONUNCIATION (2.11) Listen to the words. If you don't hear the *r*, cross it out. Listen again and repeat.

a da~~r~~k
b farm
c round
d miner
e scruffy
f servant
g hair
h freckles
i fisherman
j first-born
k earrings
l worker

Grammar

4 Match the questions and answers.

1 What does he look like?
2 What is he like?
3 What does he like?

a Cycling, reggae music and films.
b He's tall and handsome, with dark wavy hair.
c He's one of the nicest people I know.

5 Number the people from 1 (the oldest) to 6 (the youngest).

a ☐ I'm Charlie. I've got five brothers and sisters.
b ☐ Jack is slightly younger than me.
c ☐ Emily is much older than me.
d ☑ Julia is the oldest of us.
e ☐ Grace is a lot younger than all of us.
f ☐ Tom is a little older than me.

6 Complete the sentences with the prepositions below.

> as   than   from   in   of   to ✓

1 He looks similar _to_ Leonardo DiCaprio.
2 They look different _____ their parents.
3 Charlie's hair is much darker _____ Luke's.
4 Ruby is the most talkative person _____ the class.
5 My hair looks the same _____ my father's.
6 Jack's one _____ the nicest people I know.

7 Choose the correct form.

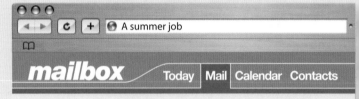

Hi Katie

Do you know that Jessica's got a summer job in America? She lives with a very strange lady and helps her around the house. The lady makes her ¹_____ for walks with her fat ugly dog. Jessica also ²_____ to prepare food for the dog. She isn't allowed to go out after nine p.m. and 'male friends' ³_____ visit her in her room. But on the other hand, the lady is quite nice to her. She lets her ⁴_____ her piano and listen to all the CDs in her huge collection. Jessica ⁵_____ get up early on Saturdays and Sundays, and she ⁶_____ phone her parents in the UK as often as she likes! I ⁷_____ find myself a job like that next summer.

1 ⓐ go   b to go   c goes
2 a must   b makes   c has
3 a mustn't   b doesn't have   c isn't allowed
4 a to play   b play   c playing
5 a don't have to b doesn't have to c mustn't
6 a must   b has to   c is allowed to
7 a must   b have to   c let

How children see their parents' jobs

How much did you know about your parents' work when you were little? What did you think of it? Share your memories here.

A My dad works in radio, but when I was little I didn't understand what he did until he once took me with him. Some companies here in the USA do this thing called Take Your Child to Work Day. The idea is that when children visit their parents at work, they get to see what mom and dad do when they're not home. I saw the studio with all the equipment, I was allowed to put on headphones and speak into a microphone. It was great fun.

Adam

B As a child, I had no idea what my mum did at work. All I knew was she left early and came home late. The words 'financial analyst' meant nothing to me. In nursery school, when we had to draw pictures of 'My Mum at work', other children drew nurses in a hospital or shop assistants selling things, or stay-at-home mums cooking. I thought those jobs were much more interesting. I just drew a plump woman in a suit with big earrings and a laptop.

Bridget

C My mum writes children's books. I liked it when she read me stories, but I wanted her to play with me and not to sit in front of a computer and write. Then one day at school everyone had to do a presentation about a book, and I decided to talk about one of hers. My classmates were really impressed. They asked me a lot of questions, such as, 'Did you actually see your mum writing this book?' Suddenly mum's work seemed glamorous!

Chris

D Being a biologist's daughter was fun. I enjoyed birdwatching with my dad. I knew a biologist was someone who knows about animals. I also thought it's someone who doesn't have to work very hard. My mum's a doctor and she was always at the hospital, all day and sometimes all night, while dad often just sat at his desk writing something. So at the age of five I decided it was better to be a scientist than a doctor.

Diane

Reading Skills

ACTIVE STUDY | Read for gist

8 Read four teenagers' stories of what they thought of their parents' jobs when they were children. Match 1–5 to the people A–D in the text above. The people may be chosen more than once.

Who:

1 appreciated his/her parent's work more thanks to other children? ____

2 did not find his/her parent's job interesting? ____

3 enjoyed learning more about his/her parent's work? ____

4 had a parent who worked long hours? ____ ____

5 compared different jobs? ____ ____

Listening Skills

ACTIVE STUDY | Listen for specific information

9 (2.12) Read statements 1–6 and listen to a conversation between Grace, who wants to do some babysitting, and Mrs Gilbert, a mother of two children. Tick (✓) true and cross (✗) false or write (?) if there is no information.

1 ☐ Grace has got three younger siblings.

2 ☐ Mrs Gilbert says being on time is the most important thing.

3 ☐ Sam is so energetic that he often gets hurt.

4 ☐ Lily wants to watch scary programmes on TV.

5 ☐ Grace agrees to babysit until midnight every night.

6 ☐ The children are allowed to have ice cream after dinner.

Speaking Skills

10 You and your friend want to find holiday jobs together. In pairs, act out the following roleplay, using the *Phrases2know* from page 26, the *Words2know* from page 30 and the list of jobs below. Student A begins.

- work in a call centre
- do some babysitting
- work on a farm
- be a human statue
- work in a shop (*what kind?*)

A: Suggest a job.

A: Disagree with B's suggestion. Say why. Suggest a third option.

A: Give details of your suggestion.

B: Disagree with A's suggestion. Say why. Suggest something else.

B: Ask for more details.

B: Agree.

5 getting there

Grammar	Future tenses
	Time clauses
	First conditional
Vocabulary	The environment
	Transport
	Holidays
Functions	Directions

Listening & Vocabulary

1 In pairs, think of five things that protect the environment and five things that damage it. Compare your ideas with the class.

Protect — recycling bottles
Damage — travelling by plane

2 **Words 2 know** (2.14) Check the words in blue in the text. What does 'carbon footprint' mean? Read the introduction to the text and check.

3 Put the activities in the text in order from 1 (biggest saving) to 8 (smallest saving). Compare your order with a partner.

4 (2.15) Ben and Alice have just done the same activity and are checking the answers. Listen and check your answers.

5 (2.15) Listen again. Tick (✓) true and cross (✗) false. Correct the false statements.

1 ☒ Pigs create more carbon dioxide than any other farm animals.

2 ☐ The quiz suggests that everyone should become a vegan.

3 ☐ Saving energy can also mean a healthier lifestyle.

4 ☐ Alice's mother doesn't like recycling.

5 ☐ Alice's family travel a lot by plane.

6 ☐ Low-energy light bulbs don't help the environment very much.

6 Find the opposites of these verbs in the text.

1 protect the environment
   destroy the environment
2 throw paper away
3 turn your heating up
4 switch your computer on
5 save energy

7 SPEAKING Discuss the questions.

• Which lifestyle changes in the text are easiest to make?

• How can you reduce your carbon footprint?

❝ I'll try cycling.

MINI WORKBOOK exercise 7 page 109

Do you know how to . . . Reduce your carbon footprint?

Every day we produce carbon dioxide, this is our 'carbon footprint'. Scientists believe that this causes global warming and is destroying our environment. But do you know the best ways to save energy and reduce pollution?

❖ Saving fuel by using the bus or train, instead of the car.

❖ Recycling your cardboard, paper, cans, glass and plastic instead of throwing them away.

❖ Becoming a vegan.*

❖ Cycling or walking instead of travelling by car.

❖ Switching off computers, TVs, etc. at night so that you don't waste energy.

❖ Using energy-saving light bulbs.

❖ Turning your central heating down by 1°C.

❖ Going on holiday by train instead of flying.

A person who does not eat any animal products including milk and eggs.

Grammar Focus

Future with *will* and *going to*

8 Look at the photos. What do you think these people are protesting about?

9 (2.16) Read and listen to the extract from a TV news programme and answer the questions.

  1 Underline three reasons why Jamie Doyle thinks the new road is a bad thing.

  2 What are the protestors going to do? What are the police going to do?

News presenter: Now the latest news from Waytown where protestors want to stop the building of a new motorway. First, an interview with Jamie Doyle from the environmental group, Green Planet. Jamie, why are you against this road?

Jamie Doyle: A new road is bad for the environment and bad for the people of Waytown. We believe that it will create pollution and destroy local wildlife, and that it will also make life noisier and more dangerous for local families.

NP: So, what are you going to do to stop this road?

JD: It's very simple. We're going to stay here – we're not going to move. The builders plan to start work tomorrow but they won't be able to do anything.

NP: That was Jamie Doyle speaking a little earlier. Now let's go to our reporter in Waytown. Jane Fry, what's happening now?

Jane Fry: Well, things are getting very tense. About twenty protestors are refusing to move and about thirty riot police are moving slowly towards them. The police are obviously going to remove the protestors … oh and people are throwing objects at the police … ow! That nearly hit me! This is really dangerous … someone's going to get hurt!

---

10 a Circle the verbs with *going to* and *will* in the dialogue. Find one example of an intention and one example of a prediction.

  b Read *Grammar2know* to check your answers.

Grammar **2 know**

Future with *will* and *going to*

Intentions

a Use *going to* to talk about intentions:
*What **are you going to** do?*
We're going to stay here … we're not going to move.

Predictions

b Use *going to* for predictions based on evidence, or something we can see:
*The police are **going to** remove the protestors.*
(they're moving slowly towards the protestors)
*Someone's **going to** get hurt.*
(people are throwing objects at the police)

c Use *will* for predictions based on what we think or believe:
*We believe that the new road **will** create pollution.*
*I'm sure they **won't** be able to do anything.*

Use these phrases for predictions with *will*:
I think (that), I'm sure (that), I believe (that)

---

11 Complete the sentences with *will* or *going to* and the verbs in brackets.

  1 The new government _____ (improve) transport – they have some interesting plans.

  2 'Green Planet' believe that better public transport _____ (reduce) traffic.

  3 All our evidence shows that global warming _____ (increase) considerably.

  4 World leaders _____ (have) a big conference about the environment soon.

  5 Many people think that we _____ (have) milder winters because of global warming.

12 Read tasks 1–4 and make notes. Then discuss your answers in pairs.

  1 Use the prompts to make three predictions about life in twenty years' time.

> more/less traffic   people travel more/less
> people waste more/less energy

     I think there will be less traffic in twenty years' time, fuel will be too expensive.

  2 Tell your partner about three intentions you have for the next few years.

  3 Look at the sky outside and make a prediction about the weather in the next hour.

  4 Make a prediction about the weather next summer.

MINI WORKBOOK exercises 1–3 page 108

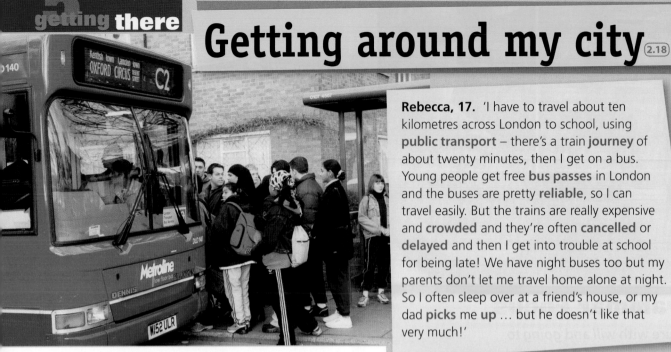

Getting around my city (2.18)

Rebecca, 17. 'I have to travel about ten kilometres across London to school, using **public transport** – there's a train **journey** of about twenty minutes, then I get on a bus. Young people get free **bus passes** in London and the buses are pretty **reliable**, so I can travel easily. But the trains are really expensive and **crowded** and they're often **cancelled** or **delayed** and then I get into trouble at school for being late! We have night buses too but my parents don't let me travel home alone at night. So I often sleep over at a friend's house, or my dad **picks** me **up** … but he doesn't like that very much!'

Vocabulary & Speaking
Transport and the environment

1 WORD RACE How many forms of transport can you write down in one minute? Which forms of transport on your list are the greenest/least green? Why?

2 Look at the photos and discuss the questions.
- What are the people doing? Which cities are they in?
- How easy is it to travel around your city/town?
- Which form of transport seems the greenest from the photos?

3 **a** In groups, decide which of these statements are true (✓) for your town.
1 ☐ People drive everywhere and don't use public transport very much.
2 ☐ The government encourages people to walk, cycle and use public transport.
3 ☐ Public transport is expensive and unreliable.
4 ☐ Some forms of public transport are free.
5 ☐ A lot of teenagers drive.
6 ☐ Traffic is not a big problem.

b Check your ideas with the rest of the class.

4 **a** Words **2** know (2.17) Check the words in blue in the texts. Then read about how three teenagers use transport in their city.

b Match the statements in exercise 3a to what the teenagers say.

1 Joel

5 Discuss the questions. Use the *Words2know*.
- What problems does each person have with transport? Do you have the same problems?
- Why do you think Californian teenagers aren't allowed to carry teenage passengers? Do you think this is fair or not?
- What is the government doing in each city to help the environment? What about in your town?

6 WRITING Write about your experiences with public transport, using the *Words2know* to help you. Include information about:
- your journey to school and any problems you have
- other problems you have with transport
- transport in your city, and how green it is.

MINI WORKBOOK exercise 8 page 109

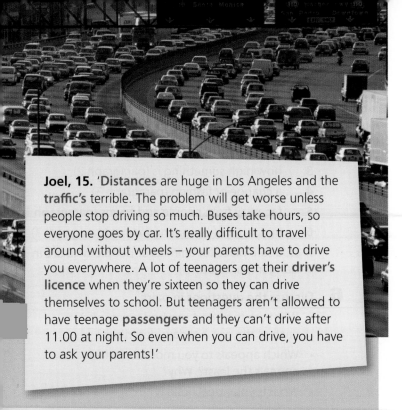

Joel, 15. 'Distances are huge in Los Angeles and the traffic's terrible. The problem will get worse unless people stop driving so much. Buses take hours, so everyone goes by car. It's really difficult to travel around without wheels – your parents have to drive you everywhere. A lot of teenagers get their **driver's licence** when they're sixteen so they can drive themselves to school. But teenagers aren't allowed to have teenage **passengers** and they can't drive after 11.00 at night. So even when you can drive, you have to ask your parents!'

Thierry, 16. 'There are a lot of problems with transport in Paris because of **traffic jams** and strikes … so people try to get around by themselves – they walk, they **cycle**, or they **rollerblade** … like me. The government encourage this because they want people to drive less. We have a lot of **cycle lanes** and there are special bicycles you can borrow to cycle around the city – they're called 'Velib'. When you reach your **destination**, you just get off and leave them! And Parisians are crazy about rollerblading, we have special rollerblade rides every Friday night and thousands of people **skate** around the city. We even have police officers on rollerblades!'

Grammar Focus

First conditional and future time clauses

7 Read the three texts above again. Then guess who said these things: (R) Rebecca, (J) Joel or (T) Thierry.

1. As soon as I'm sixteen, I'll learn to drive. ☑
2. I won't be able to drive my friends if I pass my driving test. ☐
3. I'll have to pay more for public transport when I'm eighteen. ☐
4. I'll be on time for school today unless the train is delayed. ☐
5. When I'm older, I'll use the night buses more. ☐
6. If I stop rollerblading, transport will be much more expensive. ☐

8 **a** Each sentence in exercise 7 has two clauses. <u>Underline</u> the verb in each clause.

b Are the sentences in exercise 7 about the present or the future? Read *Grammar2know* to check.

Grammar 2 know

First conditional

Use the first conditional to talk about possible future situations.

Form

if/unless + present simple, future simple:
*If I **stop** rollerblading, I **will** have to pay for transport.*

*I'**ll** be on time for school today **unless** the train **is** delayed.*

Future time clauses

After time expressions (*when, after, before, as soon as, until*), we also use the present simple to talk about the future:
*When I'**m** sixteen, I'**ll** start learning to drive.*

*I'**ll** have to pay more for public transport **after** I'**m** eighteen.*

9 Complete the sentences with the correct tense for future situations.

1. There (be) a lot more pollution after they (open) the new airport.
2. Until public transport (improve), most people (use) their cars.
3. People (not cycle) to work unless they (build) more cycle lanes.
4. As soon as the new road (open), traffic (get) worse.
5. If all the trains (be) cancelled, I (not be able to) go to school today!

10 Complete the sentences about yourself.

1. I (not) be) late home tonight unless …
   I'll be late home tonight unless my mum picks me up.
2. I (not) be) home by … o'clock unless …
3. I (not) learn) to drive when I …
4. I (not) walk) home from school unless …
5. I (be able to) relax more once …
6. I (not) go out) at the weekend if …
7. I (continue) learning English until I …

MINI WORKBOOK exercises 4–6 pages 108–109

getting there

39

Reading & Speaking

1 Put the holiday activities in order from 1 (most important) to 5 (least important). Compare your order with a partner.

- staying in a luxury hotel or villa ☐
- sightseeing ☐
- adventure ☐
- seeing exotic places and beautiful scenery ☐
- being green ☐

2 Look at the three pictures on page 41 and answer the questions.

- Describe what you see in each of the pictures. Is there anything surprising or unusual? Why?
- How do you think these places and objects are connected with holidays?

3 Read the text on page 41 quickly. Match the photos A–C to Simon's answers 1–3.

4 Read the text again and choose the correct answer.

1 Holiday pods
   a cannot be moved from one place to another.
   b do not damage the environment.
   c have to stay in the same place for fifteen years.
   d are a way of recycling the waste that tourists produce.

2 Carl Jenkins thinks that holidays pods
   a are bad for the environment.
   b are not really a new idea.
   c will eventually replace caravans.
   d are a very original idea.

3 The airship hotels
   a need to stop often.
   b travel faster than aeroplanes.
   c provide a more eco-friendly way to sightsee.
   d will be cheaper than travelling by plane.

4 Ecoteering is
   a a good way of relaxing.
   b a way of attracting more tourists to remote places.
   c becoming more and more popular with young people.
   d is very dangerous.

5 Laurence Ford
   a enjoyed all aspects of his holiday.
   b couldn't sleep because the wolves were so noisy.
   c went searching for wolves.
   d didn't enjoy his visit to the wolf sanctuary.

5 GUESSING MEANING FROM CONTEXT Find a word in the text that means:

1 … different possibilities (paragraph 1)
2 … completely new and different (paragraph 2)
3 … how high something is (paragraph 2)
4 … a change or fashion (paragraph 3)
5 … far away from people and towns (paragraph 3)
6 … in danger of becoming extinct (paragraph 3)
7 … a safe place for animals or people who are in danger (paragraph 3)

6 Discuss the questions in pairs.

- What are the good and bad points about each of the eco-holidays described?
- Which appeals to you most and which appeals the least? Why?
- What is your ideal holiday?

7 Read the postcard Laurence sent to his flatmates at college. What do you learn about his working holiday at the wolf sanctuary?

Hi guys!

Having an amazing time here in the New Mexico desert!!!! The wolves are awesome, and the people are really cool, too. We work eight and half hours a day – feeding the wolves and giving tours to visitors. At night you can camp in the desert, and at the weekend all volunteers travel somewhere together.

Hope all is well with you guys.

Take care and see you soon!

Laurence xx

Lizzie, Steve, Gemma and Will,
Flat 4, Seaview House,
New Rd,
Portsmouth.

8 WRITING Write a postcard. Imagine that you are on one of the holidays in the text. Include information about:

- the place/the other people
- how you spend your time
- whether you are enjoying yourself. Why? Why not?

✳ Future trends ECO-TOURISM (2.19)

Readers often ask us if travel will become more environmentally friendly in the future. We put your questions to our travel correspondent, Simon Lace, and look at some of the latest ideas.

A

B

1. ☐ *Will we be able to have luxury holidays in exotic places without damaging the environment? (Steve Southall, Manchester)*

SIMON: Building hotels and villas permanently affects the environment, that's why many holiday companies are looking for alternatives. One possible answer is luxury 'holiday pods'. You can assemble them anywhere in the world, from the South Pacific to the Sahara Desert, and they can remain in place for up to fifteen years. Then they can be packed up and moved to another location. The damage to the environment is almost zero: all the waste produced in the pods is collected and recycled. But some people don't believe there's anything particularly new in this. As travel writer Carl Jenkins has said, 'Lots of people already have similar pods, they're called caravans.'

2. ☐ *Will I be able to travel by air without producing carbon dioxide? (Kathy Price, USA)*

SIMON: Why not try a holiday on a helium-filled airship hotel? As we all know, air travel creates more carbon dioxide than any other form of travel but this revolutionary airship might change that. It will be able to travel for 3,100 miles without stopping, and combines the experience of travelling by cruise ship, hot air balloon and aeroplane. Yet it requires no fuel or runways. The engines use hydrogen and the airship travels at a lower speed and altitude than a normal plane, giving passengers the opportunity to sightsee from above. As the designers say, 'Passengers can see fantastic places without landing and buying a ticket.'

C

3. ☐ *What are the options for young people who care about the environment but also want adventure? (Neeta Madahar, London)*

SIMON: A big trend for young people is 'ecoteering': a combination of voluntary work and environmentally-friendly holiday. Choices include replanting tropical forests in India, working as a jungle tourist guide in remote parts of Cambodia, or working with endangered wild animals. According to student Laurence Ford, who spent two months working at a wolf sanctuary in New Mexico, USA, 'The whole experience was awesome. I formed a real bond with the wolves and I loved waking up to the sound of their howling!'

Whatever you decide to do, I think the days of choosing a holiday without thinking about the environment will soon be over. Eco-tourism is growing three times faster than any other kind of tourism!

DIRECTIONS

1 Read the online conversation between Lori and Greg and answer the questions.

1 What does Greg suggest?
2 Where and when do Lori and Greg decide to meet?

From Greg	19 Sep 15.01

Hi lori how r u? How abt that guided tour? Greg x

From Lori	19 Sep 15.07

Hi greg! Good idea! 2morrow maybe? Lori

From Greg	19 Sep 15.12

Gr8! Meet @ Scott Monument 1pm G xx

2 (2.20) Read the three conversations Lori had on the way to meet Greg and put each one in order. Then listen and check.

a ☐ **Man 1:** I can't find the Scott Museum.
b ☐ **Lori:** Oh, no problem. Thanks anyway. I'll ask someone else.
c ☐ **Man 1:** I have a map, maybe I can find it for you.
d ☑ **Lori:** Excuse me. How do I get to the Scott Museum, please?
e ☐ **Man 1:** Okay. Sorry I couldn't help.
f ☐ **Lori:** Can you find it on the map? I'm really late!

a ☐ **Lori:** Okay, and how do I get there?
b ☐ **Woman:** Sorry, do you mean the Scott Monument?
c ☐ **Woman:** Ah, yes, it's in Princes Street – next to the station.
d ☐ **Woman:** It's really easy. Go past the castle and straight on. Then go down the steps to the National Museum, turn right onto Princes Street and it's on your right.
e ☐ **Lori:** Excuse me, do you know the Scott Museum?
f ☐ **Lori:** Oh, yes! the Scott Monument.

a ☐ **Man 2:** No problem young lady. Watch the road!
b ☐ **Lori:** Oh yeah! There it is and there's Greg! Thanks!
c ☐ **Man 2:** Yes, it's just there opposite the station.
d ☐ **Lori:** The Scott Monument, I think that's its name.
e ☐ **Lori:** Excuse me, is the Scott Monument near here?
f ☐ **Man 2:** Sorry, what did you say?

3 (2.21) Listen and practise saying the *Phrases2know*.

Phrases **2** know

Asking for directions
Excuse me …
How do I get to the Scott Monument/there?
Do you know …?
I'm looking for …
Giving directions
At the traffic lights, turn left.
Cross the street opposite the bank.
It's five minutes from here.
It's just there/next to/opposite the station.
Go past the castle/and then/straight on until you get to the bridge.
Apologising and responding to an apology
Sorry I couldn't help.
No problem. Thanks anyway.
Thanking and responding to thanks
Thank you./Thanks very much.
You're welcome.

4 Look at the map on page 124. In pairs, ask for and give directions from the Scott Monument to:

CAN YOU DO IT IN ENGLISH?

- the National Gallery
- Palace of Holyroodhouse
- Waverley Station

Use the *Phrases2know* to help you.

A
Attract B's attention and ask how to get to … ↘
Thank B.

B
Give a positive response.
Give A directions.
Respond to A's thanks.

Lori gets lost on her way to meet Greg and has to ask for directions.

DESCRIPTION OF A PLACE

5  **Listen and choose the correct answer.**

1 Greg and Lori hear a noise coming from *the Castle/ the Scott Monument*.

2 People in Edinburgh know it's one o'clock because they *hear a gun/hear a bell*.

3 Sir Walter Scott was *a politician/a writer*.

4 The Royal Mile leads to *the Old Town/Parliament*.

5 Greg and Lori decide to visit *the Castle/the Old Town*.

6 **Lori looked at an internet site about Edinburgh. Read and find out:**

- how many people live in Edinburgh.
- which part of Scotland it is in.
- the names of two famous Edinburgh residents.
- what happens in the Old Town at the weekend.

Edinburgh is the capital city of Scotland. It's an important industrial, political and business centre, with a population of about 450,000 people, and it's also a busy tourist city. It's on the east coast of Scotland, on the river Forth.

There are many landmark buildings in the city such as Edinburgh Castle and the Scottish Parliament, as well as many interesting museums and art galleries. People sometimes call it 'The Athens of the North'.

Edinburgh is also an important centre for culture. The Edinburgh Festival takes place every July and attracts people from all over the world. Edinburgh is also famous as the home of well-known writers such as J.K. Rowling, who wrote Harry Potter, and Sir Walter Scott, who wrote many novels about Scottish life. There is a statue of him in the centre of the city, the Scott Monument.

The Old Town is a very good area for shopping. The streets are very narrow, and it's always crowded with tourists and shoppers, especially at weekends. There's also a street market on Saturday mornings where you can find all sorts of arts and crafts.

Edinburgh is a great place to visit, or to live. But if you come to visit, bring some warm clothes, because it can get cold, especially in the evening!

Phrases 2 know

Introducing the town or city and its location
Edinburgh is a busy city/town.
It has a population of one million.
It's in the north of/near the coast.

Describing famous buildings and monuments
There are many famous buildings such as …
You can see Holyrood Palace in Edinburgh.

Giving other reasons to visit the town/city
Edinburgh is also an important centre for …
It is famous as the home of the Edinburgh Festival.
There's also a street market.

Describing your favourite area
My favourite area is the port.
It's a very good area for shopping/night life.
The streets are narrow/wide/crowded/busy.

Concluding
I love/like Edinburgh because it's so beautiful.
It's a great place to live or to visit.
If you come to/visit Edinburgh, bring warm clothes.

7 **Think of a town you know well. Make notes using these headings:**

- introduction to the town and its location
- description of famous buildings and monuments
- other reasons why the town is famous
- the best part of the town and why you like it
- advice for visitors.

8 **Now write your description of a town. Use your notes from exercise 7, the *Phrases2know* and the text in exercise 6 to help you. Write about 200–250 words.**

6 meeting up

Grammar	Present perfect with *for* and *s...*
	Present perfect continuous
Vocabulary	Relationships
	Feelings
Functions	Starting and maintaining pol...
	conversations

Vocabulary & Listening

Social relationships

1 **a** WORD RACE Work in pairs. How many relationship words can you write down in one minute?

1 **Family:** *aunt, grandparents*

2 **Friends and acquaintances:** *classmate,*

b Check the *Words2know*. Add them to the correct list in exercise 1a.

Words 2 know (2.23)

next-door neighbour   distant cousin
ex-boyfriend   old school friend   stepsister
great-uncle   colleague   team mate
close friend   the family pet

2 **a** Look at the photos on Sophie's phone. Guess what her relationship is with them.

" *I think Harold and Joan are her grandparents.*

b (2.24) Listen and check your answers. Note down one more piece of information about each person.

Billy — the family pet — he's very lazy.

Compare your answers in pairs.

IMAGES

1 Billy   2 Ellie   3 George   4 Harold and Joan   5 Natalie

3 **a** Match the verb phrases in blue 1–11 to the explanations a–k below.

Words 2 know (2.25)

1 **adore** each other.
2 **got to know** each other on a school trip.
3 **fell out** on the school trip.
4 **split up** six months ago.
5 **doesn't get on with** Sophie any more.
6 **is going out with**
7 someone who Sophie **can't stand**.
8 **looked after** Sophie when she was little.
9 **have a good laugh** together.
10 **makes fun of** his partner a lot.
11 **keeps in touch with** Sophie online.

a ☐ are boyfriend and girlfriend
b ☐ hates
c ☐ doesn't have a good relationship
d ☐ love very much
e ☐ stays in contact
f ☐ ends a relationship
g ☐ makes jokes about
h ☐ had an argument
i ☐ have fun together
j ☐ took care of
k ☐ became friends

b Match the people 1–5 in exercise 2b with the phrases 1–11 in *Words2know*. There are three extra phrases.

4 **a** SPEAKING Work in pairs. Describe Sophie's relationship with each of the people in the photos, using the *Words2know*.

" *George is her ex-boyfriend. She went out with him …*

b Think of six people you know from exercise 1. Write sentences about them, using phrases from exercise 3a. Give reasons for what you say.

" *I can't stand my next-door neighbour — he's really rude.*

MINI WORKBOOK exercise 6 page 111

Grammar Focus

Present perfect with *for* and *since*

5 (2.26) **Match the questions 1–5 about Sophie's friends and family to answers a–f. There is one extra answer. Listen and check.**

1 [e] How long have you known your best friend Ellie?

2 ☐ Were you at school with Natalie for a long time?

3 ☐ How long did you go out with your ex-boyfriend, George?

4 ☐ Have you seen your old school friend Natalie recently?

5 ☐ How long have you had your cat Billy?

a We were together for about six months.

b We've had him for thirteen years, I think.

c They've been married since about 1960.

d Yes, we were in the same class at primary school for seven years.

e We've been friends since we started secondary school.

f No, I haven't seen her for ages.

6 a Look at answers a–f in exercise 5 and answer the questions.

1 Which situations are finished now? Which still continue?

2 Which use the present perfect and which use the past simple?

b Read *Grammar2know* and check your answers. Find an example of each rule in exercise 5.

7 Complete the sentences using *for* or *since* and the present perfect or past simple.

1 Billy isn't very well, he _hasn't eaten_ (not eat) anything __for__ three days.

2 I _____ (be) in the school basketball team _____ last Christmas.

3 I _____ (play) basketball _____ several years at primary school too, before I started secondary school.

4 My grandpa _____ (be) a gardener _____ forty years, but he's retired now.

5 My grandparents _____ (live) in their house _____ they got married.

6 George _____ (be) with his new girlfriend _____ three months now.

Grammar 2know

Present perfect and past simple

a Use the present perfect with *for* to describe situations and actions that started in the past and continue in the present:
We've had Billy for thirteen years. (we still have him now)

b Use the past simple with *for* to describe situations/actions that are now finished:
We went out together for a year. (we don't go out together now)

for and *since*

c Use *for* and *since* with the present perfect. *For* tells us how long the action continues:
for sixty years   for ten minutes

d *Since* tells us when the action started:
since last summer   since 2008

Questions with *How long*?

e Use *How long?* with both the present perfect and the past simple:
How long have you known Ellie? (you still know Ellie now)

How long did you go out with George? (you and George aren't going out now)

8 a (2.27) **Use the prompts to make questions with *how long*. Listen and check.**

1 live/is this area
How long have you lived in this area?

2 be/at primary school

3 know/your oldest friend

4 have/your school bag

5 be/your journey to school today

6 be/in this English lesson

b (2.27) **Listen to the questions again and write answers for yourself, using *for* or *since*. Ask and answer the questions in pairs.**

9 a Choose three people you know and prepare short talks about them, similar to Sophie's talks in exercise 2b:

❝ *This is Max. He's my oldest friend. I've known him for ten years. We met because we live in the same street. We get on really well because …*

b Present one person to the class.

MINI WORKBOOK exercises 1–2 page 110

meeting up

Reading & Vocabulary

1 Discuss the questions.

- Do you socialise online? Which chat rooms and social networking sites do you use?
- Have you ever had any problems with people online? What happened?

2 Read about problems that teenagers have had socialising online and answer the questions.

1 Who has Maya met online, and what does this person want?

2 Why is her friend worried? Why is Maya worried?

3 How did Andy meet Alex?

4 What is the problem with Alex?

5 Who is the victim of an online bully?

6 How did the bullying start?

3 Match the readers' answers below to the problems. Which problem has two answers?

Answer 1

You're too nice! He's just a melodramatic teenager and it's not your problem. He'll be fine – stop worrying!!!

Answer 2

You're crazy! NEVER meet up with people you meet online – it's a stupid, dangerous thing to do!!!

Answer 3

What has this boy been writing in his emails? Is it really so terrible? Words can't hurt you – just delete the emails and texts and ignore him. He'll soon get bored!

Answer 4

If you really want to meet him, be very careful. Take your friend with you to check that he's really the person in the photos. Always meet in a public place, and tell other people where you're going and when you'll be home.

4 SPEAKING Discuss the questions.

- What does each person in exercise 3 advise? Are they sympathetic or not?
- What do you think Andy, Maya and Jasmine should do?

❝ I agree with answer 1 …

I don't think Maya should …

shareyourproblems.com ⟨2.30⟩

friends | relationships | index

problem

I've been talking to this boy, Jason, online for three months, and today he's asked me to meet him. I'm really excited about the idea because he looks really nice in his photos, but my best friend's worried about it. She says he might not really be the person in the photos. But if I don't meet him, Jason might not be interested in me any more. What should I do?

Maya, 15

problem

Not long ago, I met a friend of a friend, Alex, at a party. He seemed fine and since the party I've been chatting to him on Facebook quite a lot. But he's always depressed about something – he hasn't got a girlfriend, nobody loves him, the usual stuff. At first I felt sympathetic but I've been getting annoyed with him lately. I don't really know him and I'm bored of his problems. I've deleted him on Facebook but I now feel guilty about it. What if he's seriously depressed?

Andy, 17

5 Check the *Words2know*. Which people in the texts do they describe?

depressed – Alex

Words 2 know ⟨2.28⟩

depressed   embarrassed   excited   annoyed
frightened   guilty   jealous   sympathetic
nervous   upset   bored   worried

6 a ⟨2.29⟩ Listen to six situations. What emotions are the people feeling?

❝ Claudia probably feels nervous and worried.

b ⟨2.29⟩ Listen again. How would you feel in these situations? Use the *Words2know* in your answers.

❝ I usually feel worried before an exam …

MINI WORKBOOK exercises 7–8 page 111

I went out with a boy from school for a few weeks, but I haven't been seeing him recently, because I've realised that he isn't a very nice person, and he's become really jealous. In the last few days he's been sending me really nasty text messages and emails – sometimes he sends me twenty or thirty a day. I feel upset and nervous every time I get a text or email. I can't tell my parents because I'm frightened they'll stop me going on the computer, and I'm embarrassed about the things that he's been writing in the emails. I don't know what to do.

Jasmine L

Grammar Focus

Present perfect continuous

7 **a** **Read sentences 1–6. Who said them?**

1 I**'ve been talking** to this boy online for three months.

2 Today he**'s asked me** to meet him.

3 What **has** this boy **been writing** in his emails?

4 I **haven't been seeing** him recently.

5 I**'ve been getting** annoyed with him lately.

6 I**'ve deleted** him on Facebook.

b **Which verbs in exercise 7a are present perfect simple and which are present perfect continuous? Read Grammar2know to check.**

Grammar **2 know**

Present perfect continuous and present prefect simple

Both tenses describe actions that started in the past and are still important in the present.

The present perfect simple is used for single completed actions:

I've deleted him on Facebook.

(one completed action)

The present perfect continuous emphasises that actions are repeated or continue for a period of time:

I've been talking to this boy online for three months.
He's been sending me nasty emails.

(a repeated action)

Form of present perfect continuous:
have/has + been + verb + ing

+	–	?
I've been talking …	I haven't been talking …	Have you been talking … ?
He's been talking …	He hasn't been talking …	Has he been talking … ?

Time expressions with present perfect continuous:

How long …? for, since, all day/week, lately, recently.

8 **Complete the sentences with the correct tense.**

1 Anna (go out) with Paul for six months.

Anna has been going out with Paul for six months.

2 I (met) Ben's new girlfriend – she's really nice.

3 I (not go) to the gym much recently, and I feel really unfit.

4 (you hear) the news? Gemma and Alex (split up).

5 My cousin's (learn) to drive for over three years, but she (not pass) her test yet!

9 **a** **Write the names of five of the following.**

1 a book you are reading

2 someone you know who can drive *Peter*

3 a language you are learning

4 a couple who are going out together *Mateo & Maria*

5 the street where you live street *New Road*

6 an extra class you go to

7 a sport you play

b **In pairs, swap your lists. Take turns to ask and answer questions with *How long*?**

" *How long has Peter been driving?*
Since last summer, I think.

MINI WORKBOOK exercises 3–5 pages 110–111

meeting up

Reading & Listening

1 Look at the photo. What do you think the people are talking about?

2 Read the introduction to *Strangers on a Train* and answer the questions.

1 What kind of novel is it and who is it by?

2 When was it published?

3 Where is it set?

4 What do you know about the main character?

5 Which famous director made the book into a film?

> **STRANGERS ON A TRAIN** is a crime thriller by the American novelist Patricia Highsmith, published in 1950, and set in the USA. The main character, Guy, is separated from his wife, and now wants to marry another girl, Anne. His wife, Miriam, won't divorce him. Guy has just got into a train compartment. The director Alfred Hitchcock made a famous film of the book in 1951.

3 Read extract 1. Tick (✓) true and cross (✗) false. Correct the false information.

1 ☐ Guy and Bruno are travelling to the same place.

2 ☐ Bruno is an architect.

3 ☐ Guy is travelling on business and Bruno is going on holiday.

4 ☐ Bruno gets on well with his mother.

5 ☐ Bruno gets on well with his father.

6 ☐ Guy left his wife a few years ago.

4 Read extract 1 again and answer the questions in pairs. <u>Underline</u> the parts of the text that give you the answers.

1 What are Guy's first impressions of Bruno?

2 Does he want to get involved in a conversation with him?

3 Do you think Bruno comes from a rich or poor family?

4 How would you describe Bruno's relationship with his mother?

5 What problems does Bruno have with his father?

6 Is Guy comfortable about discussing his life with Bruno?

7 What do you think of Bruno, by the end of this extract? Why?

(2.31)

STRANGERS ON A TRAIN

EXTRACT 1

Guy opened his book but his mind wandered after half a page. There was a young man opposite him, asleep. He had an interesting face, though Guy did not know why. It looked neither young nor old, neither intelligent nor entirely stupid. His skin was smooth as a girl's.

Guy moved in his seat and accidentally touched the foot of the young man. He watched as his eyes opened.

'Sorry,' Guy murmured.

'It's all right,' the other said. He sat up. 'Where are we?'

'Getting into Texas.'

The young man brought a small bottle from his pocket and offered it to Guy.

'No, thanks,' Guy said.

'Where are you going?' asked the young man with a smile.

'Metcalf,' Guy said.

'Oh. Nice town, Metcalf. On business?'

'Yes.'

'What business?'

Guy looked up reluctantly from his book. 'Architect.'

'Oh,' with interest. 'You build houses and things?'

'Yes.'

'Let me introduce myself.' He half stood up. 'Bruno. Charles Anthony Bruno.'

Guy shook his hand briefly. 'Guy Haines.'

'Pleased to meet you. Do you live in New York?'

'Yes.'

"I live in Long Island. I'm going to Santa Fe for a little vacation. Have you ever been to Santa Fe?'

Guy shook his head.

Later on, Guy and Bruno have dinner and start to get drunk together.

'What are you building in Metcalf, Guy?' Bruno asked, his mouth full of food.

'Nothing,' Guy said. 'My mother lives there.'

5 **a** Later on, Bruno suggests a crime. Guess what it is. Compare ideas with the class.

Perhaps he wants to ...

b (2.32) Listen to extract 2 and answer the questions.

• What is the plan? Did you guess correctly?

• Why is it a 'perfect crime'?

• How does Guy respond?

6 **a** (2.33) Check the words in the box. Then listen to extract 3.

> amusement park   rides   lake   island   throat

'Oh. Do you get on with your mother okay?'
Guy said that he did.
'Oh. I get on okay with my mother too,' Bruno said.
'She's coming to Santa Fe in a few days. We have a lot of fun together sitting around, playing golf. We even go to parties together.' He laughed. 'Do you think that's strange?'
'No,' said Guy.
'I have to ask for a hundred dollars now and then from my mother. My father doesn't give me any money because he says I don't want to work, but that's a lie.' Bruno put his hands in his pockets. 'If my father had a nice quiet son like you everyone would be happy.'
'Why do you think I'm nice and quiet?'
'I mean you chose a profession. Me, I don't feel like working.' Bruno laughed again.
'My father still hopes I'll enter his business. My father doesn't like me. He doesn't like anybody. He doesn't like anything but money. Sometimes I'm so angry with him I want to kill him. Did you ever want to murder somebody, Guy?'
Guy wasn't listening. He was thinking about Anne and Miriam. It was all mixed up in his head.
'Are you married, Guy?'
'No, er yes. Well I'm separated. I left three years ago,' Guy said. He didn't want to tell Bruno these things.
'Why is that, Guy?'
'I think we were too young ...'
'Do you love her?'
Guy didn't answer this.

b (2.33) In pairs, answer as many questions as you can. Listen again and complete your answers.

1 Where is Bruno going and why?
2 How does Bruno feel towards Miriam?
3 Where does Bruno go when he arrives in Metcalf?
4 Who comes out of the house?
5 Where does he follow Miriam and her friends to?
6 What happens after they've had an ice-cream?
7 When he speaks to Miriam, is she alone?
8 What happens next?

7 a In groups, decide how Guy responds to what Bruno does, and how the story ends. Compare ideas with the class.

b The book and the film of *Strangers on a Train* end differently. Read both endings on page 135. Was your ending more similar to the book, or the film?

8 You are going to act out a conversation in pairs. Read the instruction card and then spend a few minutes inventing interesting information.

CAN YOU DO IT IN ENGLISH?

Imagine! You are fifteen years older than you are now and have a new, completely different life! You are currently living or staying in the USA and meet another English-speaking foreigner on a train or plane. Invent the following:
• a career that is very glamorous or very unusual
• an interesting personal life – hobbies, family
• where you live, and why you are travelling
• other details!

9 (2.34) Listen and complete the *Phrases2know*.

Phrases 2 know

Having a polite conversation with a stranger
Starting a conversation
1 Excuse me, do you mind if I **a** _____ .
2 Sorry to bother you but **b** _____ ?
3 Let me introduce myself, I'm **c** *Anna Brown* .
4 Pleased to meet you.

Asking polite questions
5 I hope you don't mind me asking but **d** _____ ?
6 Which part of **e** _____ do you come from?
7 How long have you been living **f** _____ ?
8 What do you do for a living?
9 How long have you been working **g** _____ ?
10 Do you have a family?

Responding politely
11 And how about you?
12 Really, how **h** _____ !
13 Sorry, I didn't catch what you said.

10 a Write the start of the conversation, using the *Phrases2know*. In pairs, practise your conversation and then continue for as long as you can.

b Act out the conversation in front of the class. Whose conversation did you like best? Whose continued for the longest?

meeting up

activestudy3 (EXAMS)

Vocabulary

ACTIVE STUDY | Learn collocations

1 Choose the words a–c that can complete each phrase 1–6. There are two correct answers for each.

1 waste _____
   (a) energy (b) fuel c the environment
2 recycle _____
   a pollution b waste c glass
3 switch on/off _____
   a the computer b fuel c the lights
4 protect _____
   a wildlife b the environment c energy
5 reduce _____
   a pollution b carbon emissions c the heating

ACTIVE STUDY | Learn words in groups

2 Complete the text with the words a–h below. There is one extra word.

> a cancelled b crowded c reliable d distance
> e licence f pass g transport ✓ h traffic

What a day!

I use public ¹ _transport_ a lot. The buses in my city are ² _____ and a bus ³ _____ is not very expensive. But yesterday there was some important political event with a lot of visitors and everything was wrong. The main streets were closed, and everywhere else there were terrible ⁴ _____ jams. Many buses were ⁵ _____ and the rest were so ⁶ _____ it was difficult to breathe. A lot of people were late for school. My friend who's just got his driver's ⁷ _____ was two hours late, because he tried to drive. In fact, the only people who came on time were the ones who cycle to school.

3 Match sentences 1–6 to the reasons a–f.

1 ☑ Sophie's really depressed.
2 ☐ I've never been so embarrassed in all my life.
3 ☐ Miss Ross looks really annoyed.
4 ☐ The children are very disappointed.
5 ☐ Luke is terribly nervous.
6 ☐ Charlie's very jealous.

a Emily's been dancing with another guy.
b He thinks he's been learning the wrong things for the exam!
c I've done something really silly.
d She's split up with her boyfriend *and* lost her job!
e The school trip has been cancelled.
f Tom has been rude to her.

ACTIVE STUDY | Notice sentence stress

4 a PRONUNCIATION (2.35) Listen to the sentences and underline the stressed part of each phrasal verb.

1 They **fell <u>out</u>** after the party.
2 They **split up** two weeks ago.
3 I don't **get on with** him any more.
4 She's **going out with** a very nice guy.
5 My little brother's ill and I have to **look after** him.

b (2.35) Listen again and repeat.

Grammar

5 Choose the correct verb form to complete the text.

Holiday of a lifetime

I ¹ ___ my best friend Alfie since we were five. We ² _____ to primary school together for six years. Now we're in different schools, but we keep in touch. If everything goes well, we ³ _____ on a cycling trip around Europe this summer. We ⁴ _____ this trip for a year. We ⁵ _____ all the equipment. As soon as school ⁶ _____ , we'll get on our bikes and be off! We're going to Normandy first. If we ⁷ _____ it there, we'll stay for a week. We'll camp in a tent unless it ⁸ _____ . I can't wait!

1 a know   b knew   (c) 've known
2 a went   b have gone   c have been
3 a go   b 'll go   c are going
4 a have   b plan   c 've been
   planned   planning
5 a 've already b already   c 've already
   prepared   prepared   been preparing
6 a will finish b finish   c finishes
7 a like   b likes   c will like
8 a will rain b doesn't rain   c rains

6 Complete the second sentence so that it means the same as the first.

1 Grace started going out with Patrick five months ago.

Grace _has been going out_ with Patrick for five months.

2 I've lived in Budapest from the day of my birth.

I've lived in Budapest _____ born.

3 There may be traffic jams on the roads tomorrow. Then we'll cycle to school.

If there _____ on the roads tomorrow, we'll cycle to school.

4 I won't come if she doesn't invite me.

I won't come unless _____ me.

5 He'll get home and he'll switch on his computer at once.

He'll switch on his computer as _____ home.

Listening **Skills**

ACTIVE STUDY | Listen for specific information

7 (2.36) Listen to a radio talk about how to make a relationship a success. Choose the best answer.

1 The first piece of advice is to

a look after your relationship.

b take care of yourself.

c try to look more attractive.

d avoid being bored.

2 To get to know your partner better, Helen advises you to find out

a about his/her favourite bands.

b about his/her long-term plans.

c how he/she feels about different things.

d if he/she really likes you.

3 You should talk about your feelings

a to help you understand them.

b when you fall out.

c when you think he/she doesn't care about you.

d without making him/her feel bad.

4 If you and your partner have fun together,

a it's good for your health.

b the relationship will feel more important.

c you can make fun of the other person.

d you have a better chance of staying together.

5 Choose the best title for this talk.

a Four Ways to Make a Relationship Work

b Getting to Know Each Other

c You Don't Have to Split Up

d Finding the Perfect Boyfriend

Speaking **Skills**

8 In pairs, act out the following roleplay, using the *Phrases2know* from page 42.

> **A:** You're a tourist visiting your town. You're looking for a building/monument (decide which one).
> • Ask where it is.
> • Ask the way.
> • Thank the person who helped you.

> **B:** You're in your home town. A tourist asks you for directions.
> • Say where the place is.
> • Give directions to get there.
> • Respond politely.

9 Look at the photos of people going on holiday using different means of transport. Compare and contrast them. Include the following points:

• the advantages and disadvantages of the different means of transport

• how you think the people are feeling

• which way of travelling you think will be more popular in the future

• your favourite ways of travelling.

SKILLS STRATEGIES back cover

7
fast food

Grammar	The passive
	Causative *have*
Vocabulary	Food and cooking
	Diet and health
Functions	Requests and offers

Grammar Focus

The passive

1 Which fast foods are most popular with teenagers in your country? Which do you like?

2 Read the fast food facts. Tick (✓) true and cross (✗) false.

1 ☐ The 'Pizza Margherita' was invented in the USA.

2 ☐ Coca-Cola™ was a big success immediately.

3 ☐ The average Mexican drinks more Coca-Cola™ than the average American.

4 ☐ People who eat a lot of fast food are generally slimmer than other people.

5 ☐ Fast food creates a lot of rubbish.

3 Discuss the questions.

• Is it a good or bad thing that fast food is spreading around the world?

• Do you agree with the 'slow food' campaign?

4 Look at the verbs in bold in the text. Which are passive and which are active?

5 Read *Grammar2know* and complete the table with the verbs from exercise 4.

Grammar 2know

The passive

Use the passive when the action is the most important thing in the sentence, not the doer:

*A billion drinks **are sold** every day.*
(It doesn't matter who sells them.)
*Food **should be grown** locally.*
(Obviously farmers grow it.)

To say who does the action we use *by* + person:
*Coca-Cola™ was invented in 1886 **by Dr Pemberton**.*

Form: correct form of *be* + past participle

	active	passive
present simple	*drink*	*are sold*
past simple		
present continuous		
present perfect		
modal		

fast food ... fast facts!

Ten things you didn't know about fast food ⓷.5

○ A kind of pizza **was eaten** in Ancient Greece, although the modern pizza was only invented in the nineteenth century.

○ The first 'Pizza Margherita' was prepared for King Umberto and Queen Margherita of Italy when they **visited** Naples in 1889. They loved it!

○ Coca-Cola™ was invented by Dr John Pemberton, in Atlanta USA, in 1886. In the first year, about eight drinks a day were sold.

○ Today over a billion drinks of Coca-Cola™ **are sold** every day. Mexicans **drink** the most Coca-Cola™ in the world: 533 drinks per person, per year!

○ On average, a person who eats two fast food meals a week weighs five kilos more than a person who eats one or less.

○ Sales of fizzy drinks **are going down** in the USA, but more drinks **are being sold** in the developing world.

○ The first McDonald's restaurant was opened in California in 1940. Today there are 32,000 McDonalds around the world, and 58 million customers are served every day.

○ Since 1992, over 1,000 McDonald's restaurants **have been opened** in China.

○ Around twenty-five grams of plastic packaging is used in a fast food meal. Most of this packaging is not recycled.

○ The Italians **have started** a 'slow food' campaign Campaigners believe that people **should eat** local specialities, and that food **should be grown** locally.

6 (3.1) Underline the correct answer. Listen and check.

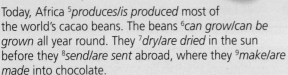
The dark side of chocolate

Chocolate ¹*makes/is made* from cacao beans. These ²*originally find/were originally found* in South America, and chocolate ³*drank/was drunk* by the Aztecs for hundreds of years, before it ⁴*brought/was brought* to Spain, in the sixteenth century.

Today, Africa ⁵*produces/is produced* most of the world's cacao beans. The beans ⁶*can grow/can be grown* all year round. They ⁷*dry/are dried* in the sun before they ⁸*send/are sent* abroad, where they ⁹*make/are made* into chocolate.

However, there is a dark side to the chocolate trade. In the last few years, African farmers ¹⁰*have found /have been found* it difficult to make money, because they ¹¹*are not paying/are not being paid* much for their product. As a result, many African children ¹²*have sold/have been sold* to cacao farms as slaves, where they work in terrible conditions. However, more and more customers ¹³*are buying/are being bought* 'fairtrade'* chocolate, and campaigners ¹⁴*hope/are hoped* that working conditions on cacao farms will get better soon.

*'fair trade' companies promise to pay a good price to their producers.

7 a Make true sentences in the passive using the prompts and your own ideas.

❝ *Hamburgers weren't eaten in this country a hundred years ago.*

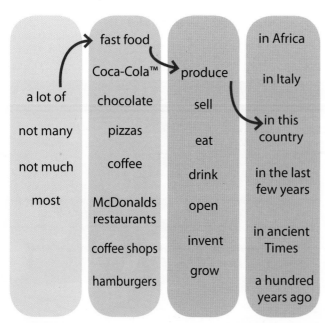

	fast food		in Africa
	Coca-Cola™	produce	in Italy
a lot of	chocolate	sell	
not many	pizzas	eat	in this country
not much	coffee	drink	in the last few years
most	McDonalds restaurants	open	
	coffee shops	invent	in ancient Times
	hamburgers	grow	a hundred years ago

b (3.2) Listen to what other students said.

MINI WORKBOOK exercises 1–3 page 112

Vocabulary&Listening
Preparing food

8 Look at the cover of a cookbook and discuss the questions.

- What kind of recipes does the cookbook contain?
- What dishes can you see in the photos? What are the ingredients, do you think?
- Can you cook your favourite snacks?

9 a Words 2 know (3.3) Check the words in blue. Put the instructions for each recipe in the correct order.

Quick smoothie
- ☐ **Pour** in the orange juice and **mix** with the fruit.
- ☐ **Add** some ice and **serve** immediately.
- ☐ **Blend** with an **electric blender**.
- ☐ **Peel** the mango and pineapple, **chop** and place in a **bowl**.

Fast pizza
- ☐ **Spread** the tomato paste onto the pizza base.
- ☐ **Grill** for about ten minutes, or until the cheese **melts**.
- ☐ **Slice** the pepperoni and onions and put them on top.
- ☐ **Add** some **grated** cheese.

b (3.4) Listen and check.

c Memorise the instructions for one of the recipes. Test each other in pairs.

MINI WORKBOOK exercise 6 page 113

Vocabulary & Listening

Nutrition and health

1 Discuss the questions.

- What kind of health problems are caused by eating too much fast food?
- Do you think people in the past ate more healthily than we do? Why? Why not?

2 Look at the photos and read about the TV series, *A Taste of the Past*. Answer the questions.

- What happens in each week's programme?
- Who are Sadie, James, Jackie and Steve, and what kind of experience did they have?

3 **Words 2 know** (3.6) Check the words in blue. Listen to part 1 of a TV series and complete the table about what rich people and poor people ate in the Elizabethan diet.

	Rich people	Poor people
vitamins	✗	✓
fibre		
protein		
fat		
alcohol		
caffeine		

4 **Words 2 know** (3.7) Listen to part 2 and tick the things that happened to the Lawrences.

- ☐ They **put on weight**.
- ☐ They **lost weight**.
- ☐ They **had headaches**.
- ☐ They didn't **have any energy**.
- ☐ They **felt sick**.
- ☐ They got **skin diseases**.
- ☐ They **felt fit** and **healthy**.

5 (3.8) Listen to both parts again and answer the questions.

1 Which of these Elizabethan dishes does Martina mention?
  ☐ live frog pie ☐ roasted peacock
  ☐ baked blackbird ☐ liver and heart

2 Why did poor Elizabethan people have a more balanced diet than rich people?

3 Why didn't rich people eat vegetables?

4 Why did children drink beer?

5 Why did Sadie lose weight during the programme?

6 Why did Sadie's mum get headaches?

7 In what way was the Elizabethan diet similar to a modern fast food diet?

6 Would you like to try Elizabethan food? Why? Why not?

I'd like to try Elizabethan food because they ate lots of meat.

MINI WORKBOOK exercise 7 page 113

T V Listings

Programmes >Food >A Taste of the Past

A Taste of the Past

Many experts are worried about the modern diet, but was it any better in the past? Each week in *A Taste of the Past*, volunteers try food from a different period of history, and find out how it compares with what they normally eat. In this week's programme, teenage fast food fans Sadie and James Lawrence, and their parents Jackie and Steve, experience Elizabethan food for two weeks.

Grammar Focus

have something done

7 Before the TV programme, the Lawrences had a lot of health checks. Read a description of the checks and find one mistake.

> Sadie and her family had their health checked carefully before they appeared on *A Taste of the Past*, because it was important that they were fit and healthy. Sadie had her blood pressure taken, she had her heart and liver checked, she had her ears pierced, and she was weighed. Luckily, Sadie and all her family were in good shape.

8 Read the text again. Who checked Sadie's heart, Sadie or someone else? Read *Grammar2know* and check your answer.

Grammar **2 know**

have something done

Use *have* + object + past participle when someone does something for us but we do not say who:

The doctor checked Sadie's heart. > *Sadie **had** her heart **checked.***

The jeweller pierced your ears. > *You **had** your ears **pierced.***

Form and tenses

Present continuous: *Sadie **isn't having** her ears **pierced.***

Present perfect: *My granny **has had** a lot of tests **done.***

going to: *Am I **going to have** my blood pressure **taken?***

will/won't: *You'll **have** your heart **checked.***

9 Use the prompts in A to say one thing you have done and one thing you don't have done in the places in B.

A

eyes/test   teeth/whiten hair/cut
legs/wax clothes/clean shoes/repair

B

the optician's   the dentist's
the hairdresser's   the drycleaner's
the cobbler's   the beautician's

❝ *At the optician's you have your eyes tested but you don't have your teeth whitened.*

10 Use the ideas in brackets to write sentences in the correct tense about the people in the pictures.

Last summer Will decided to change his image so he:
• (ear/pierce) • (hair/dye) • (a tattoo/do)
He had his ear pierced.

Chloe is going on her dream holiday tomorrow. So this afternoon she:
• (nails/do) • (legs/wax) • (hair/restyled)

Max's car was in a bad state, but now it is looking good because he:
• (windscreen/mend) • (engine/check)
• (whole car/clean)

MINI WORKBOOK exercises 4–5 pages 112–113

Reading & Speaking

1 Do you buy snacks in the street very often? What are your favourites?

2 Look at the photos. What snacks are being sold, and which country do you think they are from?

3 Check the *Words2know*. Then find which food in the text they describe. There are two extra adjectives.

Words 2 know (3.9)

sour   crispy   tender   grilled   fried
spicy   sweet   savoury   rich   boiled

4 Read the text and <u>underline</u> the ingredients of these snacks, how they are cooked and what they are served with.

French fries

Pho soup   Tacos

Harira   Pie floaters

5 Which snacks in the text sound tasty? Which sound disgusting? Use phrases from the text to explain your opinion.

6 Read *Active Study*.

ACTIVE STUDY

Guess meaning from context

You can sometimes guess what a word means from the words round it:

*The food **stalls** in the streets of Ho Chi Minh City open early in the morning and stay busy until late, selling snacks to hungry **passers-by.***

A 'stall' sells things, so it is probably some kind of shop. It is in the street and sells food, so we can guess what kind of shop it is.

Sometimes the actual words help. 'Passers-by' buy the food, so they must be people. The words tells us exactly what kind of people they are: the people who 'pass by'.

(3.11)

Street food around the world: the original fast food!

1 BELGIUM: Home of French Fries

You can find French fried <u>potatoes</u> all over the world, but as Belgians will tell you, they, not the French, invented this popular street food, back in the seventeenth century. The Belgian city of Antwerp has the world's only French fries museum. Crispy French fries, <u>eaten</u> from a **paper cone** <u>with salt and plenty of mayonnaise</u> are the Belgians' favourite snack. They are sold at special kiosks all over major towns. The secret of perfect French fries is that <u>they are fried not once, but twice, in hot oil</u> – the first time to cook the inside, and second time to give a perfect, golden outside.

2 VIETNAM: Soup for breakfast

The food stalls in the streets of Ho Chi Minh City, Vietnam, open early in the morning and stay busy until late at night, selling snacks to hungry passers-by. The most famous dish is pho*, a noodle soup with slices of tender beef or chicken and a variety of vegetables. It's usually eaten for breakfast – many Vietnamese people say they cannot start the day without this delicious savoury snack! Many Vietnamese live and work abroad, and pho has been exported all over the world. There are now **chains** of pho restaurants in the United States, Australia and Canada.

* pronounced /fɜʊ/

3 MOROCCO: Food as theatre

Street food in the main square of Marrakesh, Morocco is like an exciting performance. As the sun sets at the end of the day, street sellers set up their **charcoal** grills and the air is filled with smoke and delicious smells of cooking. Crowds of locals and tourists sit on wooden **benches** and eat off paper plates, surrounded by the sights, smells and tastes of African culture: *harira*, for example, a rich soup made with lamb and spices. Or how about sheep's head or tiny boiled snails, served with a **toothpick**?

4 AUSTRALIA: Fancy a pie floater?

Feeling hungry? No visit to South Australia is complete without trying the local speciality – a pie floater. They are traditionally sold at roadside kiosks, some of which stay open all night. It consists of a meat pie floating (usually upside down) in a thick green pea soup. Finally, the pie is covered with plenty of bright red tomato ketchup. Enjoy!

5 MEXICO: The food of the people

It's lunchtime in Mexico City and everywhere people are queuing up for Mexico's favourite fast food – *tacos*. They're soft corn pancakes served with a variety of **fillings**, such as chicken, beef or vegetables, and then covered with spicy sauce, lettuce and sour cream. 'The best Mexican food is the food of the people,' says José Iturriaga, who has written more than twenty books on Mexican food. And the city's best taco? 'It's a taco made from cows' eyes,' says José. 'It's extraordinary.'

7 GUESS MEANING FROM CONTEXT. Look at the words in bold in the text. Match each word to an explanation below. Use *Active Study* to help you.

1 Fuel used to cook food outside. (on barbeques)
2 A small stick you use to remove food from between your teeth.
3 Food you put inside something, for example a sandwich.
4 A group of similar restaurants owned by one company.
5 Paper folded so that it can hold food.
6 A simple seat for several people, usually found outside.

8 Discuss the questions with the class.

- What 'street food' is popular in your country?
- Are there any local specialities?
- What are the ingredients and how is it made?
- What's your favourite?

9 **a** Work in pairs, A and B. Choose a local dish or street snack to discuss. Read the instruction cards and prepare your ideas, using the *Phrases2know*.

CAN YOU DO IT IN ENGLISH?

A is an English-speaking visitor. You are going to ask questions about the local dish.

B You are going to explain the local dish to the visitor, and answer his/her questions.

Phrases 2 know (3.10)

Asking about typical dishes

Have you tried harira yet?
What's it made of?
How is it cooked?
What does it taste like?
Where is it sold?
When is it usually eaten?

Describing dishes

It's a kind of pie/pancake/soup.
The main ingredients are fish and rice.
The potatoes are grilled/boiled/fried.
It tastes spicy/sour.
It's sold at kiosks.
It's usually eaten at home.
People eat if for lunch in the winter.

Responding

It sounds delicious/interesting/nice!
I'd like to try it!

b Act out the conversation. You can start like this:

" *Have you tried harira yet?*
No, what's that?
It's a kind of soup. It's made of....

MINI WORKBOOK exercise 8 page 113

fast food

REAL TIME

REQUESTS AND OFFERS

LORI, Nick and Kate are getting ready for an audition for a new drummer.

1 (3.12) **Listen to the conversation between Lori, Kate and Nick and answer the questions.**

1 Who is going to arrive at two o'clock?
2 What does Kate ask Nick to get from the van?
3 What does Kate ask Nick to move?
4 Does Lori do anything to help?

2 (3.12) **Listen to the conversation again. Put the expressions in bold in the _Phrases2know_ box:**

Lori: Okay, we've got ten minutes to get ready. Henry's going to be here at about two o'clock so we need to move some chairs.

Kate: Right.

Lori: Oh, my phone's ringing. Just a minute. Hello? Oh, hi!!

Kate: Okay, move the chairs – I'm sure Nick will help. NICK?

Nick: Just a minute, this is really heavy!

Kate: Oh! Be careful with that!

Nick: **Shall I** put it over here?

Kate: Yes, **please**. Actually, no, **can you** put it over there for now? Right, thanks a lot. Oh, Nick, **would you mind** getting my saxophone from the van?

Nick: Sure, **no problem**. Is there anything else?

Kate: … oh, and the microphones!

Nick: Okay, fine.

Kate: Thanks, Nick. That's **very kind of you**. And after that, **could you** move those chairs?

Nick: Yes, all **right**.

Lori: All right, bye! Okay, guys. Sorry about that. **Do you want me to** do something?

Kate: No, it's **all right**. Nick's doing everything. Who was that on the phone?

Phrases 2know

Requests and offers

Making a request

Shall I put it over there?
_____ getting my saxophone?
_____ move the chairs?

Responding to a request

Yes/Sure, _____ /okay./Yes, all _____ .

Making an offer

_____ put it over here?
_____ do something?

Responding to an offer

Yes, _____ /No, it's _____ .

Thanking

Thanks a lot.
That's _____ .

3 (3.13) **Listen to the _Phrases2Know_ and practise the intonation.**

4 **In pairs, take turns to act out the conversation. Use the _Phrases2know_.**

You need to arrange a room for a party. Think of some things you need to do, e.g. move tables and prepare music.

A

Ask your friend to come and help you move something and to organise the music.

Thank your friend and respond to his/her offer to help at the party.

B

Respond positively. Offer more help.

Respond and ask if you can help later.

CAN YOU DO IT IN ENGLISH?

5 **(3.14)** Listen and tick (✓) true, cross (✗) false and write (?) if there is no information.

1 ☐ Lori and Nick are both very enthusiastic about the new drummer.
2 ☐ They have found a new guitarist for the group.
3 ☐ Lori wants the group to play at the Fresher's Festival.
4 ☐ She has found a rehearsal room.
5 ☐ Nick has written a song about Lori.

Lori and Nick are going home after the audition.

A FORMAL LETTER OF ENQUIRY

6 Lori sees an advert for a studio. Read it and complete Lori's notes. Write (?) if there is no information.

- Name   *Sound Place Studios*
- Address
- Price? What's included?
- Number of studios
- Studios available in June/July?
- Name of contact person

> **The Sound Place:** a rehearsal and recording studio in Leith, Edinburgh.
> We have three studios available with all modern recording facilities. There is also a refreshment area with hot and cold drinks. For further info please contact:
> **Sound Place Studios, 5–7 Dock Place, Leith, EH6 6MV**
> **Contact: Andy Curtis**

7 Read the letter and find another <u>underlined</u> phrase for each heading in the *Phrases2know* box.

Phrases **2**know

Giving your reason for writing
I saw your advertisement for the recording studio.
I am writing in connection with your advert.
  I am writing to enquire …

Asking for information
Please send me details of prices.
Could you tell me if it is available next week?

I'd like to know more about the equipment there.
I'd like further information on the prices.
Can you give me more details on your music?

Concluding
I look forward to hearing from you.

73B George Terrace
Edinburgh
EH2 8NR
6 October 2010

The Sound Place
5–7 Dock Place,
Leith, EH6 6MV

Dear Mr Curtis,

I saw your advertisement for The Sound Place and <u>I am writing to enquire about your rehearsal facilities</u>.

We are a new five-piece band and we urgently need rehearsal space. Please send me details of your prices, and <u>could you also tell me if the rehearsal rooms are available in June/July</u>. I would also like to know what equipment is included in the price, the minimum number of hours we can book and the opening times of the rehearsal rooms. Finally, <u>please can you tell me if there is any food available at the studio</u>, or if we need to bring our own.

I look forward to hearing from you,

Yours sincerely,

Lori Ash

Lori Ash

8 Use the information below to write a formal letter of enquiry. Use the letter in exercise 7 and the *Phrases2know* to help you.

You are planning a camping holiday. You have seen an advertisement for camping spaces at a farm and decide to write a letter of enquiry (The address is: Mrs. Jane Parker, Oxted Farm, Sheldon, Lancashire PR7 8GD).

Give your reasons for writing and ask for further information about:

- prices
- if there are spaces available in September
- if there are any facilities for eating or drinking
- if there are any shops or supermarkets nearby.

8 living space

Grammar	First and second conditional
	wish + past simple/*would*
Vocabulary	Describing buildings
	Living together
Functions	Giving your opinion
	Agreeing and disagreeing

Vocabulary & Speaking

Describing buildings

1 Look at the photos. Which building do you think is the strangest? Which do you like best? Why?

2 Check the *Words2know*. Which of these things can you find in the photos?

House A has a balcony.

House C is semi-detached.

Words 2 know (3.15)

a balcony   a chimney   an attic room
the ground floor   the first floor   a roof
a detached house   a semi-detached house
an apartment block   a four-storey house
a terrace   a basement   a traditional house

3 (3.16) Read and listen to the description and <u>underline</u> five of the *Words2know*. Which building does it describe?

It's a four-storey building and it's got an attic room. I think there might be a basement too, but it's difficult to see. It's semi-detached and it's in a traditional style – it's painted a grey-green colour with a black or brown roof. It's in a normal street, but it's very strange because it's incredibly thin. It's probably only about two or three metres wide so I imagine it's quite small inside. I really like it because it's so unusual – I think I'd like to live there.

4 (3.17) Listen and practise saying the *Phrase2know*.

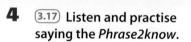

Describing buildings

Asking for description

What kind of house is it?

What colour is it painted?

How big is it?

Is there a chimney?

Does it have any other unusual features?

Describing a house

It's painted bright colours.

The balcony is curved.

It's a two-storey house.

The chimney's in the middle.

There's a balcony on the first floor.

It looks very unusual.

It's probably quite small inside.

The balcony overlooks the park.

5 **a** Work in pairs. Student A looks at the picture on page 124. Student B looks at the picture on page 135. Find five differences between the two buildings, using the *Phrases2know*.

Has it got a balcony?

b Describe the differences to the class.

House B has a balcony but House A doesn't.

6 **a** WRITING Write a description of one of the six buildings.

b Swap descriptions with a partner. Which building is your partner describing?

MINI WORKBOOK exercise 7 page 115

D

Grammar Focus

First and second conditional

7 Discuss the questions.
- Would you like to live in any of the buildings in the pictures? Why? Why not?
- What kind of house would you like to live in?

8 (3.18) Read and listen to what some teenagers say about where they would like to live. What does each teenager want?

1 I'm looking for somewhere to live at the moment, because my parents are moving to another town and I want to stay here, with my friends. I'll be happy if I can find a place in a nice apartment block in the town centre – I want to be near the action. (Liam, 18)

2 If I could live anywhere in the world, I wouldn't stay in my home town, that's for sure! I'd live somewhere hot, next to the beach, with a balcony that overlooks the sea. In my perfect house, I'd have a swimming pool and lots of bathrooms, so I wouldn't have to share. (Sue, 16)

3 I'm going away to uni soon, but it's very hard to find accommodation. If I can find somewhere near my college, I won't spend so much on bus fares, and life generally will be much easier for me. (Joe, 17)

4 I've got this picture of my dream home, I'd have horses and other animals everywhere. If I had enough money, I'd have a huge detached house, maybe with five storeys, in the country! (Imogen, 14)

9 Which people are talking realistically about the future and which ones are just imagining? Read *Grammar2know* to check your answers.

10 Complete the sentences about where people would like to live.
1 If I ___*have*___ (have) children when I'm older, I won't live in a city.
2 If I _____ (inherit) a lot of money, I'd buy a house in the mountains.
3 I'd travel around the world if I _____ (win) a lot of money!
4 If I can't find a cheap flat, I _____ (stay) at home with my family.
5 My brother _____ (move) abroad if he could.
6 If I can save enough money, I _____ (buy) an apartment.

11 Use the prompts to complete sentences of your own. Tell your partner your plans.
1 If I (can live) anywhere in the world, I (go) to …
If I could live anywhere in the world, I'd go to Miami.
2 If I (have) enough money, I (buy) …
3 If I had lots of money, I (not) … any more.
4 If I (can) meet one famous person, I (choose) …
5 If I (can change) anything in my life, I …

12 a WRITING Write a short description of your ideal home using *would* and vocabulary from exercises 2 and 4. Use the *Phrases2know* to help you.

My ideal home would be on an island in the Tropics. It would be next to the beach and it would have a huge balcony overlooking the sea.

b Work in pairs. Imagine if you could design your ideal home. Tell your partner about it.

MINI WORKBOOK exercises 1–3 page 114

living space

Listening & Vocabulary

1 Discuss the questions.
- What do you think the relationship is like between the brother and sister in the photos?
- How do you think they feel about the situation?
- Do you get on well with the people you live with?
- What kinds of things cause trouble?

> *I sometimes argue with my sister because she ...*

2 **a** **Words 2 know** 3.19 Check the words in blue. Put the annoying habits in order from 1 (most annoying) to 10 (this doesn't bother me).

b Compare answers with other students.

IT DRIVES ME CRAZY – ANNOYING HABITS

Do your mum and dad drive you mad? Do your brother and sister make your life miserable? We asked one hundred readers about the annoying habits of the people they live with. Here are the top ten.

- ☐ Borrowing things **without asking**.
- ☐ **Not letting** other people use the computer or television.
- ☐ Being too **fussy** and **tidy**.
- ☐ Making a **mess** around the house.
- ☐ Spending a **long time** in the bathroom.
- ☐ Coming into your room without **knocking** on the door.
- ☐ Not **sharing** the **chores**.
- ☐ **Nagging** you to tidy up **all the time**.
- ☐ Playing **loud music** that you **don't like**.
- ☐ Making **annoying noises**.

3 3.20 **LISTENING FOR GIST** Listen to the radio phone-in. Which callers does the DJ sympathise with?

Lizzy ☐ Daniel ☐ Steve ☐ Alison ☐

4 3.20 Listen again and choose the best summary of each complaint.

1 Lizzy is unhappy because her brother
  a never cleans the bathroom.
  b never tidies up in the bathroom.
  c spends too much time in the bathroom.
  d has horrible clothes.

2 Daniel is annoyed with his flatmate because
  a he makes annoying noises.
  b he comes into his room without knocking.
  c he plays loud music late at night.
  d he hates noise.

3 Steve is annoyed because
  a he has to tidy up himself.
  b his mother nags him.
  c his mother is very untidy.
  d he can't find things in his house.

4 Alison's husband annoys her because he
  a can't cook well.
  b always makes a mess in the kitchen.
  c never helps with the cooking.
  d cooks meals she doesn't like.

5 Discuss the questions.
- Does anyone in your family have these annoying habits?
- Do your family think you have got any annoying habits?

MINI WORKBOOK exercise 8 page 115

Grammar Focus

wish + past simple/would

6 a Read the chat room comments. Complete the gaps with the people in the box.

> my flatmate   my elder brother
> my little sister   my dad

b What is the problem in each case? Who do/don't you sympathise with?

haveyourmoan.com

What are the worst things about the people you live with?

1 _____ is the most annoying person in the world. She's really spoilt and is allowed to do what she wants. I have to do loads of chores in the house and my parents always criticise me for doing things wrong, but she never has to do anything. Sometimes, I wish I was an only child!
Freddie, 15.

2 I share a room with _____ and he's driving me mad at the moment! He makes a lot of noise when he comes to bed and then when he goes to sleep, he snores really loudly so I can't get back to sleep! I wish I had my own bedroom!
Ryan, 14.

3 I can't stand the way _____ is behaving. He treats me as if I was six. He asks me loads of questions about where I'm going, who I'm going with, when I'm going to my homework … I wish he would leave me alone!
Melissa, 17.

4 I'm finding _____ really difficult at the moment. She's just finished with her boyfriend and now she spends every hour of every day crying and telling me how heart-broken she is. She doesn't go anywhere or do anything. I wish she would go out and find some new friends!
Nehar, 18.

7 a What does each person in the chat room wish? <u>Underline</u> the sentence that shows this.

b Do you think these things are going to change or not? Read *Grammar2know* to check your ideas.

wish

Use *wish* to describe situations that we want to change. Often they are situations that cannot change or that we do not think will change.

wish + past simple

Use *wish* + past simple to describe present situations that we want to change:

*I **wish I was** an only child.* (but I have a sister)

*I **wish I had** my own bedroom.* (but I don't)

wish + *would* + verb

Use *wish* + *would* + verb to describe situations that we want to change in the future:

*I **wish** my dad **would leave** me alone.* (but I don't think he will)

*I **wish** she would find some new friends.* (but I don't think she will)

We cannot use *wish* + *would* with state verbs:

*I **wish** I **was** an only child.*   NOT: ~~I wish I would be an only child.~~

8 Read the situations and make sentences with *wish*, using the prompts.

1 Lucy would love a pet dog, but pets aren't allowed in her flat. (have/a pet dog)

   Lucy wishes she had a pet dog.

2 Jamie is an only child and feels lonely. (have/ some brothers and sisters)

3 Sarah does a lot of chores in the house but her brother doesn't do any. (her brother/help/more)

4 Matt's sister borrows his CDs all the time, and never puts them back. (his sister/not borrow/his CDs)

5 Angie's son leaves dirty plates all over the house. (wish/wash them up)

9 a Use the prompts to make four true sentences and two false sentences about yourself.

• I wish … would/wouldn't

   I wish my parents would go out more.

• I wish I had/didn't have …

   I wish I had black hair.

• I wish I was/wasn't …

b Read your sentences to a partner. Can he/she guess which ones are false?

MINI WORKBOOK **exercises 4–6 pages 114–115**

living space

Reading & Listening

1 Look at the photo and discuss the questions.

- What is happening in the photo?
- What kind of TV programme does the photo come from?
- Which reality TV shows are popular in your country?

2 Read the text and tick (✓) true and cross (✗) false.

1 ☐ *Big Brother* has been shown all over the world.

2 ☐ It was the first reality show in which strangers lived together.

3 ☐ Lots of programmes since *Big Brother* have used the same idea.

4 ☐ The writer suggests that viewers find personality problems entertaining.

5 ☐ Jo Barnett thinks that shows like *Big Brother* reflect real life.

6 ☐ Bart Spring is very pleased that he appeared on *Big Brother*.

3 Find the missing word (or phrase) in the text to match the definitions.

1 _____ : organise (paragraph 2)

2 _____ : badly behaved because they have been given too much (paragraph 2)

3 _____ : disagreement (paragraph 3)

4 _____ : not nice (paragraph 3)

5 _____ : thinks something is good (paragraph 4)

6 _____ : stupid, without any real reason (paragraph 4)

4 Discuss the questions.

- Do you think reality TV reflects real life?
- Do you agree that contestants 'become famous for being stupid'?
- Would you ever appear on a reality TV show? Why? Why not?

Living in front of the cameras 3.22

1 Say the words 'reality TV' and the show that comes into most people's minds is *Big Brother*. Love it or hate it, the programme is a global phenomenon: there have been versions in more than seventy countries! The basic format is simple: put a group of strangers into a house, record everything they do and watch how they manage to live together.

2 Actually the idea wasn't original. A similar show, *The Real World*, was broadcast in 1992 on MTV. But the format really became popular with the success of *Big Brother*, and it has been copied again and again, including celebrity versions. In similar shows, contestants have been sent to the jungle or put on a desert island. In *Wife Swap* a mother goes to live with a family of strangers and tries to run their home; in *Young, Dumb and Living off Mum* a group of spoilt teenagers with no life skills learn to live together and look after themselves.

3 So what makes these shows so addictive? Inevitably, living with strangers is stressful and personality problems are common. Contestants often have to share tasks and chores and this also brings conflict. 'It's all about relationships,' says TV critic Jo Barnett. 'Some characters are pleasant, and some are unpleasant but they are all real people. If you aren't interested in reality TV, you aren't interested in people.'

4 But is it healthy to be this interested in other people's private lives? And what kind of people want to appear in front of TV cameras twenty-four hours a day? Not everyone approves of such shows, including the first ever winner of *Big Brother*, Bart Spring. 'I'm not a fan of the programme or of people becoming famous for being stupid. If I helped to create this mindless monster, then I'm not proud of it,' he says.

5 a Read about a new reality TV show. What do contestants have to do?

REAL TV

ARE YOU A 'STAR FLATMATE'?
Would you make the perfect flatmate for a mystery celebrity? TV company seeks outgoing young people to take part in new reality TV show! Send us a 45 second presentation and convince us that you would be the perfect 'star flatmate'!

b (3.21) In pairs, A and B, listen to four possible contestants, Caroline, Kat, Dale and Jed. A make notes on Caroline and Dale. B make notes on Kat and Jed.

Caroline: nice, gets on well with people …

6 a Read your notes and decide what the positive and negative points about each person are. Compare ideas in pairs.

b Who would you choose as a flatmate? Why?

I'd choose … because she's …

I wouldn't like to live with … because he …

7 Prepare a two minute presentation about yourself, explaining why you would make a 'star flatmate'. (You can invent as much as you like!)

❝ *I think you would enjoy living with me because I'm very …*

Writing & Speaking

8 Read the essay about Reality TV. Which points do you agree with?

'Reality TV is bad for society' discuss.

a Reality TV is popular everywhere nowadays but it is also controversial. Some people say it is a harmless way to relax. Others believe that it has a bad influence and that there are too many reality shows nowadays.

b There are several reasons why people think reality TV is harmful. Firstly, it often shows bad behaviour, because contestants will do anything to get viewers' attention. Also, reality TV shows don't need writers or actors, so these people cannot find work.

c On the other hand, people watch reality TV because they are interested in other people, which is a good thing. It is true that reality TV is not educational, but neither are soap operas or game shows. People watch these shows for fun and surely everyone should relax in their own way.

d In conclusion, I don't think we should have too much reality TV, we need a variety of programmes. Personally I think that people should be free to watch what they want. If you don't like reality TV, you can always read a book instead.

9 a Match descriptions 1–4 to paragraphs a–d in the essay.

1 ☐ Reasons why people agree with the statement

2 ☐ A summary and the writer's own opinion

3 ☐ Introduction of the topic and explanation why the statement is controversial

4 ☐ Reasons why people disagree with the statement

b Underline the *Phrases2know* in the essay. Which three aren't there?

Phrases 2 know

Introducing an argument
There are several reasons why …
Firstly …
Also …
Surely everyone should …

Introducing opposite arguments
On the other hand …
However …

Summarising
To sum up
In conclusion …

Giving your opinion
Personally I think that …
I don't think (we) should …
In my opinion …

10 a In pairs, choose a statement below. List the arguments *for* and *against*. Then think of examples and reasons to explain your argument.

• Young people should live away from their parents before they get married.

• It's a good idea for children to share a bedroom.

• Teenagers should not be allowed to watch TV after 10p.m.

b Decide what to put in the introduction and how to sum up.

c Write an essay (200-250 words). Use the *Phrases2know* and the model text in exercise 8 to help you.

activestudy4 EXAMS

Vocabulary

ACTIVE STUDY Learn words in groups

1 Put the words below into the categories in the table. Add one more word in each category.

> blend fibre spicy melt protein ✓
> peel sour savoury vitamins

Verbs: preparing food	Adjectives to describe food	Nouns: nutrients
		protein

2 Complete the email with the words below.

> attic chimney detached ✓
> floor storeys terrace

```
000
← → ✕ ↻ ⌂  ✎ 🖨 ✉
Back Forward Stop Refresh Home  AutoFill Print Mail
Address: @
```

Hi Katie

Let me tell you about our new home. It's lovely. It's a
¹ *detached* house with a garden. It's got two
² _____ , plus an ³ _____ at the top.
There's a ⁴ _____ in the middle of the roof,
and a big ⁵ _____ on the first ⁶ _____,
where we sit and have drinks when the weather's
good. Come and visit us!

Love,

Sophie

ACTIVE STUDY Learn collocations

3 Match the words to make collocations.

1 lose ———— a sick
2 have —— b weight
3 feel   c a headache
4 make   d on the door
5 share   e a mess
6 knock   f the chores

4 PRONUNCIATION 3.23 Listen to these two-word noun phrases and put them into the right group in the table. Then read the two lists aloud.

- fizzy drink
- refreshment area
- sour cream
- grated cheese
- rehearsal room
- dry cleaner's
- blood pressure

Main stress on the first word	Main stress on the second word
refreshment area	*fizzy drink*

Grammar

5 Read the blog and choose the correct verb form.

myblog

The big day

This has been the busiest week of my life.
Today is my elder sister's wedding day. A
hundred people ¹ _____. We ² _____ tons
of food. Yesterday a big tent ³ _____ in our
garden. That's where the meal ⁴ _____ . Our
parents have allowed our little sister Ruby, who
is eleven, to ⁵ _____ !
My sister's got nothing more to do. She
⁶ _____ her dress made a long time ago. Now
she just needs ⁷ _____ her hair styled. But I've
got my hands full! The guests must ⁸ _____
and directed to their seats. Right now, the
sound system ⁹ _____. I wish it ¹⁰ _____ over!

1 a is invited   b have invited   ⓒ have been invited
2 a have ordered   b have been ordered   c were ordered
3 a put up   b was put up   c has been put up
4 a is served   b will serve   c will be served
5 a have her ears pierced   b pierce her ears   c have pierced her ears
6 a 's had   b has got   c had
7 a have   b to have   c to be
8 a welcome   b be welcomed   c have welcomed
9 a is being checked   b was checked   c is checked
10 a is   b was   c has been

6 Match the sentence beginnings 1–5 to the endings a–e.

1 If it rains, *b*
2 If no guests came to the wedding,
3 If we were incredibly rich,
4 Unless it rains,
5 If my sister and her husband didn't have a flat,

a my sister would be very sad.
b the wedding guests will get wet.
c the party will take place in the garden.
d they'd live with us.
e we'd organise the wedding on a tropical island.

Reading Skills

ACTIVE STUDY Listen for gist

7 Read the text about pasta. Match the titles A–F to the paragraphs 1–5. There is one extra title.

A Different ways to serve pasta

B A great choice

C Pasta in culture

D The ingredients of good pasta

E The origins of pasta

F Try for yourself

Listening Skills

ACTIVE STUDY Listen for specific information

8 (3.24) Listen to two women talking about a restaurant. Choose the best answer, a–c.

1 Michael enjoys

  a going out to restaurants.

  b celebrating birthdays.

  c unusual food.

2 Bulgarian food

  a is based only on vegetables and cheeses.

  b is similar to food from other countries in the same part of the world.

  c is quite rich.

3 Michael

  a eats a lot of meat.

  b doesn't like vegetables.

  c likes a variety of foods.

4 The restaurant is

  a in a detached house.

  b on the first floor.

  c in a garden.

5 Lily and Michael are

  a close friends.

  b siblings.

  c girlfriend and boyfriend.

Speaking Skills

9 Choose one of the topics and talk about it to the class for about three minutes.

- Food in my country – the traditional and the modern.

- Sharing a flat with someone is the best way to stop liking them – discuss.

SKILLS STRATEGIES back cover

Forty centuries of pasta (3.25)

1 ___

Pasta is tasty, healthy, and very easy to cook. There are dozens of shapes, such as spaghetti, penne, fusilli and tagliatelle, and hundreds of sauces. If you cooked a different shape with a different sauce every day, you could eat pasta 365 days a year and never have the same dish!

2 ___

According to legend, the Italian traveller Marco Polo brought pasta from China in 1295. This is not true, though; in his *Travels,* Polo described a Chinese food similar to pasta by comparing it to a dish he already knew. However, it is true that the oldest noodles we know of have been found in China. They are 4000 years old! 2000 years ago various pasta-like foods were eaten by Greeks, Romans and Arabs.

3 ___

Pasta has been an important part of Italian culture for centuries. In the fourteenth-century literature classic *Decamerone*, Giovanni Boccaccio described a fantasy land in which there is a mountain of grated Parmiggiano cheese. The people living on it spend their whole time making macaroni and ravioli. In the 1930s the futurist poet Filippo Tommaso Marinetti tried to start a campaign against spaghetti. He claimed it 'killed the noble spirit of the Neapolitans'. The campaign became a joke when he was seen in a restaurant one evening enjoying a plate of spaghetti! Later in the 20th century, characters eating pasta appeared in films by great Italian directors such as Luchino Visconti and Federico Fellini.

4 ___

Italian pasta is generally eaten with some kind of savoury sauce. Chinese, Japanese and Vietnamese noodles can also be served in soup. In Poland, soft noodles called 'kluski' are sometimes served as a sweet dish, with fruit, sugar and sour cream.

5 ___

If you'd like to start cooking your own pasta dishes, here's a simple recipe for you to try: Cook some penne according to the instructions on the packaging. Chop some parsley and 100 grams of smoked salmon. In a big bowl, mix the salmon and parsley with green pesto sauce and olive oil. Add the cooked pasta.

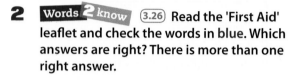

Grammar	*used to*
	Past continuous
	Past perfect
Vocabulary	**First Aid**
	Accidents and adventures
	Adverbs for telling a story
Functions	**Making arrangements**
	Telling a story

Vocabulary & Listening

Accidents and First Aid

1 Look at the photos and discuss the questions.

- What is happening in each photo?
- What injuries might happen in these situations?
- Would you know what to do to help?

+ FIRST AID

Do you know what to do if you have an accident?

1 You **cut** yourself quite badly with a kitchen knife. What should you do?
   a Wash the cut.
   b Stop the **bleeding** with a plaster or bandage.
   c Go to hospital immediately.
   d Go to hospital if it doesn't stop bleeding.

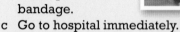

2 You **burn** yourself on a pan while you are cooking. What should you do to the burn?
   a Put a **plaster** on it.
   b Put it under cold water for a few minutes.
   c Put ice or cream on it.
   d Put a loose **bandage** on it.

3 You **sprain** your ankle while you are playing tennis. What should you do?
   a Give it plenty of exercise.
   b Put ice on it to stop the **swelling**.
   c Put it up and rest it.
   d Take **painkillers** if it hurts.

4 You fall off your skateboard and **hit** your head. How do you know if you have **concussion** and need to go to hospital?
   a You have a headache and feel **dizzy**.
   b You feel **sick**.
   c You can't remember what happened.
   d You have any of these **symptoms**.

2 ☐ Words 2 know ☐ (3.26) Read the 'First Aid' leaflet and check the words in blue. Which answers are right? There is more than one right answer.

3 (3.27) Listen to a lecture about First Aid and check your answers.

4 **a** Read the leaflet again and complete the collocations with the correct verb in the box.

> burn ✓   cut   feel   have   hit   put
> stop   sprain   take

1 _____ dizzy/sick
2 _____ concussion/a headache
3 _____ painkillers
4 _____ your head on something
5 _____ a plaster/bandage on it
6 _____ your ankle
7 _____ the swelling
8 *burn* yourself
9 _____ yourself

b Which collocations describe problems and which describe treatments? Put them in the correct column.

Problem	Treatment

5 (3.28) Listen to the test at the end of the lecture. Are the answers correct or incorrect? Listen to the end of the lecture to check.

MINI WORKBOOK exercise 6 page 117

Grammar Focus

used to and past continuous

6 Read about Jack and Tara's childhood accidents. What happened? What injuries did they get?

7 **a** Which sentence in bold in text 1 describes:

- a single action in the past
- a past habit
- an action in progress in the past
- a past state

b Read *Grammar2know* to check. Find another example of rules a–d in text 2.

Grammar **2** know

Past simple and past continuous

a Use the past simple to describe the main events in a past story:
*Will **pushed** me.*

b Use the past continuous to describe actions in progress at the time these events happened:
*I **was sitting** on a wall when Will pushed me.*

Time expressions: We often use past simple and past continuous together in sentences with *when, while* or *as*:
*My back was bleeding **when** I got home.*

used to

Use *used to* :

c to describe a past state:
*The river **used to be** really dirty.*

d to describe a past habit:
*We **used to play** in the park all the time.*

NOT: We ~~were playing~~ in the park all the time.

8 Put the verbs into the correct tense. Use the past simple or the past continuous.

1 Josh _broke_ (break) his leg when he _was skiing_ (ski).

2 Ellen _____ (burn) herself while she _____ (do) a science experiment.

3 Bella _____ (fall) downstairs as she _____ (run) to answer the phone.

4 When she _____ (come) home from school, Lily _____ (fall) off her bike.

5 Ben _____ (cut) himself while he _____ (shave).

6 Oliver _____ (break) his nose when he _____ (play) football.

Childhood Accidents

1 Jack

'My friend **Will and I used to play in the park** near our house all the time when we were young. There was a little river, and I remember **it used to be really dirty**. Anyway, one day **I was sitting on a wall** by the river and suddenly **Will pushed me**! I fell into the water and hit my back. It was bleeding quite badly when I got home, and I was really sick because of the dirty water ... Will's mum was so angry!'

2 Tara

'When I was little **I used to love swimming**, and I learned how to dive when I was really young. I was very proud of myself and **I used to practise all the time**. Unfortunately, I didn't realise that you have to dive into water! So one day, **I was playing in the garden**, and **I decided to dive off the garden wall**! I landed right on my nose and it started bleeding, but luckily it wasn't broken.'

9 (3.29) Read story 3 and <u>underline</u> the correct answers. Listen and check.

3 Melanie

'When my little sister and I were young, we [1] *used to play/were playing* hospitals ... I was always the doctor and she [2] *used to be/was being* the patient. One day, she [3] *was lying/used to lie* in bed, and I [4] *was putting/used to put* some cold water and a bandage on her leg. But the water was so cold that she [5] *jumped/was jumping* out of the bed and she [6] *hit/used to hit* her head on a radiator and [7] *cut/was cutting* it open. My parents [8] *took/used to take* her to a real hospital to have some stitches! '

10 Use the prompts to make sentences with *used to* about your childhood. Compare answers in pairs.

" *When I was little, I used to play with my cousins a lot.*

When I was little ...

- I/play with ... a lot.
- I/pretend ...
- I/go to / with my mum / dad
- I/love going to ...
- I/be very good at ...
- I not/like ...

11 Write a short description of an accident you had as a child.

When I was little I used to love the snow. One day, while I was playing in the snow ...

MINI WORKBOOK exercises 1–2 page 116

help! help!

69

Grammar Focus

Past perfect

1 Look at the pictures. What do you think is happening in each picture? Read and check.

2 Match the correct endings a–c to the stories 1–3. Which story is the strangest?

Unfortunate accidents and incredible escapes!

1 Seventeen-year-old twins, Luke and John Little, crashed their cars into each other as they were driving home.

2 An umbrella saved the life of a Chinese schoolgirl when a strong wind blew her off the top of a six-storey building. The umbrella acted as a parachute, slowing her fall.

3 Giuseppe Plantini was doing his driving test when his mother stopped beside him and started shouting and waving at him. Distracted, he crashed into a wall, breaking both the examiner's legs.

a … She had gone up to the roof of the building to rescue her pet cat from the bad weather!

b … His mother had followed him because she hadn't wished him good luck before he left the house! Giuseppe, of course, failed his test!

c … The brothers had just passed their driving tests, and were going home to tell their parents the good news!

3 a Which of these actions in story 1 happened first?
- They **crashed** their cars.
- They **had passed** their driving tests.

b Read *Grammar2know* to check and <u>underline</u> three more past perfect verbs in the endings to the other stories.

Past perfect

Use the past simple to describe the main events in a story:
*The wind **blew** the girl off the roof.*

Use the past perfect to describe events that happened before the main events:
***When** the twins **crashed**, they **had** just **passed** their driving tests.*

Time expressions: *when, before, after*

Form: had + past participle

+ I **had gone** on the roof.

– She **hadn't wished** him luck.

? **Had** he **passed** his test?
Yes , he **had**./No, he **hadn't**.

4 <u>Underline</u> the correct tense, past simple or past perfect.

1 Andrew *had run/<u>ran</u>* to the bus stop, but the bus *already left/had already left*.

2 I *hadn't been/wasn't* hungry because I had *just eaten/just ate* breakfast.

3 The match *already started/had already started* when I *arrived/had arrived* at the stadium.

5 Complete the text with the past simple, past perfect or past continuous.

A Lucky Escape

My brother often sleepwalks, and he ¹ *had* (have) a lucky escape two summers ago. We ² _____ (just/move) to a new house. One night, after all the others ³ _____ (go) upstairs to bed, I ⁴ _____ (watch) TV in the living room. It was a warm summer night so we ⁵ _____ (leave) some of the upstairs windows open. I ⁶ _____ (begin) to fall asleep in front of the TV when ⁷ _____ (hear) footsteps coming from my brother's room upstairs. A few moments later, there was a crash outside the window. I ⁸ _____ (look) out and I ⁹ _____ (see) my brother – he ¹⁰ _____ (lie) outside on the grass… while he ¹¹ _____ (sleepwalk), he ¹² _____ (fall) out of an upstairs window and he _____ (land) on a pile of leaves … and he ¹³ _____ (not wake up)! When my parents ¹⁴ _____ (come) downstairs to see what ¹⁵ _____ (happen), he ¹⁶ _____ (still/snore)!

MINI WORKBOOK exercises 3–5 pages 116–117

REAL LIFE EMERGENCIES!
Brian Howard and Darryl Jones were flying to Knoxville in the USA, when disaster struck!

1

2

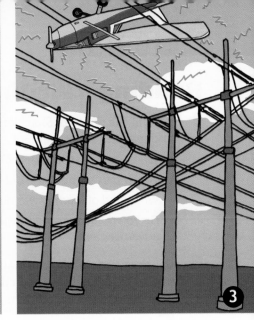

3

4

5

Listening & Vocabulary

6 a Look at the pictures that show the true story of what happened to two young men. Match the words and phrases to the pictures.

> a crane   to run out of fuel   firemen
> power lines carrying electricity   sparks
> a two-seater plane   to land upside-down
> to call for help

b (3.30) In pairs, decide what happened. Then listen and compare your ideas to the real story.

7 (3.30) Listen again. Tick (✓) true and cross (✗) false.

1 ☐ They ran out of fuel at the beginning of the journey.
2 ☐ The plane crashed into some trees.
3 ☐ The firemen arrived quite quickly.
4 ☐ They rescued the two men immediately.
5 ☐ Brian isn't going to give up flying.

8 a Check the *Words2know*. Then <u>underline</u> the correct word to complete the sentences from the story.

Words 2 know (3.31)

a few minutes later   at first   eventually
fortunately   unfortunately   meanwhile   finally
suddenly   after that   in the end   immediately

1 *In the end/Suddenly,* the engine stopped.
2 *At first/Fortunately,* I didn't know what had happened, but *eventually/meanwhile* I realised we had hit some power lines.
3 *Fortunately/Unfortunately,* Darryl managed to find his cell phone and he called for help.
4 *At first/After that,* we just sat there and waited.
5 *Unfortunately/A few minutes later,* the firemen arrived.
6 *Meanwhile/At first,* the weather conditions were getting worse.
7 We were in the plane for six hours but a crane arrived *immediately/in the end.*
8 *At first/Finally,* the door opened and we just fell out of the plane.

b (3.32) Listen and check.

9 Imagine you are either Darryl or one of the firemen. Use the *Words2know* and the vocabulary in exercise 6 to tell the story.

10 a SPEAKING Do you know any stories of emergencies or lucky escapes? Spend a few minutes thinking about how to describe what happened.

b Tell the story using the *Words2know.*

❝ *A few years ago, when we were coming home from holiday …*

MINI WORKBOOK exercise 7 page 117

help! help!

Reading & Writing

1 Look at the photo of Shackleton and the map, and read the advertisement.

- Who was Ernest Shackleton?
- Which part of the world did he explore? When?
- What kind of journey was he expecting?
- Do you think many people replied to his advertisement?

2 Use the words below, the map and the photos to make three predictions about what happened to the expedition.

> to abandon   to melt   to get stuck   to sink
> to rescue   remote   exceptional   the crew
> a lifeboat   a wave   ice

3 Read the account and check your predictions.

4 Look at the map below. Draw Shackleton's actual route from point A when the *Endurance* sank until the crew were rescued.

5 In pairs, answer the questions.

1 Are you surprised by the response to Shackleton's advert?

2 Why was Shackleton's plan ambitious?

3 After they got stuck in the ice, how long did the crew wait in the ship? What were conditions like?

4 Give four reasons why Shackleton's journey to South Georgia was difficult.

5 What did Shackleton discover when he returned to Elephant Island to rescue his men? How long had the men been in the Antarctic by then?

Sir Ernest Shackleton (1874-1922) was a famous British explorer. In 1914, he placed the following advertisement in a newspaper.

MEN WANTED FOR HAZARDOUS JOURNEY.

Small wages. Bitter cold. Long months of complete darkness. Constant danger. Safe return doubtful.

ENDURANCE (3.33)

The story of Ernest Shackleton, hero of the Antarctic.

The story began in 1914, with an advertisement in a British newspaper:
'Men wanted for hazardous journey. Small wages. Bitter cold. Long months of complete darkness. Constant danger. Safe return doubtful.'

The man who had placed the advertisement was the explorer, Ernest Shackleton. He planned to cross Antarctica from the Weddell Sea to the Ross Sea, via the South Pole, something no one had ever done before. More than 5,000 men applied to join the expedition. Only twenty-eight were chosen.

Shackleton's ship, the *Endurance*, left England on 8 August 1914, and it reached the Weddell Sea in December, the Antarctic summer. But the weather was exceptionally bad, and on 17 January 1915, *Endurance* got stuck in ice. Unable to move, Shackleton and his men had to wait for eight months, in complete darkness and freezing cold.

Finally, spring came, but it brought disaster. As the ice melted, the ship broke in half. The crew had to abandon ship and camp on the ice for two months. When the *Endurance* finally sank, on 21 November 1915, Shackleton and his men tried to survive by floating on the ice. Eventually the ice melted and Shackleton put his men into three small lifeboats and headed for the nearest land.

After five days at sea, they reached Elephant Island. The men were cold and exhausted, and weak from the journey and the lack of food. There was no chance of rescue in this remote place, so Shackleton decided to continue to South Georgia. He knew there was a Norwegian whaling station* there, where he could get help, but it was a journey of 1,300 kilometres. Leaving the others on Elephant

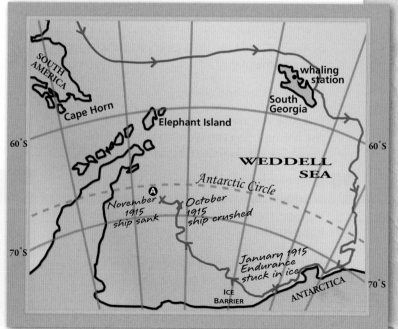

Island, Shackleton chose five men to accompany him to South Georgia in a tiny seven-metre lifeboat. After fifteen exhausting days with winds of sixty kilometres an hour and waves of up to fifteen metres, they arrived in South Georgia. The weather was so bad they couldn't land for two days. Even when they landed, their journey wasn't over. The whaling station was sixty kilometres away on the other side of the mountainous island. No one had ever crossed South Georgia on foot before.

The men marched continuously for 36 hours. They had no tent and could not stop to rest for more than a few minutes – if they fell asleep they would die of cold. Starved and frozen, they finally reached the station. On 30 August 1916, two years after the expedition began, they returned to Elephant Island in a small boat provided by the Chilean government. The other twenty-three men were still waiting. Miraculously, not one person had died.

Shackleton even returned to Antarctica. In 1921, he set out again to sail round the continent, but died during the journey in 1922. He is buried in South Georgia, remembered by history as a man who showed exceptional leadership … and unbelievable endurance.

* A place from which fishermen go out to catch whales.

6 Read extracts from letters the youngest sailor wrote to his 'sweetheart'.

    a Which parts of the journey does each letter describe?

    b How does he feel at each stage?

(3.34)

> Southampton, England,
> 8 August 1914
>
> My Dearest Emily,
> Today the 'Endurance' leaves England. Our great adventure has begun! Imagine the stories that I shall have to tell you when I get back!

> Weddell Sea,
> 22 January 1915
>
> Dearest Emily,
> Since my last letter, we have had a disaster. We reached the Weddell Sea six weeks ago. The weather was much worse than we had expected, it was snowing constantly, and it was always light, it was impossible to sleep. It was very difficult to sail through the thick ice, and unfortunately our ship became stuck a few days ago. We must wait until spring before we can continue. You cannot imagine how cold it is here. Sometimes I wonder if I shall ever see England again.

> Elephant Island,
> April 1916
>
> My Beloved Emily,
> I do not know if you will ever read these letters, but I shall continue to write for I must believe that one day we will see each other again.
> Ten days ago, the 'Endurance' finally sank. After the ship had gone down, Captain Shackleton looked at us and said, 'She's gone, boys, but we must still have hope.'
> We got into the lifeboats, and after seven days at sea, we eventually reached a place called Elephant Island. We are all exhausted after the journey in the freezing cold, with very little food.
> Captain Shackleton plans to sail to South Georgia to get help. He says that I am a strong lad, and has asked me to join his expedition. I feel proud that he has chosen me. I pray that we shall arrive there safely …

7 Write another letter from the sailor to his sweetheart, dated September 1916. Use the letters to help you. Include descriptions of:

- the journey to South Georgia and how he felt at the time.
- the rescue at Elephant Island and how the men feel now.
- his hopes of seeing Emily again.

    Finish the letter `your loving …`

8 What do you think of Shackleton? Discuss your opinion with the class.

    I think he was brave because …
    I think he was wrong because …

REAL TIME

MAKING ARRANGEMENTS

1 Look at the photo below and answer the questions.

1 What are Kate and Lori doing?
2 When and where are 'BlueSky' playing?

2 (3.35) Listen to Kate and Lori's conversation and answer the questions.

1 Who are Kate and Lori talking about?
2 Who phones Lori?
3 How do you think Lori feels about Greg?

3 (3.36) Complete the conversation with the *Phrases2know*. Then listen and check.

Lori:	Greg, hi.
Greg:	Hi, Lori. [1] _____ ? How are things at college?
Lori:	Oh fine.
Greg:	Good. Listen. What are you doing on Saturday? [2] _____ ?
Lori:	Saturday? Oh, Greg, [3] _____ I'm busy. We're playing our first gig!
Greg:	That's a pity.
Lori:	But listen, [4] _____ ? It's at the Arts Centre – eight o'clock.
Greg:	[5] _____ ?
Lori:	Great. I'll leave you a ticket at the entrance. I hope you enjoy it. It's our first live concert together.
Greg:	Sounds good. I'll see you on Saturday.
Lori:	See you then! He's coming to the gig! Greg is coming to our first gig!! And he's in the music business!

4 (3.37) Listen and practise saying the *Phrases2know*.

5 Work in pairs. Use the prompts and the *Phrases2know* to make arrangements. Remember to give reasons when you refuse an invitation. You can invent information.

1 Go/the cinema/after school?

> *Do you fancy going to the cinema after school today?*
> *Sounds great! / I'd love to, but I have to write an essay.*

2 have/lunch/today?
3 go/shopping/at the weekend?
4 watch/DVD/tonight?
5 go/BlueSky concert/on Saturday?

6 In pairs, act out the dialogue below. Student A, use the prompts below. Student B, look at page 135.

- You are free on Saturday afternoon and would like to spend some time with your best friend. Invite your friend to do something on Saturday afternoon.
- Respond to your partner's suggestions.
- Agree what you will do and when.

Phrases 2 know

Making arrangements

Starting a conversation
Hi!
What's new?
What are you doing on Saturday?

Inviting someone
How about going out somewhere?
Do you fancy coming to the gig?
Why don't we go out on Sunday?

Accepting an invitation
Sounds good/great.
Sure, why not?
That would be great!

Refusing an invitation
I'm sorry, I can't.
I'm busy.
I'd love to but I have plans.
That's a good idea but I'm on holiday that week.

Edinburgh Arts Centre
Saturday 24th Septemb...
Doors open 7 p.m. - Band on from 8 p.m.
Tickets: £3 advanced sale/£5 pay on the night

On Saturday, Kate was cycling to the gig when she had an accident.

1   Something really annoying happened when I was going to the concert last Saturday. I was riding my bicycle along the street when I saw a woman standing on the pavement outside one of the boutique shops. She was carrying lots of shopping bags.

2   I had just passed the crossing when she suddenly stepped into the road without looking. I didn't hit her, but I fell off my bicycle. I was really scared because I banged my head and hurt my arm when I fell. It's a good thing I was wearing a crash helmet, so I wasn't badly hurt! The woman came over to me while I was sitting in the road. I expected her to apologise but she began shouting at me.

3   I felt absolutely furious! She had caused the accident. She didn't even apologise! In the end, her friend told her to calm down, and she went away. To be honest, I think she should pay for the damage to my bicycle.

4   My bicycle wheel was broken so I had to catch the bus to the concert. It seemed to take hours! Eventually, I got to the Arts Centre. Meanwhile, my friends were all very worried about me, but fortunately I wasn't badly hurt and I was still able to play my saxophone!

A NARRATIVE

7 **(3.38) Listen to the conversation. Tick (✓) true and cross (✗) false.**

1   ☐ Kate is late because she had an accident on her bicycle.

2   ☐ Kate fell off her bike because she hit the woman.

3   ☐ Kate was angry with the woman.

4   ☐ Kate walked the rest of the way.

5   ☐ She was badly hurt and can't play the saxophone.

8 **Read the blog Kate wrote about the accident. Find the paragraph where she describes:**

*   how she felt about it   *paragraph 3*
*   the main events
*   what she did after the accident
*   when and where it happened
*   what happened at the end.

9 **You are going to write a narrative. Choose one of the situations below. Then look at exercise 8, read the *Phrases2know* and make notes for each paragraph.**

a   a time when you had an accident or hurt yourself

b   a time when somebody really annoyed you or someone was rude to you.

10 **Now write your narrative. Use Kate's narrative, your notes in exercise 9 and the *Phrases2know* to help you. Write about 200–250 words.**

Phrases **2**know

Describing where and when it happened
Something really annoying happened when I was going to the concert last Saturday.
Sequencing words: at first, then, next, after that

Describing background and previous events
I had just passed the crossing when …
I was riding my bicycle when …

Describing main events
She stepped into the road without looking.
I didn't hit her but I fell off my bicycle.
Adverbs: Suddenly, Eventually, Meanwhile

Saying how you felt
I felt absolutely furious.
I was really scared/surprised.

10 in the news

Grammar	Reported speech Reported questions
Vocabulary	Newspapers Celebrities and the media
Functions	Giving opinions

Listening & Vocabulary

1 Do you read a newspaper? If so, which one?

2 Check the *Words2know*. Then put them into the categories below. Compare your answers in groups.

> **Words 2 know** (4.1)
>
> news articles   the horoscopes   cartoons
> letters to the editor   advertisements
> gossip column   film reviews
> sports news   'human interest' stories

I usually read	I don't usually read
the sports news	*'human interest' stories*

3 **a** Look at the photo and the headline. You will hear a news story about how a local newspaper helped Lisa Wicks and her father, Michael. What do you think the 'amazing coincidence' was?

b (4.2) Listen and check.

4 (4.2) Listen again and answer the questions.

1 How had Lisa and her dad lost contact?
2 Why was Michael feeling 'a bit desperate'?
3 What did he decide to do?
4 Was the editor helpful?
5 How did Lisa feel when she saw the newspaper?
6 What did Lisa's mother think she should do?
7 How did her dad react?
8 How are Lisa and her dad feeling now?

5 Do you think this is a sad story or a happy story? Why? Why not?

MINI WORKBOOK exercise 7 page 119

Amazing coincidence as dad searches for long-lost daughter
SHE'S BEHIND YOU!

Lisa Wicks. Please phone your dad on 05487659845.

Help me find my daughter!

Grammar Focus

Reported speech

6 **a** (4.2) Listen to the story of Lisa and her father again. Who said these things in the news programme, Lisa or Michael?

1 'I was completely shocked.'
2 'We certainly won't wait another five years before we see each other again.'
3 'We plan to spend more time together.'
4 'We're going out tonight to celebrate.'
5 'Can you print a photo of me in your paper?'

b Read the newspaper article describing the same story to check your answers. <u>Underline</u> the sentences that tell you what the people said in exercise 6a.

(4.3)

Londoner Michael Wicks travelled to Sunbury in Middlesex last week to look for his 17-year-old daughter Lisa, who he had not seen for five years. Lisa moved to Sunbury with her mother after her parents divorced, and she was not in contact with her father, who lived in a different town.

After days of searching, Mr Wicks asked *The Sunbury Free Press* to print a photo taken in Sunbury's main square showing his telephone number, and asking his daughter to contact him.

When the newspaper came out a few days later, Lisa was amazed to see a picture of her dad – and when she looked more closely, she saw herself too in the background!

Lisa said she had been completely shocked. 'I was just a few metres from my dad and I had no idea!' she said. She showed the paper to a friend, who told her to phone the number immediately.

'At first, my dad thought it was a joke,' she said, 'but he soon realized it was really me. It's great to be in contact again after all these years!' She said that they were going out that evening to celebrate.

Delighted dad, Michael, smiling from ear to ear, told our reporter that they planned to spend a lot more time together, and joked that it definitely wouldn't be another five years before they saw each other!

7 **a** Compare the sentences in exercise 6a with the <u>underlined</u> sentences in 6b. Which show the speaker's exact words and which show reported words?

b Read *Grammar2know* to check your answers.

 **Grammar 2know**

Reported speech

In direct speech, we give the speaker's exact words using inverted commas:
'I was completely shocked,' said Lisa.

In reported speech, we explain what the person said, without giving their exact words:
Lisa said that she had been completely shocked.

Verb tenses

In reported speech, we normally change the tense of the main verb further into the past:
*'We **plan** to spend more time together.'*
*He said they **planned** to spend more time together.*
*'We**'re going to** celebrate.'*
*She said they **were going to** celebrate.*
*'I **was** completely shocked.'*
*She said that she **had been** completely shocked.*
*'We **won't** wait another five years.'*
*He said they **wouldn't** wait another five years.*
*'We **haven't** seen each other for years.'*
*He said they **hadn't** seen each other for years.*

Pronouns

*'**We**'re planning to spend more time together.'*
*Michael said that **they** were planning to spend more time together.*

8 Here are some more things that Michael Wicks, Lisa and her friend said. Put them into reported speech and make any necessary changes.

1 'I came to Sunbury to look for my daughter,' Michael told the reporter.
   Michael told the reporter that he had come to Sunbury to look for his daughter.

2 'I haven't seen Lisa for ten years,' Michael said to the reporter.

3 'You haven't changed!' Michael said to Lisa.

4 'I go to school in Sunbury,' Lisa said to her father.

5 'I'm sorry I didn't contact you before,' Michael told his daughter.

6 'We won't lose touch again,' Lisa said.

7 'I'm planning to visit London soon,' Lisa said.

9 Change the direct speech in the news article into reported speech. Take turns to retell the story.

MINI WORKBOOK exercises 1–2 page 118 and exercise 5 page 119

Vocabulary & Listening

Celebrities and the media

1 Read the newspaper stories, 1–3, and match the celebrities to the pictures, A–C. Then answer the questions.

- Why are these people celebrities?
- Why are they in the news at the moment?
- Do you know any real-life celebrities who have done similar things? Which real-life celebrities are in the news at the moment?

❶ (4.6) Hollywood stars, **Nicolina Lorie** and **Chad Bitt**, appeared in public yesterday to show the world their new twin daughters, Astra and Galaxy. Also with them, were their four adopted children, Zula (7), Kalahari (5), Chutney (4) and Pepe (2). The child-loving couple adopted the kids while they were doing charity work in different parts of the world.

❷ Heiress **Madrid Maddison**, daughter of billionaire businessman Ron Maddison, has been released by Los Angeles police. She was arrested late last night for dangerous driving, and spent the night in a police cell. When the police stopped her, she was driving at 140 kph the wrong way down a Los Angeles freeway. Witnesses said it was a miracle that she hadn't had an accident.

❸ Manchester and England footballer, **Jason Dole**, has moved into a friend's flat. Friends say he has split up with his wife, pop singer Melanie Kim. They have been married for only three months. Photographs showing Dole and nineteen-year-old model Kelly Brains dancing in a nightclub appeared in last week's newspapers.

2 **Words 2 know** (4.4) Check the words in blue. Do you agree or disagree with the statements? Compare your answers in pairs.

1 ☐ Celebrities should have more **privacy**, photographers should be banned from following them and standing outside their houses.

2 ☐ Celebrities **deserve** the treatment they get. They want **publicity** so they can't complain when they sometimes get bad publicity!

3 ☐ It's wrong for celebrities to use their children to get publicity – they should keep them away from **the media**.

4 ☐ I don't believe most things I read about celebrities in the media. I think they **print lies**, just to sell papers.

5 ☐ Celebrities are **under** more **pressure** than other people, that's why they **behave badly** sometimes.

6 ☐ Most celebrities are **self-centred** and **desperate for attention**.

7 ☐ Celebrities **have** a strong **influence on** young people, both good and bad.

8 ☐ I'm not **influenced by** celebrities.

3 (4.5) Listen to four people discussing celebrities. Which statement in exercise 2 summarises each person's opinion?

Speaker 1 ☐   Speaker 2 ☐   Speaker 3 ☐   Speaker 4 ☐

A

Grammar Focus

Reported questions

4 Read the questions the journalists asked the celebrities. Who did they ask each question to: M (Madrid), J (Jason), N&C (Nicolina and Chad)?

1 Are you planning to have any more children? *N & C*

2 What does your father think about the incident?

3 What's happening between you and Kelly?

4 Why have you moved out?

5 When will you appear in court?

6 What do the older children think of the twins?

7 Is Chad a good father?

8 Were you drunk last night?

9 Are you going back to Melanie?

10 Are you sorry for what you have done?

5 Read part of an article written by one of the journalists in the picture. Which celebrity is it about? Do you think the celebrity is sorry for what she has done?

MINI WORKBOOK exercise 8 page 119

… suddenly Madrid Maddison and her personal assistant appeared at the police station door. I asked her when she would appear in court. Maddison remained silent. 'No comment,' answered her assistant, sharply.

Another journalist asked whether she had been drunk the previous night. 'Miss Maddison was very tired last night,' said the assistant, reading carefully from a statement. 'She was also very upset about some sad personal news.'

I asked if she was sorry for what she had done. 'Miss Maddison very much regrets that she put other people in danger. She is very glad that no one was hurt.'

Another journalist asked what her father thought about the incident. 'Miss Maddison thanks her parents for their kindness and support,' said the assistant. Then the heiress disappeared into a waiting limousine.

6 **a** <u>Underline</u> four reported questions in the article. Match them to the direct questions in exercise 4.

b Compare the four direct and reported questions. What is the difference in word order? Read *Grammar2know*.

Grammar **2** know

Reporting *Wh-* questions and *yes/no* questions

We report *Wh-* questions with *ask* + question word:
'**What** does your father think?'
I asked her **what** her father thought.

We report *yes/no* questions with *ask* + if/whether:
'Are you sorry for what you did?'
I asked her **if** she was sorry for what she had done.

Word order in reported questions

Notice the word order of subject and verb in direct and reported questions:

  1 2   2 1
'**Were you** drunk?'   I asked whether **she had been** drunk.

Tenses, pronouns and time expressions change in the same way as in other reported speech.

7 Read more questions that reporters asked Miss Maddison. Rewrite them in reported speech.

1 What time did the incident happen?
I asked her …

2 Are you worried about going to prison?

3 Is your car damaged?

4 How long did you spend in the police cell?

5 Have you ever been arrested before?

8 In pairs, choose three questions from exercise 4 and write the answers. Now write an article like the one in exercise 5. Use reported speech where possible.

I asked him … and he said … Then I asked …

MINI-WORKBOOK exercises 3–4 page 118 and exercises 5–6 page 119

Reading & Speaking

1 Look at the headlines. Read the first line of each story and match them to the headlines.

B
Police threaten teenager with bill after massive party

A
DOG BITES STUDENT £7M LOTTERY WINNER

C
California Teenagers Face Prison for Hacking Into School Computers

True life stories 4.9

1

Two high school students from Orange County, California could go to prison for crimes that some people might think are trivial. Prosecutors told the court that Omar Khan and Tanvir Singh, both 18, had broken into Tesoro High School to steal tests and had changed their own and others' grades on the school computer network.

While Singh allegedly only tried doing it once, Khan apparently did it several times. Khan could get more than 38 years in prison. Singh could get three years. 'These are very serious crimes,' said prosecutor Chuck Lawhorn.

Defence lawyer Carol Lavacol told *The Los Angeles Times* that Khan was 'a really nice kid. He's only 18 years old, it's just a very sad situation.' Tesoro High School, with 2800 students, is one of the country's best.

2

An Australian teenager could be fined 20,000 AUS$ for having a party while his family was on holiday. 'It was just a get-together with a couple of mates at first and then we thought, why not have a bit of a party,' 16-year-old Corey Delaney told reporters. 'But it got a bit out of control.'

More than 500 people came to Corey's house in Melbourne and police were called when neighbours complained about the noise. No one was arrested but 30 police officers, a helicopter and a dog squad were needed to break the party up. Police chief Christine Nixon said that Corey would have to pay for damage to neighbours' cars and gardens. 'He needs to be taught a lesson and one way or another, we'll do that,' she said.

Corey's mother, Jo Delaney, said: 'We're a good family. I'm just horrified that this has actually happened.'

3

A teenage student was bitten by her dog as she celebrated a £7m lottery win. 18-year-old Ianthe Fullagar was shocked when she heard the news. 'I was screaming so loudly with excitement that my dog, Brock, didn't know what was happening. So he bit me!'

Ianthe is currently on a gap year between school and university, and has been working as a part-time waitress at a hotel near her home in Ravenglass, Cumbria. She said she was planning to organise a holiday in Egypt for herself, her family and friends, and to buy her first car. After that, she said she was still planning to go to university to study law. 'I just plan to live like a normal student and not like a millionaire,' she told reporters.

	The Royal Bank of Scotland plc
Pay	
Ianthe Fullagar	Date **26.09.08**
Seven million, fifty five thousand, one hundred	£ **7,055,142.10**
and forty two pounds and ten pence	Camelot Group plc Prize Payment Account

2 **a** Match at least two phrases below to each headline in exercise 1.

> to get out of control   a prison sentence
> a fine   to change grades   damage
> to complain   a defence lawyer
> a prosecutor   to break in   prize money
> to scream with excitement

b PREDICTING Can you predict what each story is about? Make a list of ideas with the class.

3 **a** Work in groups of three, A, B and C. Each read one 'True life' story on page 80. Answer the questions.

- What has happened?
- What do people say about it?
- What may/will happen next?

b Tell the other students in your group about the story you have read, using the questions above to help you.

4 Read all three stories. Choose the correct answer.

1 Singh and Khan
  a only changed their own grades.
  b only hacked into the school computer once.
  c may get very different punishments.

2 The prosecutor in California thinks
  a these crimes are trivial.
  b Omar and Tanvir are nice boys.
  c these are serious crimes.

3 Corey originally planned to
  a have a small party.
  b have a big party.
  c do a lot of damage.

4 Corey's mother
  a thinks her son is horrible.
  b can't really believe what has happened.
  c thinks her son has learnt a lesson.

5 Ianthe's dog
  a was probably frightened by her behaviour.
  b was excited that she had won.
  c is always very noisy.

5 **a** (4.7) Listen to some people A–C discussing the stories and answer the questions.

- Which story is each conversation about?
- Which people in the stories, do or don't the speakers agree with?

b (4.7) Listen again and tick (✓) the *Phrases2know* that you hear.

Phrases 2 know (4.8)

Asking other people's opinion
- ☐ Do you think this punishment is fair?
- ☐ Do you feel sorry for him?
- ☐ What would you do in that situation?

Giving and explaining your opinion
- ☐ Personally I don't think …
- ☐ I definitely think she should …
- ☐ Obviously you shouldn't …
- ☐ It's not fair that …
- ☐ She's completely right.
- ☐ I think he's wrong because …
- ☐ I don't feel sorry for them because …
- ☐ She probably feels …
- ☐ Personally, I'd …
- ☐ In that situation, I wouldn't …

6 **a** Read the questions below and spend a few minutes planning how to express your opinion.

b Discuss your opinion in groups.

Story 1
- Do you have any sympathy for Omar Khan and Tanvir Singh? Why do you think they did what they did?
- Do you think the prison sentences suggested in the article are fair or not?
- If not, what would be an appropriate punishment?

Story 2
- Do you have any sympathy for Corey Delaney?
- What would you do if you had a party that 'got out of control'?
- Do you think that a $20,000 fine is the right punishment for Corey?
- Who do you think should pay the fine?

Story 3
- If you won £7m, would you 'live like a normal student' or would you do something different?
- Do you think the win will make Ianthe's life better or not?
- How can Ianthe make sure that she can lead a 'normal' life?

7 WRITING Write a short paragraph giving your opinion about one of the stories. Use the *Phrases2know* to help you.

Personally, I think the punishment for Omar Khan is fair, because … He probably did this because … However, I don't feel sorry for him and I think he should …

activestudy5 (EXAMS)

Vocabulary

ACTIVE STUDY | Learn words in groups

1 Put the words below into the categories in the table. Add one more word in each category.

concussion ✓ crash editor lifeboat
defence lawyer advertisement
bleeding prosecutor review get stuck
symptoms prison sentence fine
gossip column dizzy firemen

Health problems	Accidents & rescues	The media	The law
	concussion		

ACTIVE STUDY | Learn collocations

2 Match the words to make collocations.

1 sprain	a out of control
2 feel	b an influence
3 take	c law
4 get	d sick
5 have	e painkillers
6 study	f your ankle

ACTIVE STUDY | Word formation

3 Complete the sentences with the correct form of the word in brackets.

1 Some celebrities want __*publicity*__ so much they'll do anything to get media attention. (PUBLIC)

2 Please knock before entering my room – respect my _____ . (PRIVATE)

3 The singer's fans were screaming with _____ . (EXCITE)

4 We waited for hours and _____ our friends arrived. (FINAL)

5 It's an _____ story, but it's true. (BELIEVE)

6 I've been under a lot of _____ recently because of exams. (PRESS)

7 _____ , the firemen arrived too late. (FORTUNE)

8 Shackleton's crew survived thanks to his _____ . (LEADER)

ACTIVE STUDY | Notice silent letters

4 PRONUNCIATION (4.10) Listen to the words and cross out the letter which is silent. Listen again and repeat.

1 exhausted   2 heiress

3 advertisement   4 doubtful

5 island   6 column

Grammar

5 Read the story. Put the phrases a–f in the gaps 1–6.

Keith Moore, 45, from Kendal, has received a police award for bravery this week. On 25 July [1] __*b*__ when he noticed two men talking to his elderly neighbour, Mrs Tillis. He heard them say they would come with her to the post office so she could pick up some money. 'I realised [2] ____ ,' he said later. Mr Moore immediately called the police [3] ____ . Mrs Tillis entered the post office and the men waited outside. Mr Moore followed her and managed to persuade her to stay indoors [4] ____ . The two men were arrested and it was discovered that [5] ____ in other towns before. Mr Moore, [6] ____ , said yesterday as he received the award: 'It is really nice to be honoured in this way but I don't see myself as a hero.'

a and then followed the three people to the town centre

b Mr Moore was working in his garden

c they had committed similar crimes

d they were trying to rob her

e until the police arrived

f who used to be a Cadet as a schoolboy

6 Complete the second sentence so that it means the same as the first.

1 'I work as a driver,' the man said.

The man said _he worked_ as a driver.

2 'I'm going to study law,' Amy said.

Amy said _____ law.

3 'I'll phone you every day,' Katie said to me.

Katie said _____ every day.

4 'I'm sorry I forgot to do the shopping,' said Daniel.

Daniel said _____ the shopping.

5 'Give me that gun!' said the police officer to the robber.

The police officer told _____ the gun.

6 'Have you ever seen a real criminal?' my friend asked me.

My friend asked _____ a real criminal.

7 'Where did you spend your holiday?' Mrs Young asked us.

Mrs Young asked _____ holiday.

Reading Skills

ACTIVE STUDY | Read for specific information

7 Read the following news story. Match the sentences a–f to the gaps 1–5. There is one extra sentence.

a 'Any one of us could have been killed,' he added.

b He then gave his name and other details to the cyclists and eventually drove away.

c Mr Johnson told the media that the incident showed London needed more cycle lanes.

d The door hit a parked Ford Mondeo and started pulling it along the street.

e When the police arrived, the witness reported what she'd seen.

f The police have contacted and questioned the lorry driver.

Mayor narrowly escapes accident (4.12)

Boris Johnson, the Mayor of London, narrowly escaped a dangerous accident while inspecting the streets on his bike last Friday. Mr Johnson and several other officials were cycling down Narrow Street in Limehouse, east London, looking for new cycle routes, when the door of a passing lorry, which had not been locked properly, opened as it was crossing a speed hump. ¹ ___ . The Ford crashed into another parked car. 'There was torn metal and broken glass flying in all directions,' a witness told our reporter.

The Mayor and the group accompanying him missed the crash by a few metres. One of the cyclists said it was a miracle nobody was injured. ² ___ . Commenting on the incident later, the Mayor said his companions had remained impressively calm.

The lorry driver got out, checked that nobody was hurt and helped clear the debris off the road. ³ ___ . The incident was recorded by a security camera on one of the buildings. The Mayor can be seen in the video, walking around the crashed cars and inspecting the damage.

⁴ ___ . He may be fined for two motoring offences: driving 'without due care and attention' and keeping a vehicle in a dangerous condition.

⁵ ___ . As the summer cycling season begins, the City Council promises a £115m 'cycle revolution', which will involve, among other projects, the introduction of a network of marked 'Cycle Super Highways' on key routes through the capital.

Listening Skills

ACTIVE STUDY | Listen for gist

8 (4.11) Listen to four news items. Match headings a–e to news items 1–4. There is one extra heading.

a Art thieves arrested

b Difficult rescue

c Fatal accident

d Internet thief faces jail sentence

e Lucky escape

Speaking Skills

9 In pairs, act out the following roleplay.

A: You have seen an accident. Tell the police about it. Include details of:
- the place
- the people
- the events.

B: You are a police officer. Student A will tell you about an accident he/she saw. Ask about the details:
- the exact time and place
- what happened
- Student A's reaction.

SKILLS STRATEGIES back cover

Grammar	Gerunds and infinitives
	Modals of deduction
Vocabulary	The arts
	Responses to art
Functions	Describing a picture
	Giving advice

Vocabulary & Speaking

Cultural events

1 Think of an example of each cultural event below. Compare your answers with the class. Which events can you see in the photos?

- an opera *Carmen*
- a fashion show
- a classical concert
- a musical
- a rock festival
- a new play
- an art exhibition
- ballet
- a heavy metal gig

2 **a** Imagine you can have a free ticket to one of the events in exercise 1. What are your first, second and third choices? Which two would you least like to go to?

b Compare and explain your answers in pairs.

I'd really like to go to the fashion show. I love fashion. How about you?

3 Check the *Words2know*. Which do you find at the events in exercise 1?

At a classical concert you find an orchestra ...

> ### Words 2 know (4.13)
>
> a set   lighting   a stage   paintings   an orchestra
> sculptures   an audience   costumes   a band
> backing musicians   a conductor
> an exciting atmosphere

4 Think about a cultural event that you have been to or seen on TV. In pairs, tell your partner what it was like.

The acting/music was fantastic!
What was the set like?

5 WRITING Write a short paragraph about the event you described in exercise 4.

I went to see ... at... recently. I really enjoyed it. The acting was excellent and the set was really unusual ...

MINI WORKBOOK exercise 6 page 121

Grammar Focus

Gerunds and infinitives

6 Read about the Headley Rock Festival. Would you like to have a festival like this in your town? Why? Why not?

HEADLEY ROCK FESTIVAL

Three days of live music, major international bands.

50,000 tickets on sale for camping festival.

www.headleyrock.com

7 Read what the five town residents think of the festival. Do they have positive, negative or mixed feelings?

> I'd really like **to go** … I love **watching** live music, and some good bands are coming. It's difficult to get tickets, and they're expensive, so I'm not sure if I'll be able to go.
> *Sam, 15*

> Standing in the rain and listening to loud rock music is not my idea of fun! I don't mind having the festival here – **it's important to have events for young people**, I think, but personally, **I'm planning to go away** that weekend!
> *David, 58*

> I'm really excited about having the festival here. I'm hoping to spend all three days there – it'll be so cool! **I'm queuing to get my ticket right now!**
> *Sophie, 19*

> I think there'll be a great atmosphere in the town, we definitely want to take our kids. **Camping and meeting different people will be a great experience for them**, and **we'll enjoy listening to the music!**
> *Liz, 36*

> **I'm not keen on having the festival here.** I know there'll be trouble, people will get drunk and behave badly in the town. There'll be litter and noise. I'm writing to the council to complain about it.
> *Bridget, 74*

8 **a** Read the first comment in exercise 7. Which verb in bold is a gerund and which is an infinitive?

b Read *Grammar2know*. Find another example for each rule in the texts.

Grammar **2know**

Gerunds

a Some verbs are followed by gerunds:
*I **love watching** live music.*
Also: *like, enjoy, don't mind, hate, can't stand, start, stop*

b We can use the gerund as the subject of a sentence:
***Standing** in the rain is not my idea of fun.*

c We always use a gerund after a preposition:
*I'm really excited **about having** the festival here.*
Also: *interested in, bored of, angry about, keen on*

Important uses of infinitives

d Some verbs are followed by infinitives:
*We definitely **want to take** our kids.*
Also: *would like, plan, need, hope, expect, decide*

e We often have sentences with *be* + adjective + infinitive:
***It is difficult to get** tickets.*
Also: *it's easy, expensive, cheap, good, better to*

f We use the infinitive to give the reason for doing something:
*I'm writing to the council **to complain**.*

9 Complete the sentences using the gerund or infinitive of the verb in brackets.

1 I love ___*spending*___ (spend) the weekend with lots of other people.
2 I'm going on eBay _____ (sell) my ticket.
3 It is impossible _____ (get) tickets for the gig.
4 I can't stand _____ (go) to museums.
5 _____ (Watch) a fashion show is not my idea of fun.
6 I'd really like _____ (see) that new musical.
7 We're queuing _____ (get) a good seat.
8 _____ (Queue) is really annoying.

10 Write sentences with gerunds or infinitives about the events in exercise 1 (or other events), using the phrases below.

I enjoy/don't enjoy …   I can't stand …
I'd like/love to …   … is /isn't my idea of fun.
… is really boring/annoying
I'm (not) very interested in/keen on …
It's very expensive/difficult/fun to …

I can't stand going to art exhibitions.
It's very expensive to go to a big football match.

MINI WORKBOOK exercises 1–3 page 120

Listening & Vocabulary

1 a What are the people in the photo below doing and why?

b Think of three good and bad things that may happen to street performers:

Good: *People could give you money.*

Bad: *It may start raining.*

2 (4.14) **Listen to an interview with Ben and Kirsty, two young buskers. Tick (✓) true and cross (✗) false.**

1 ☐ Ben and Kirsty used to be music students.
2 ☐ They've played in various cities around Europe.
3 ☐ They never play their own songs.
4 ☐ They usually make £30 or £40 a day.
5 ☐ People often give them £20 or more.
6 ☐ Rush hour is the best time for busking.
7 ☐ Friday is a good day for busking.

3 a **Words 2 know** (4.15) **Check the words in blue. Tick (✓) the reactions that Ben and Kirsty have experienced.**

1 ☐ Some people **don't take any notice** of them.
2 ☐ People often **appreciate** their music even if they don't give any money.
3 ☐ Some people **react positively** and obviously find their music **entertaining**.
4 ☐ Some people are very **generous**.
5 ☐ Some people **react negatively**. They **object** to buskers asking for money.
6 ☐ Some people tell them their music is **rubbish**.
7 ☐ Some people **shout rude comments** at them.

b (4.14) **Listen to the interview again in exercise 2 and check.**

4 Discuss the questions, using the *Words2know*.

• Are there street performers in your town/other towns you know? What do they do?

• How do the public react to them? What about you and your friends?

MINI WORKBOOK exercise 7 page 121

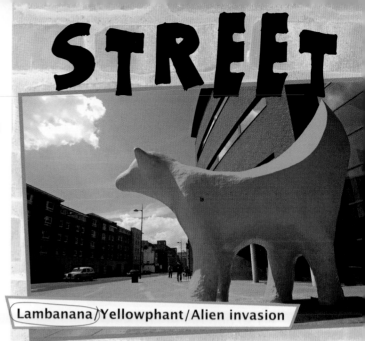

Lambanana / Yellowphant / Alien invasion

Grammar Focus

Modals of deduction

5 Look at the works of art. Which one do you think is the most interesting? Why?

6 a (4.16) Look at the possible titles for each work of art. Read and listen to some ideas about which is the correct title for each piece.

1 It **may** be *Lambanana* because it's yellow like a banana, and the front half **could** be a lamb.

2 It **can't** be *Two Sisters* because they are both men. I think they look like each other so it **must** be *The Littlewood Brothers*.

3 I don't know really … it **might** be *The Accident*, because I think the boy has just fallen into a hole in the ground. Or it **could** be *Rescue*, because when you look at it, you want to rescue him. But it **may** be untitled, because it's only a chalk drawing on a pavement, so perhaps the artist didn't give it a title?

b Which do you think is the correct title? Check on page135.

7 Answer the questions. Read *Grammar2know* and check.

• Do the speakers in exercise 6 know the titles of the works of art?

• Which speaker is sure about his/her ideas? Which speakers are not?

ART

Two Sisters/
The Friends/
The Littlewood
Brothers

The Accident/Rescue!/Untitled

Grammar **2 know**

Modals of deduction

must, might, may, could* and *can't

If you don't know something, use the verbs above to make a guess or a deduction.

a Use *must* when you are sure that something is true:

*The title **must be** The Littlewood Brothers.* (I'm sure it is.)

b Use *can't* when you feel sure that something isn't true:

*It **can't be** Two Sisters because they are both men!* (I'm sure it isn't.)

c Use *might, may* or *could* when you think something is possible but you are not sure:

*It **could/might/may be** The Rescue.* (I think it's possible.)

8 Complete the conversation about the painting below with *must, could* or *can't*.

A: Where do you think it is?

B: I'm not sure. It ¹ _can't_ be in this country because the signs are all in English, so it ² _____ be an English-speaking country.

A: I suppose so. It ³ _____ be England.

B: Hmm, I don't think so. I don't think it snows much there, and look, the cars are on the right of the road so it ⁴ _____ be England.

A: The buildings look American so it ⁵ _____ be the USA.

B: Or Canada.

A: Yes. It ⁶ _____ be one of those countries.

B: It ⁷ _____ be winter time because it looks wet and cold, and there's snow on the ground.

A: Yes, but if you look carefully, the road is wet because the snow is melting. So it ⁸ _____ be the beginning of spring, after a very cold winter. March or April perhaps?

B: Or Christmas? Those ⁹ _____ be Christmas decorations on the street lamps.

9 SPEAKING In pairs, talk about the painting on page 135 using the modal verbs. Use the prompts and your own ideas. Give reasons for your ideas.

It must be very late, because it's dark and there are no people in the street.

MINI WORKBOOK exercises 4–5 pages 120–121

for art's sake

Reading & Speaking

1 Look at the five works of art. Have you seen any of them? Find the following.

> graffiti   sheets   a shark   a portrait
> abstract swirls of colour   underwear

2 PREDICTION Which works of art do you think are the most/least valuable? Why?

3 SCANNING Read the text and complete the captions with the name of the artist and the price. Write (?) if there is no information.

4 Find the missing word or phrase in the text to match the definitions:

1 *a genius* : a person who is exceptionally clever (n) (paragraph 1)

2 _____ : a person who writes and gives their opinions about the arts (n) (paragraph 1)

3 _____ : to pay for everything that someone needs. (v) (paragraph 2)

4 _____ : to have the value of (adj) (paragraph 2)

5 _____ : causing a lot of disagreement (adj) (paragraph 3)

6 _____ : an event when things are sold (n) (paragraph 4)

7 _____ : to show something in public (v) (paragraph 4)

5 Read the text and choose the correct answer.

1 Jackson Pollock
   a was considered a genius after he died.
   b was successful when he was alive.
   c also designed wallpaper.

2 Van Gogh
   a died very poor.
   b gave all his money to his brother.
   c sold his paintings for millions.

3 Damien Hirst
   a doesn't make much money.
   b makes all his work himself.
   c says that money doesn't matter to him.

4 The exhibition of Tracey Emin's bed received a lot of publicity because
   a some people didn't think it was real art.
   b a visitor cleaned the bed up.
   c Tracey Emin laughed at the visitors.

5 Banksy
   a doesn't get paid for his work.
   b is a well-known celebrity.
   c isn't appreciated by everyone.

By _____   Price _____

By _____   Price _____

Art and Money
(4.18)

In 2006, a Mexican businessman paid $140 million for *No 5 1948*, by the American artist Jackson Pollock. It was the most expensive painting ever sold. But is any work of art worth such an incredible price? Pollock created his abstract swirls of colour by dripping paint onto the canvas, often dancing as he did it and for many in the art world, he was a genius. Not everyone agrees though, one critic has compared his paintings to wallpaper!

At least Jackson Pollock was appreciated during his lifetime. Not all great artists have been so lucky. Dutch artist Vincent Van Gogh only sold one painting in his entire career and his brother had to support him financially throughout his life. He died in poverty at the age of 37, unknown to the world. Yet a hundred years later, almost any work by Van Gogh is worth millions. His *Portrait of Dr Gachet* sold for $ 82.3m in 1990.

Other artists are more fortunate in their lifetime: Picasso and Dali were multi-millionaires when they died. The controversial British artist Damien Hirst is perhaps the most successful living artist of all: in 2008, a sale of his work raised $198 million.

By _____ Price _____

By _____ Price ___?_____

By _____ Price _____

However, he doesn't usually make the works himself – that is done by assistants. As a conceptual artist, he believes it is the artist's original idea that makes something into a work of art. Typical Hirst pieces include a dead shark, which sold in 2004 for $12 million. However, Hirst claims that he 'always ignores money.'

For some people, this is not art at all. There was great controversy when *My Bed*, a work by conceptual artist Tracey Emin, was displayed in one of London's top art galleries. Many visitors were horrified by the unmade bed, complete with dirty sheets and underwear, and one lady even tried to tidy it up! However, the artist had the last laugh – after the exhibition, the bed sold for £200,000.

Even graffiti makes money these days. Take the mysterious graffiti artist, 'Banksy', whose 'street art', with its strong political and social messages, appears on walls and buildings all over the world. No one knows who 'Bansky' actually is, but his work now sells for hundreds of thousands of dollars, and celebrity collectors include Angelina Jolie and Christina Aguilera. However, not everyone is impressed. After all, graffiti is against the law!

6 **a** Spend a few minutes deciding what you think of the works of art. Use the *Phrases2know* to help you.

> **Phrases 2 know** (4.17)
>
> **Asking for opinions**
>
> What do you think of …
>
> What do you think the artist is trying to say?
>
> Do you think this is a work of art?
>
> **Giving your opinion**
>
> I really like the style.
>
> It's very beautiful/original/sad.
>
> I don't understand what the artist is trying to say.
>
> I think it's ugly/ridiculous.
>
> It makes you think.
>
> It doesn't mean anything to me!
>
> I don't think it's a work of art.
>
> It reminds me of wallpaper.

b In pairs, discuss your opinions.

What do you think of the Jackson Pollock?

I really like … because I like the style. It's very original and interesting.

7 **a** WRITING Choose either one of the works of art in this unit or another work of art you know.

b Write a description giving your opinion of it.

This picture shows …

MINI WORKBOOK exercise 8 page 121

REAL TIME

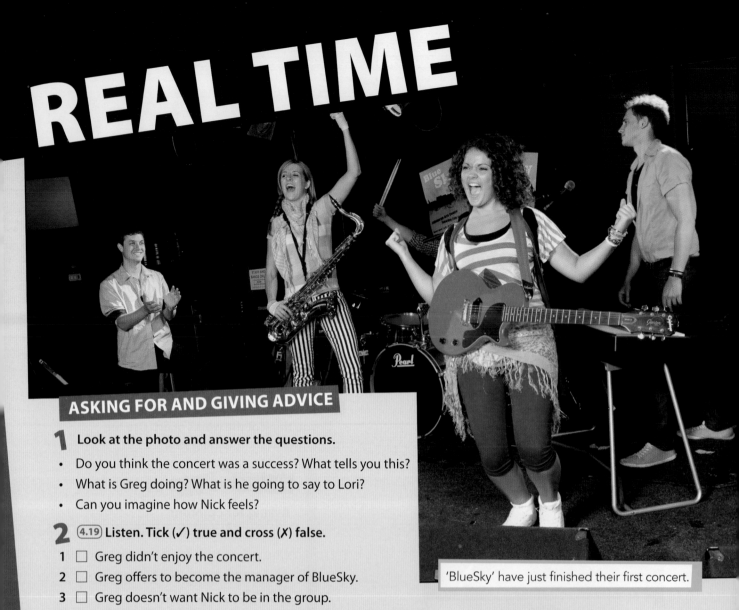

ASKING FOR AND GIVING ADVICE

1 **Look at the photo and answer the questions.**

- Do you think the concert was a success? What tells you this?
- What is Greg doing? What is he going to say to Lori?
- Can you imagine how Nick feels?

2 (4.19) **Listen. Tick (✓) true and cross (✗) false.**

1 ☐ Greg didn't enjoy the concert.
2 ☐ Greg offers to become the manager of BlueSky.
3 ☐ Greg doesn't want Nick to be in the group.
4 ☐ Lori agrees to look for a new keyboard player.

'BlueSky' have just finished their first concert.

3 (4.20) **Lori talks to Kate about Greg's suggestion. Complete the conversation with the *Phrases2know*. Then listen and check.**

> **Kate:** Lori, what's the matter? You look worried …
>
> **Lori:** Kate, ¹ _____ ? It's important, it's about the group.
>
> **Kate:** Sure.
>
> **Lori:** It's Greg. He wants to be our manager. I know he'd be fantastic for us – he knows everyone in the music business – I think he could really help us in our career.
>
> **Kate:** Absolutely! So, ² _____ ?
>
> **Lori:** Nick. Greg doesn't want Nick to be in the group. He doesn't think he's lively enough!
>
> **Kate:** In other words, he thinks we should get someone else.
>
> **Lori:** Exactly. ³ _____ ? Should I say something to Nick?
>
> **Kate:** Well, ⁴ _____ to him if I were you, you know how sensitive Nick is. He really likes you.
>
> **Lori:** Do you think so?
>
> **Kate:** Yeah, really. So, it's either Nick or Greg. I think you should do what you think is right, Lori.
>
> **Lori:** ⁵ _____ but – it's so difficult!!

Phrases 2know

Asking what's wrong
What's the matter?
What's the problem?
What's up?

Asking for advice
Can I ask your opinion about something?
What do you think we should do?
Should I say something?

Giving advice
I wouldn't say anything about that.
You should try something different.
I think you should speak to him.

Agreeing and responding sympathetically
You're right.
Sure!
Absolutely!
Exactly!

4 (4.21) **Listen and practise saying the *Phrases2know*.**

5 In pairs, take turns to act out the conversation. Student A, your friend is worried about some exams. Student B, turn to the notes on page 135.

Student B, turn to the notes on page 135.

- Student B looks worried, ask what's wrong
- Agree. Ask what the problem is.
- Respond sympathetically, give B advice about the problem.

Try the conversation again with these problems:

- worried about money
- worried about girl/boyfriend.

CAN YOU DO IT IN ENGLISH?

6 (4.22) Listen to Greg and Lori's conversation and answer the questions.

1 What did Lori decide to do in the end?
2 How does Greg respond to this?
3 What was Greg's real reason for coming to the gig?
4 Do Lori and Greg finish their conversation in a friendly way?
5 Do you think Lori made the right decision? Why? Why not?

After asking Kate's advice, Lori speaks to Greg.

A CONCERT REVIEW

7 A few days, later a review of the concert is posted on *musiclive.com*. Read the review quickly. In which paragraph do you find:

☐ the name of the group/singer and some background information about the type of music/people in the group
☐ where and when the concert happened and how many people were in the audience
☐ information about some of the songs and how the audience reacted
☐ the introduction
☐ a summary of the concert.

Phrases 2 know

Giving information about the group
'BlueSky' are a great new/well-known rock group from …
The group has … members.
The real star is …
Where and where the concert happened
The band played at … on … to an audience of …
Information about the songs and the audience
They began with …
The audience really loved …
Their last song was …
Summing up and the reviewer's opinion
To sum up …
This was a brilliant/awful/exciting gig.
I recommend … for anyone who likes …

What's new on the local scene …

1 This week we sent our reporter to listen to an exciting new group on the Edinburgh music scene.

2 BlueSky are a great new rock group from Edinburgh. The group has five members, but the real star is singer-guitarist Lori Ash. Lori was born in England, but she is now a student at the Edinburgh College of Performing Arts. Lori writes many of their songs, with keyboard player Nick Wallace writing the lyrics.

3 The band played at the Edinburgh Arts Centre, one of the city's best small venues with its low ceilings and great sound, on Saturday night to an audience of more than a hundred people.

4 They began with a song Lori wrote called *From the Inside*. Lori definitely looks like a star of the future! The others seemed nervous at first, but they soon became more confident. The highlight of the performance was *I Do It All For You* – a romantic duet between Lori and Nick which the audience loved! Their last song was the Coldplay hit *Yellow* – by the end everyone in the audience was singing and dancing.

5 To sum up, this was a brilliant gig by a really exciting new group. I recommend BlueSky for anyone who likes music with heart, soul and plenty of energy. Go and see them live and tell your friends!

8 a Prepare to write a review of a concert in your town (you can use real information, invent a group, or look at the notes on page 135). Write some notes about:

look at the notes on page 135

- the name of the group/singer and some background information about the type of music/people in the group
- where and when the concert happened and how many people were in the audience
- information about some of the songs and how the audience reacted
- adjectives of opinion, positive and negative.

b Write your review. Use the model in exercise 7, your notes and the *Phrases2know* to help you. Write about 200–250 words.

Grammar	Third conditional
	Quantifiers
Vocabulary	Abstract nouns
	Physical description
Functions	Describing objects

Listening & Vocabulary

1 **a** Look at the list of some of the world's most important inventions. Which can you see in the photos?

- the rocket
- gunpowder
- the telephone
- penicillin
- time zones
- the wheel
- the World Wide Web
- the printing press

b Add five more inventions to the list.

2 (4.23) In pairs, answer the quiz questions. Then listen and check.

The world's most important inventions

★**1** The invention of gunpowder led to the creation of many great empires. Who originally invented gunpowder?
a The Chinese
b The Americans
c The Spanish

★**2** The invention of the printing press gave information and knowledge to millions of people. When was it invented?
a 1040 b 1440 c 1740

★**3** Standard time zones are important for successful modern business and travel. How many time zones is the world divided into?
a twelve b twenty-four c thirty-six

★**4** Penicillin was the first drug that cured many dangerous diseases. What was penicillin used to develop?
a vaccines b painkillers
c antibiotics

★**5** Everyone uses a mobile phone to communicate these days, but when did they first become available?
a 1950s b 1970s c 1980s

★**6** Tim Berners-Lee created the important modern system for communication, education and entertainment. What was it?
a the World Wide Web
b television c radio

3 (4.23) Listen again and answer the questions.

1 When was gunpowder first invented?

2 Why was education difficult before the invention of the printing press?

3 Before 1884, what did you find if you travelled to a different town or country?

4 What *can't* antibiotics cure?

5 How much did the first mobile phones weigh?

6 What important decision did Tim Berners-Lee make?

4 **a** Which five inventions in exercise 1 are most important in your opinion? Compare your lists with other students.

b What will be the next great invention, do you think?

5 Read *Active Study* and complete the table. How many forms can you complete **without** using a dictionary?

Notice word families

Some words have several forms:

noun: creation   verb: to create
adjective: creative

A dictionary can help you to find these:

cre·ate /kri'eɪt/ v
1 to make something exist that did not exist before: *Some people believe the universe was created by a big explosion.*

cre·a·tion /kri'eɪʃən/ n
1 [U] the act of creating something: **[+of]** *the creation of 2,000 new jobs*

cre·a·tive /kri'eɪtɪv/ adj
1 involving the use of imagination to produce new ideas or things: *This job is so boring. I wish I could do something more creative.*

ACTIVE STUDY

verb	noun	adjective
a *communicate*	communication	b _____
c _____	development	——
d _____	discovery	——
e _____	education	f _____
g _____	entertainment	h _____
i _____	information	j _____
k _____	invention	l _____
m _____	knowledge	n _____

MINI WORKBOOK exercise 6 page 123

Grammar Focus

Third conditional

6 Read about Antonio Meucci and then close your book. In groups, what can you remember about his life? Think about:

- where and when he was born and the different places he lived
- the problems he had in his life
- his achievements and his reputation today.

★ The man who (nearly) invented the telephone (4.24)

Ask most people who invented the telephone and they say it was the Scot, Alexander Graham Bell. However, the U.S. Congress has now agreed that the true inventor of the telephone was an unknown Italian inventor, who died in poverty in New York. Antonio Meucci was born in Florence in 1808. In the 1830s, he got into trouble with the authorities for his political views and, after a period in prison, he decided to move to Cuba. There he continued working on his inventions and discovered that sounds could travel through copper wire. In 1850, Meucci moved to the United States, where he thought he would have more opportunities to develop his ideas. When his wife became ill, he developed a primitive telephone system so that she could 'phone' him from her bed while he was working. Around 1860, he demonstrated his latest invention, the *teletrofono*, but because he didn't speak English well, few people were interested. Then in 1870, he became ill himself and had to sell his plans to pay for doctors. Meanwhile, another inventor, Alexander Graham Bell was working on a similar idea, and the rest is history …

---

7 **a** Read three imaginary sentences about Meucci. Do the sentences describe situations in the past, present or future?

- If Meucci hadn't gone to prison, perhaps he wouldn't have left Italy.
- If Meucci's wife hadn't been ill, he wouldn't have invented his first telephone.
- If Meucci had spoken better English, people would have taken more notice of him.

b Read *Grammar2know* to check.

Third conditional

Use the third conditional to describe hypothetical (imaginary) situations in the past and their imaginary consequences:

*If Meucci **had spoken** better English …*

(he didn't speak good English, so we are imagining)

*more people **would have listened** to his ideas.*

(they didn't listen because he didn't speak good English)

Form

*If + **had** + past participle, **would** + **have** + past participle*

+ *People **would have listened** to him if he'**d spoken** better English.*

− *He **wouldn't have sold** his plans if he **hadn't been** ill.*

? *__Would__ he **have invented** the telephone if his wife **had been** well? Yes, he **would**./No, he **wouldn't**.*

---

8 Complete the sentences about Meucci and the inventions on page 92.

1 Meucci (not be able) to develop his ideas if he (stay) in Cuba.

2 He (not sell) his plans for a telephone if he (not become) ill.

3 If he (sell) his ideas, he (become) a very rich man.

4 If Meucci (publish) his ideas, Alexander Graham Bell (not become) so famous.

5 If Gutenberg (not invent) the printing press, ordinary people (not have) books.

6 If European countries (not have) gunpowder, they (not build) such big empires.

7 If Fleming (not discover) penicillin, we (not find) a cure for many diseases.

8 If someone else (invent) the World Wide Web, perhaps they (not make) it free.

---

9 **a** Think of some events in your life that are linked to each other.

I got up late – I forgot my homework – I got detention

b Write sentences about the events, like this:

If I hadn't got up late, I wouldn't have forgotten my homework.

If I hadn't forgotten my homework, I wouldn't have got detention.

MINI WORKBOOK exercises 1–2 page 122 and exercise 5 page 123

Vocabulary & Speaking

Describing objects

1 WORD RACE In one minute think of five everyday objects that you find in these places.

1 A desk: *a pencil sharpener*
2 A kitchen: *a knife*
3 Your bag or pockets: *an umbrella*

2 **a** (4.25) Listen to Ali and Bella playing a guessing game. Number the questions in *Phrases2know* in the order that you hear them in the recording.

> **Phrases 2 know**
>
> **Asking about objects**
> ☐ How big is it?
> ☐ What shape is it?
> ☑ What is it made of?
> ☐ What's it used for?
> ☐ Has it got any special features?
>
> **Giving descriptions**
> It's made of plastic.
> It's got speakers.
> It's for measuring things.
> It's about 30 cm long.
> It's long and rectangular.

b (4.25) Listen again. Which answer in *Phrases2know* is different from the recording? What object is Ali thinking of?

3 (4.26) Match the answers in *Phrases2know* to the questions. Listen and practise the phrases.

4 **a** **Words 2 know** (4.27) Check the words in blue and then decide which question in *Phrases2know* they answer.

- It's two metres **high/wide**.
- It's made of **leather/metal/wood/ fabric**.
- It's got a **handle/switch/pocket**.
- It's **cylindrical/round/flat/ long and thin**.
- It's for **storing/spreading/cutting/holding** things.

b Write six sentences about everyday objects, three true and three false. Your partner decides which are true and which are false.

" *Scissors are usually made of wood.*   *False!*
Pencils are long and thin.   *True!*

5 Play the guessing game on the recording in exercise 2. Take turns to think of an everyday object and answer your partner's questions.

MINI WORKBOOK exercise 7 page 123

Grammar Focus

Quantifiers

6 Match the inventions A–E in the pictures to their names. What are they used for?

☐ Butter stick   ☐ Office tie
☐ iPod cushion   ☐ Umbrella headband
☐ Stair drawers

7 Which inventions do you think are the most and least useful?

8 (4.28) Which invention(s) are the speakers below discussing? Are their reactions positive?

① This is brilliant! If you're carrying **a lot of** stuff, and if **both** your hands are full it's really hard to hold an umbrella … I'm going to buy one for these as a present for all my friends!

② This is a fantastic idea! **Every** one holds **several** pairs of shoes. I've got **no** storage space in my house, and I've got **a lot of** shoes. If I had **a few** drawers like this in my stairs, I'd have **plenty of** space for my shoes!

③ I'm not sure about this one … **none of** the pockets are big enough for a wallet or a purse … and there's **no** reason to carry a pair of scissors around with you, is there? I don't think it's very useful.

④ Hmm … I suppose if you just want **a little bit** of it on your bread, it's a good idea … but I think **a lot of** people will think it's disgusting, so I don't think it'll catch on!

⑤ I'd love to have the cushion – it's really cool, but I think the tie and the umbrella thing are a bit weird, **neither of** them are things that I would want!

I'd never thought of that!

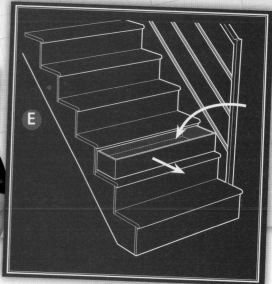

9 a Find the quantifiers in **bold** in exercise 8. Mark them C if they are followed by a countable noun and U by an uncountable noun. Which are followed by both?

a lot of <u>*stuff*</u>   *U*   *both* <u>*your hands*</u>   *C*

b Read *Grammar2know* to check your answers.

Quantifiers

	countable nouns	uncountable nouns
100%	**all** my friends	**all** your stuff
	every drawer	
	a lot of shoes	**a lot of** stuff
	plenty of drawers	**plenty of** space
	several pairs	
	a few drawers	**a little (bit of)** butter
0%	**no** reason	**no** butter

a Use *both* and *neither* to talk about two things:

(+) *Both your hands are full.*

(–) *Neither of them are things that I would want.*

b Use *all* or *none* to talk about more than two things:

(+) *I'm going to buy one for all my friends.*

(–) *None of the pockets are big enough.*

10 Complete the sentences with *both, neither, all* or *none*.

1 Helen's mum and dad are _____ art teachers.

2 _____ the students in my year have to study design technology.

3 I've got two mobile phones but _____ of them is working at the moment!

4 It was such a difficult exam that _____ of the students passed.

5 I tried two pairs of shoes but _____ of them was the right size.

6 Claudia and Irena _____ speak Spanish very well.

7 He spoke so quietly that _____ of the people in the audience could hear him.

8 My sister keeps _____ her CDs in order.

11 a (4.29) Underline the quantifier that best completes each sentence. Listen and check.

Is your bedroom a mess? Mine is. I can never find things. [1]*All/Every* morning before I leave the house I waste [2] *a few/a lot of/all* time looking for things – my keys, my purse, my iPod. So last week I decided have a big clear out. There's [3] *a little/no/a lot of* space in my room for anything new, so I decided to throw away [4] *all/a little/a few* the things I don't use any more – old books, games and magazines. It was really interesting! As I was looking under the bed I found [5] *all/a bit of/a little* my old school reports and [6] *all/every/several* CDs which I thought I'd lost! [7] *A few/A little/Every* hours later, I'd managed to fill [8] *several/a little/every* plastic bags with [9] *all/a few/every* my old things. Now, I've got [10] *a lot of/no/a few* space in my room … but I still can't find anything!

b Write a short description of your bedroom, using quantifiers to describe it.

MINI WORKBOOK exercises 3–4 page 122

Reading & Speaking

1 Look at the pictures of five robots. Which are from movies and which show real-life robots?

2 **a** Check the words below. Which things do you think robots can already do?

> assemble cars   dispose of bombs
> explore under the sea   do housework
> give medicine to hospital patients
> respond to greetings   serve drinks
> change facial expression   fight in wars
> show emotions like compassion and pity

b Read the text quickly and check your answers.

3 Read the text again. Tick (✓) true and cross (✗) false. Write (?) if there is no information in the text.

1 ☐ *Star Wars* showed life in the 1980s.

2 ☐ One twentieth-century scientist thought that robots would replace human beings.

3 ☐ Robots are only used to do jobs which are dangerous for humans.

4 ☐ New robots in Japan are being designed to resemble human beings.

5 ☐ Robots will replace doctors in many hospitals by 2030.

6 ☐ Many car workers are angry that robots have taken their jobs.

7 ☐ The military expert believes that robots will replace soldiers.

8 ☐ He mentions three disadvantages of robots over human soldiers.

4 Discuss the questions. Give reasons for your answers.

- Which things should robots do, and which things shouldn't they do?
- Is there anything in the text that you find worrying?
- Do you think robots will ever take over the world?

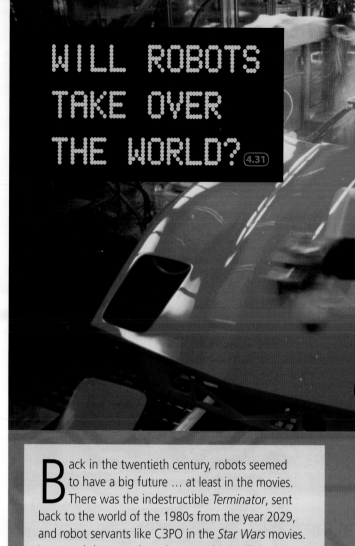

WILL ROBOTS TAKE OVER THE WORLD? 4.31

Back in the twentieth century, robots seemed to have a big future … at least in the movies. There was the indestructible *Terminator*, sent back to the world of the 1980s from the year 2029, and robot servants like C3PO in the *Star Wars* movies. It seemed that one day robots would do all the boring or dangerous jobs while the humans sat around doing something more interesting. But there was also a fear that robots might become the bosses, not the servants. 'Unless mankind redesigns itself by changing our DNA, computer-generated robots will take over our world,' wrote one famous scientist.

Has it happened? You're still unlikely to see a robot walking around your town but that doesn't mean they don't exist. Robots are used in car manufacturing, and in areas which are dangerous for humans, in bomb disposal and deep-sea exploration, for example. There are even robots which carry drinks at fashionable parties! According to one estimate, there are 750,000 working robots in the world today.

These working robots definitely look like machines but many scientists are now trying to make robots look more similar to humans. Hiroshi Ishiguro, a professor at Osaka University, has created a new generation of robots, including an exact robot copy of himself. At Tokyo Science University there are robot receptionists which respond to greetings and even look upset if you speak to them rudely!

So what will robots be able to do by, say, the year 2030? There are already plans to use robots in hospitals and old people's homes. Robot nurses will remind patients to take their medicine or tell a doctor if the patient needs attention. But many people are worried about the idea of robots looking after the old, the sick and the very young, depriving them of important human contact. It could also create unemployment. Robots have already replaced workers in the car industry and there is a real possibility that robots will be used for many jobs in areas like fast-food service and retail sales.

An even bigger concern is the use of robots for military purposes. Robots have already been used in several war zones, and according to one prediction, thirty percent of all frontline soldiers will be robots by the year 2050. Robot soldiers have several advantages over humans. 'Robots don't get hungry, they don't get tired, and they can kill without pity,' says one military expert. 'It's not a question of whether robots will replace humans, it's a question of when.'

But can we be sure that the next generation of robots will always obey human orders? Or will we be able to create robots that have human emotions, such as kindness and compassion? Only the future will tell. But have a good look at the person sitting next to you on the bus home. He or she might just be a robot!

CAN YOU DO IT IN ENGLISH?

5  Sophie has designed her own personal robot servant. Listen and tick the features below that it has.

1 ☐ It looks like Brad Pitt.
2 ☐ It looks like a cute little puppy.
3 ☐ It can do her homework.
4 ☐ It can tidy her bedroom.
5 ☐ It can play computer games with her.
6 ☐ It can serve her drinks and heat up snacks for her.
7 ☐ It can put on her make-up for her.
8 ☐ It can choose music to suit her mood.
9 ☐ It can choose clothes for her.
10 ☐ It can chat and tell her interesting gossip.

6 **a** Spend a few minutes designing your own personal robot. You can include features from exercise 5, but include at least four ideas of your own.

b Is there anything that you wouldn't like your robot to do?

7 **a** Take turns to present your robot either to the class or in groups.

b Decide whose robot you like best and why.

> *I'd like a robot that can wake me up in the morning with a cup of coffee.*
>
> *I wouldn't like my robot to choose music for me because I prefer to choose music myself.*

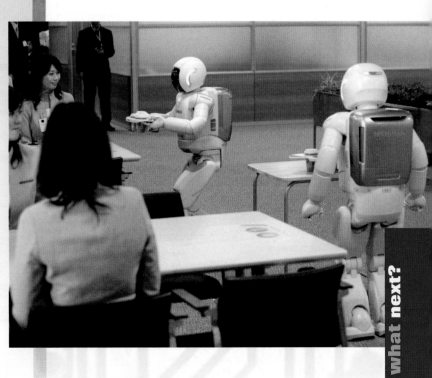

what next?

97

Vocabulary

1 Match the words below to the sentences in which they could be used. Add one more word to each group.

> **a** an audience **b** ballet performance
> **c** costumes **d** cylindrical **e** exhibition
> **f** fabric **g** flat **h** gig
> **i** leather **j** lighting **k** metal
> **l** penicillin **m** play **n** the wheel
> **o** the printing press **p** rectangular
> **q** round **r** a stage **s** wood

1 I went to see a(n) … at the Centre of Modern Culture. _b_ ___ ___ ___

2 At the theatre you have … ___ ___ ___ ___

3 The object is made of … ___ ___ ___ ___

4 The object is … in shape. ___ ___ ___ ___

5 … is one of the world's most important inventions.

___ ___ ___

2 Complete the sentences with the correct prepositions.

1 The audience shouted angry comments _at_ the band.

2 Most people didn't take any notice ____ the new sculpture in the park.

3 My friend objects ____ conceptual art. She thinks it's rubbish.

4 I'm not keen ____ opera.

5 He didn't respond ____ my greeting.

6 There's plenty ____ space in these drawers.

3 Use the words in brackets to build words which complete the text.

'Educating the whole person

The world is changing faster than ever before. Nobody knows what the future will look like, and exactly what skills you will need to be [1](SUCCESS) _successful_ . Unfortunately, nearly all educational systems focus too much on [2](KNOW) _____ and intellectual skills. The importance of [3](CREATE) _____ is not always appreciated. But if you don't get a chance to discover your creative side, your [4](DEVELOP) _____ is not complete. Of course not everyone will become an actor or a [5](MUSIC) _____ , but we need to explore our different abilities to discover what we're best at. Another important area that everyone needs to learn is 'people skills,' such as being [6](COMMUNICATE) _____ and sensitive to others.'

4 PRONUNCIATION (4.32) Listen to the words from exercise 3 and write each word next to its stress pattern. Listen again and repeat the words.

1 ■▪ _____

2 ▪■▪ _successful_ _____

3 ■▪■▪ _____

4 ▪■▪■▪ _____

5 ▪▪■▪▪ _____

Grammar

5 Number the quantifiers from 1 (the largest) to 5 (the smallest).

I've seen ☐ **several of** his paintings.

☐ **none of** his paintings.

☐ **just a few** of his paintings.

☐ **all of** his paintings.

☐ **plenty of** his paintings.

6 Complete the sentences with the correct form of the verb, gerund or infinitive.

1 I hope _to get_ (get) tickets for the film festival.

2 I'm fed up with _____ (look) at paintings. Let's do something different tomorrow!

3 _____ (Listen) to classical music is not my idea of fun.

4 It's not very expensive _____ (make) your own video.

5 I'm phoning the theatre _____ (ask) about tickets.

6 My parents gave up _____ (go) to gigs after the age of forty.

7 Complete the second sentence so that it means the same as the first.

1 Perhaps he's a singer.

He ____ _might be_ ____ a singer.

2 We didn't go to the exhibition because we didn't know about it.

If we _____ to it.

3 I'm sure he's not an actor.

He _____ be an actor.

4 There were two new films on at the cinema, but both looked uninteresting to me.

There were two new films on at the cinema, but _____ them looked interesting to me.

article   discussion

search

Street Art at Tate Modern (4.33)

On 23 May 2008, six enormous graffiti appeared on the red wall of the Tate Modern gallery, which overlooks the river Thames. Did the management call the police to report this act of vandalism? No. In fact, they had paid large sums of money for the pictures to be placed there. The artworks were part of an exhibition entitled Street Art, the first major public museum show of such art in London. They'd been created by six internationally famous artists working in different urban environments.

All the works showed large human or human-like figures. Those by Sixeart from Barcelona were very colourful, painted in a childlike style. Nunca from São Paulo, Brazil, was inspired by the traditional art of his country. Os Gêmeos ('The Brothers'), also from São Paulo, had painted a yellow giant wearing a red mask. The graffiti by Blu from Bologna showed a large white head cut open to show what was inside – a lot of small, detailed scenes.

Not all the pictures were strictly graffiti. Some were 'paste-ups', which means they had been painted on several large sheets of paper or canvas and then pasted onto the wall. The piece I liked best was a large paste-up by JR from Paris. It showed a black man holding what at first seemed to be a gun, but was actually a camera pointed at the viewer. It made me think about the stereotypes we sometimes uncritically accept.

More urban art was on show in the streets around Tate Modern. You could join a guided tour or just pick up a map from the gallery to see work by five artists from Madrid in the kind of city environment where it would normally appear. The exhibition was accompanied by talks and discussions on issues such as: Is 'street art' a real art form or just a nicer word for vandalism? Who does public space belong to and who should decide how it's used? The show closed in August 2008, but here's the good news: if you weren't there, you can still see all the pictures, go on an interactive tour, and read about all the artists, on the Tate Modern website!

Reading Skills

ACTIVE STUDY | **Read for specific information**

8 **Read the text and choose the correct answer.**

1 The wall of the Tate Modern

a can be seen from the river.

b was vandalised.

c displayed six paintings from the gallery.

d was very expensive to build.

2 All the works

a used the same technique.

b were very colourful.

c showed people or similar creatures.

d had been pasted on the wall.

3 What makes the six artists similar is that

a they are all from Europe.

b they all work in cities.

c they paint in the same style.

d they are inspired by traditional art of their countries.

4 The picture by JR

a was supposed to make you think.

b showed a black man with a gun.

c was not clear.

d had been made in Paris.

5 The pictures by artists from Madrid

a could only be seen by organised groups with a guide.

b were difficult to find without a map.

c were shown in the gallery.

d were in places similar to those where you would ordinarily see them.

6 If you haven't seen the exhibition, you can still

a get a map with all the pictures on it.

b visit the gallery's website.

c go on a guided tour of the gallery.

d listen to a talk on street art.

Speaking Skills

9 **Choose one of the topics and talk about it on your own for about three minutes.**

- 'People who dislike modern art just don't understand it.' Do you agree?

- 'Robots will take over the world some day.' Do you agree?

SKILLS STRATEGIES back cover

1miniworkbook

✳ easy to do
✳✳ a bit harder
✳✳✳ extra challenge

Grammar

1 ✳ Present continuous

Complete the sentences with the correct form of the verb in brackets.

1 It is _becoming_ (become) very difficult to find a good job these days.

2 My uncle _____ (not come) back from Spain until next week.

3 'How _____ (your driving lessons/go)?' 'Great! I _____(learn) how to park the car this week!'

4 It's nearly April – the days _____ (get) longer and the weather _____ (improve).

5 '_____ (you/enjoy) your meal?' 'Yes, thanks!'

6 My sister is an actress but she _____ (not work) at the moment.

2 ✳✳✳ Present simple and present continuous

Complete the interview with the correct form of the verb in brackets.

Interviewer: I ¹ _'m talking_ (talk) to Larry Bailey, who's an English teacher with a difference … Larry, what kind of people ² _____ (you/teach)?

Larry: I ³ _____ (teach) footballers. More and more foreign players ⁴ _____ (come) to play in England these days, so English ⁵ _____ (become) more and more important for them.

I: I see. How many students ⁶ _____ (teach) at the moment?

L: I ⁷ _____ (work) with three students right now – they ⁸ _____ (have) lessons two or three times a week. Next Monday I ⁹ _____ (start) with a new student – he ¹⁰ _____ (come) from Russia and he ¹¹ _____ (not speak) a word of English!

I: One more question, ¹² _____(like) football, Larry?

L: Oh no! I ¹³ _____ (hate) it! But I like footballers!

3 ✳✳ Read *Grammar Plus*. Then underline the correct answer.

Grammar + Plus

Time expressions

• When we talk about how often we do things we use phrases like:

once/twice/three times a day/week/month
every day/week/month etc.

We usually put these phrases at the end of the sentence:

*We go to the cinema **three times a month**.*

• We can also use phrases with *most* and *some*:

most days/weeks
some weeks/years

These phrases usually go at the beginning of the sentence.

1 We go skiing *every/most/once* weekends.

2 Ali has piano lessons three times *a/in a/in the* week.

3 Lisa goes to Goa *every/most/some* summer.

4 *All/Every/Some* days it's really difficult to wake up.

5 You should brush your teeth *all/some/twice* a day.

6 *Every/In/Some* evenings I meet my friends in the town centre.

4 ✳ State verbs

Complete the sentences with the correct form of the verb in brackets.

1 ' _Do you like_ (like) Chinese food?'
'I _____ (not mind) it but _____ (prefer) Thai. I _____ (love) green curry … it _____ (be) my favourite!'

2 'I _____ (not believe) it!'
'What's the matter?'
'_____ (remember) John Barnes from our old school? He's got a new job.'
'Hmm, well I _____ (not care).'

3 '_____ (need) any help with your coursework?'
'Everything _____ (seem) fine but if there's anything I _____ (not understand) I'll tell you.'

4 My mum's lasagne _____ (look) good, it _____ (smell) fantastic and it _____ (taste) delicious!

5 (✱✱) State and activity verbs

Complete the sentences with the correct form of the verb in brackets.

1 My cousin _has_ (have) a fantastic new guitar.
2 I _____ (not think) Charles is going to pass his exams.
3 I can't talk now. I _____ (have) lunch with my family.
4 What _____ (you/think) about? You look very happy!
5 How many brothers and sisters _____ (you/have)?
6 _____ (you/think) this dress looks good on me?

Vocabulary

6 (✱) Education

Complete the definitions with the words below.

[mixed   private   single-sex   state ✓]

1 A _state_ school gives free education and receives money from the government.
2 A _____ school has either only girls or only boys.
3 At a _____ school parents have to pay for their children's education.
4 A _____ has both boys and girls.

7 (✱✱) Secondary school

Complete the speech with the words below.

[compulsory   discipline   head teacher ✓
optional   pupils   responsibilities   rules
specialise   staff   subjects   uniform]

'Welcome, everyone, to parents' evening at Edwin Hall School. My name is Ruth Mullin and I'm the
¹ _head teacher_ here. As you know, here at Edwin Hall we ² _____ in science, I can show you our fantastic labs later. During the first year, Maths, English and a science are all ³ _____ . Other
⁴ _____ such as Art, History and Languages are
⁵ _____ – the students can choose to do them. There aren't many ⁶ _____ here at Edwin Hall – we believe that ⁷ _____ should come from the
⁸ _____ themselves, and that everyone should know their ⁹ _____ . But we do insist that all the children wear the school ¹⁰ _____ : a green jacket with yellow stripes. If you have any questions for me – or any other members of the ¹¹ _____ please ask!'

8 (✱✱) Education and work

Write in the missing letters to complete the texts.

A

Petra's a keen student. She started
¹ _secondary_ school five years ago, but this is her most important year so far. At the moment, she's doing her Art ² c _ _ _ _ _ _ _ k but she's also
³ r _ _ _ _ _ _ g for her exams next June. She hopes to ⁴ p _ _ s them all! After that she'd like to go to university, get a good ⁵ d _ _ _ _ e and maybe study abroad.

B

Jack never liked school – he didn't get good
⁶ m _ _ _ s and often missed class. He couldn't wait to get a job and start earning a ⁷ s _ _ _ _ y, so it wasn't surprising that he ⁸ f _ _ _ _ d all his exams. He ⁹ a _ _ _ _ _ d for a lot of jobs, but it wasn't easy because he didn't have any
¹⁰ q _ _ _ _ _ _ _ _ _ _ _ s. He got the ¹¹ s _ _ k from his first job because he was always late. Finally, he found a job in a clothes shop. He worked hard, and he soon got ¹² p _ _ _ _ _ _ n and a pay
¹³ r _ _ e: now he has a successful ¹⁴ c _ _ _ _ r as a shop manager.

9 (✱✱) Are you becoming a 'digital goldfish'?

Choose the correct answer.

1 Some people say that chewing gum can _____ your concentration.
   a ignore   b improve ✓   c solve
2 Don't waste time on things that aren't worth _____ .
   a study   b studying   c to study
3 It's important to set yourself _____ while you're revising.
   a goals   b problems   c skills
4 I've learned a lot of very useful _____ on my computer course.
   a decisions   b distractions   c skills
5 We all need to work together to _____ the problem of global warming.
   a make sense   b set   c solve

2 mini workbook

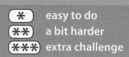

* easy to do
** a bit harder
*** extra challenge

Grammar

1 (**) **Relative clauses**

<u>Underline</u> the correct answer.

Formula 1: Did you know ...

1 The F1 season consists of seventeen races *which/who/ø* all take place in different countries.

2 The 'Formula' in Formula One is a set of rules *where/who/ø* all the teams must follow.

3 *Grand Prix* is a French phrase *that/who/ø* means 'Large Prize'.

4 Silverstone, England, is the place *where/who/whose* the world's first F1 race took place.

5 Italian Giuseppe Farina was the man *which/who/ø* won the first race.

6 A mechanic is a person *that/who/whose* job is to change the tyres.

7 Jenson Button is the driver *which/whose/ø* most people expect to win this year.

2 (**) **Read *Grammar Plus*. Then rewrite the sentences using reduced relative clauses.**

Grammar + Plus

Reduced relative clauses

We can omit the relative pronoun and auxiliary verb *be*:

The man ~~who is~~ sitting next to you has fallen asleep.

To talk about possession and physical characteristics, we can use *with* instead of *who* or *that* and the auxiliary verb *have*:

*I met a girl **who had** beautiful blue eyes.*

*I met a girl **with** beautiful blue eyes.*

1 The guy who is waiting outside is my cousin.

The guy waiting outside is my cousin.

2 London is a city which has a lot of parks.

3 I asked the woman who was sitting next to me for the time.

4 My brother is the young man who has a beard.

5 People who have tickets can go inside.

6 Passengers who are travelling on the 20.00 train should go to Platform 8.

3 (*) **Present perfect**

Complete the sentences with the present perfect form of the verb in brackets.

1 '*Have you finished* (you/finish) that book I gave you?'

'No, *I haven't started it yet* (not start it/yet)!'

2 Hurry up! The match _____ (already/begin).

3 '_____ (you see/Anthony) recently?' 'No, I haven't.'

4 My cousin _____ (just/sell) his motorbike.

5 Valentine's Day is next week, but Jane (already/buy) _____ a card for her boyfriend.

6 '_____ (you/ever/visit) Rome?' 'No. In fact, I _____ (never/go) to Italy.'

4 (**) **Past simple: Time expressions**

Complete the sentences with the correct form of the verb in brackets and a word from below.

> ago   at   hour   in ✓   night   on   last
> when   yesterday

1 Sam _*was*_ (be) born _*in*_ 1990.

2 He _____ (start) playing tennis _____ he was eight.

3 He _____ (enter) his first tournament two years _____ .

4 He _____ (win) his first tournament _____ month.

5 He _____ (arrive) in Australia _____ Sunday.

6 He _____ (practise) for eight hours _____ .

7 He _____ (not sleep) well last _____ .

8 He _____ (wake up) _____ five o'clock this morning.

9 His first match _____ (begin) half an _____ ago. Now he's losing 0–6, 0–6, 0–5.

5 (***) Present perfect and past simple

Complete the sentences with the correct form (present perfect or past simple) of the verb in brackets.

1 '*Have you already met* (you already/meet) Bianca?'
'Yes … we _met_ (meet) last week.'

2 I _____ (get) here half an hour ago but my friend _____ (not arrive/yet).

3 '_____ (you/ever/see) snow in Madrid?'
'Yes, there _____ (be) a lot of snow last winter, actually.'

4 I _____ (love) reading about Africa when I was a child but I _____ (never/go) there.

5 '_____ (you/hear) any news from Josh recently?'
'Yes, he _____ (phone) me a few days ago.'

Vocabulary

6 (**) Sporting activities

<u>Underline</u> the correct answer.

1 Danny wants to *get/go/join* fit, so now he *does/gets/goes* running every morning.

2 It was a very bad start for United: they *entered/lost/scored* their first match and they didn't *beat/support/win* a game until October.

3 My mother *entered/joined/went* a gym a few weeks ago: she's not the best in her class but she always *does/gets/goes* her best!

4 Roberto *did/scored/won* the first goal for City but then he *did/got/lost* injured and had to leave the field.

5 Andrew was a very keen chess player from an early age: he *entered/scored/supported* his first competition at the age of just eight, and he *beat/lost/won* a player thirty years older than him.

6 'Which football team does Elana *beat/support/win*?'
'Arsenal, of course! She loves them!'

7 (***) Likes and dislikes

Complete the online profiles with the words below.

> about ✓ find love into mind not
> point quite stand

I'm passionate [1] _about_ life! I'm looking for fun people to chat with! I [2] _____ clubbing, and I'm also really [3] _____ travelling and generally having a great time!

Welsh girl!
From: Cardiff
Age: 18

I'm a football hater looking for other people who can't [4] _____ football!! I can't see the [5] _____ of running around, kicking a ball … does anyone else [6] _____ sport incredibly boring???????!!!!!!

Football hater!
From: Leeds
Age: 20

Sorry, but I'm [7] _____ really into exercise (although I [8] _____ enjoy a romantic walk by the sea. I don't [9] _____ watching other people exercise, BTW. … any other lazy people out there????

Lazy guy!
From: Brighton
Age: 17

8 (**) How the English invented sports

Complete the sentences with the words below.

> champion hold ✓ rules record spread

1 The committee has decided that London will _hold_ the 2012 Olympic Games.

2 From an early age, Khan's ambition was to be world _____ .

3 The Jamaican runner Usain Bolt holds the world _____ for the 100 m – 9.69 seconds.

4 Rugby began in England but the game soon _____ to the rest of Britain.

5 United broke the _____ by putting an extra player onto the field.

3miniworkbook

* easy to do
** a bit harder
*** extra challenge

Grammar

1 (**) **Making comparisions**

Read about Tom. Choose the correct answer.

Tom is in Australia looking for a job during his gap year.

So here I am in Australia after ¹ _____ far the longest plane journey ever! The weather's ² _____ better than it was in England. It's 25 degrees and they say tomorrow will be even ³ _____! Sydney is ⁴ _____ city in Australia and for me it's also ⁵ _____ exciting! It's a busy place but the traffic isn't as bad ⁶ _____ London.

Love to everyone ... hope Grandma's feeling ⁷ _____ after her flu.

Tom

PS Please send some money — I'm afraid things here are ⁸ _____ more expensive than I thought!

1 a as   b by ✓   c with
2 a as   b much   c more
3 a hot   b hotter   c more hot
4 a the big b the bigger c the biggest
5 a the most b most   c more
6 a as   b than   c like
7 a best   b better   c the best
8 a than   b little   c much

2 (**) **Other phrases for comparing**

Complete the sentences. Write ONE word only in each gap.

1 People in the north of my country are completely different _from_ people in the south.

2 Marta is _____ of the nicest people I know.

3 People say my sense of humour is the same _____ my father's!

4 Thomas' eyes are very similar _____ his mother's.

5 Who's the tallest person _____ your class?

3 (**) **Asking for descriptions**

Read the information about George and Melissa. Then write the correct question for each answer.

1 _What's Melissa like?_
   She's a very calm and relaxed person.

2 _____?
   He's got short dark hair and a moustache.

3 _____?
   She's got pale skin and she's very tall.

4 _____?
   He likes playing chess and Melissa's cooking.

5 _____?
   He's charming and romantic.

6 _____?
   She likes gardening and playing the piano.

4 (**✱✱**) Read *Grammar Plus*. Then complete the sentences with the correct form of *look* or *look like*.

Grammar + Plus

look and *look like*

To talk about appearance, we can use *look* + adjective: You **look tired.**

To talk about similarities we use *look like* + noun/person: Ewa doesn't **look like her mother.**

1 Ben's only sixteen but he _looks_ older.

2 Nobody believes we're related – I _____ my brother at all.

3 Gemma thinks that her teacher _____ Johnny Depp.

4 Our teacher has just arrived … and he _____ really angry!

5 My cousin's only fifty but he _____ an old man!

6 Zoe _____ Italian but in fact she comes Scotland.

Vocabulary

5 (**✱**) Physical description

Which of the words and phrases below go with *be* and which go with *have got*?

> a strong personality ✓   dark hair   quiet
> very tall   nice clothes   in his twenties
> blue eyes   an earring   in her teens

be	have got
	a strong personality

6 (**✱✱**) Physical description

Match the definitions with the words below.

> bald ☐   elegant ☐   glamorous ☑
> medium-length ☐   plump ☐   round ☐
> scruffy ☐   straight ☐   wavy ☐

1 attractive in a rich, exciting, wealthy way

2 (of hair) not long or short

3 a little fat (in a nice way)

4 dirty and untidy

5 shaped like a circle

6 (of hair) with curves, not straight

7 with a graceful and attractive appearance

8 (of hair) without curls or curves

9 with little or no hair on your head

7 (**✱**) Describing people

Unscramble the letters to complete the definitions.

1 Someone who is (mugratentiave) often disagrees with other people!
   argumentative

2 (creklefs) are light brown marks on a person's skin. _____

3 A (bosicale) person is friendly and enjoys being with other people. _____

4 If you are (hys), you are not confident when meeting new people. _____

5 (glith) brown is the opposite of dark brown. _____

8 (**✱✱**) How birth order affects your personality

Match the sentences to the adjectives below.

> ambitious ☐   bossy ☐   easy-going ☐
> conscientious ☐   indecisive ☑
> dynamic ☐   organised ☐   punctual ☐
> self-centred ☐   sensitive ☐

1 'I'd like this one – no, that one. I'm not sure!'

2 'I always arrive at school at 8.55 exactly'.

3 'I don't mind. You can play music late at night if you want to.'

4 'I'm not interested in what anyone else says, the only thing that's important here is *me*!!'

5 'I've made a list of thirty things to do before we go on holiday.'

6 'One day I want to be President!'

7 'I always cry when I see a sad film!'

8 'I'm not going out until I've finished my homework and done the washing-up.'

9 'I've got three jobs, I run for two hours every day and I'm writing a novel!'

10 'Don't argue with me! Just do what I tell you!'

4 miniworkbook

✱	easy to do
✱✱	a bit harder
✱✱✱	extra challenge

Grammar

1 ✱ Obligation: negative and question forms

a Make the sentences negative.

1 Pupils have to wear a uniform at this school.

   Pupils don't have to wear a uniform at this school.

2 Ana was allowed to stay out late when she was fifteen.

3 We're allowed to eat our sandwiches here.

4 Sean had to get up early on Saturday.

5 We have to bring our passports.

6 They were allowed to use their parents' computer.

7 You must ring the doorbell late at night.

b Make sentences 1–6 into questions.

1 Do pupils have to wear a uniform at this school?

2 ✱✱ Obligation: *have to, don't have to, (not) be allowed to*

Read the information about riding a moped in the UK. Then complete the sentences with *have to, don't have to* or *(not) be allowed to.*

Riding a 50 cc moped
Minimum age: 16

Compulsory:
Crash helmet
Full driving licence
(100 cc bikes <u>only</u>)

Remember the speed limit
(30 mph in towns)

Not compulsory:
'L' plates*
Driving theory test

* L = Learner

1 In the UK, you *'re allowed to* ride a moped when you're 16.

2 You _____ drive faster than 30 mph in towns.

3 You _____ wear a crash helmet.

4 You _____ use 'L' plates.

5 You _____ take a driving theory test to ride a 50 cc moped.

6 You _____ pass a test before you can ride a 100 cc bike.

3 ✱✱ Obligation

Choose the correct answer.

1 We missed the last bus, so we _____ walk home.

   a have to   **b** had to ✓   **c** mustn't

2 The rules say you _____ use your hands when you're playing football.

   a aren't allowed to   **b** don't have to   **c** must

3 We _____ play football on the grass when we were children.

   a didn't have to   **b** mustn't
   c weren't allowed to

4 Silvia _____ to borrow her parents' car until she's passed her test.

   a doesn't have to   **b** have to
   c isn't allowed to

5 There were only a few people in the queue, so we _____ wait for very long.

   a didn't have to   **b** had to
   c weren't allowed to

6 You _____ wear smart clothes: it's a very informal party

   a aren't allowed to   **b** don't have to   **c** must

4 ✱✱ Read *Grammar Plus*. Then complete the sentences on page 107 with the correct form of *have got to* or *must (not).*

Grammar + Plus

Obligation

Have got to is another way of saying that something is necessary, especially in informal spoken English: *Sorry, I can't come out tonight. **I've got to** finish my essay.*

Must and *must not* are often used to say things are necessary or forbidden in formal, written English (e.g. signs):

*All visitors **must** report to reception.* (= it is necessary to do this)

*Members of the public **must not** enter here.* (= it is forbidden to do this)

1 'I *'ve got to* visit my grandmother on Sunday … it's her 70th birthday.'

2 Passengers over the age of sixteen _____ pay the full adult fare.

3 Visitors to the museum _____ take photographs without permission.

4 'My brother's not at school today. He _____ go and see the doctor.'

5 'It's nearly eleven o'clock … we _____ be home in half an hour.'

6 All applicants for a parking permit _____ complete an application form.

5 (**) *make* and *let*

Complete the text with the correct form of *make* or *let*.

'I love babysitting for my little sister Ellie and she loves it too! Here's why; my dad always [1] *makes* Ellie go to bed at exactly 8.30 but I [2] _____ her stay up later. (But I always [3] _____ her promise to tell Mum and Dad it was 8.30.) If she wants to watch a TV programme, I think it's good [4] _____ her watch it. It's easier that way. I'm happy if she [5] _____ me play on my computer in peace. But I think it's important to [6] _____ her put away her things before bedtime. I don't want to clean up her mess!

Vocabulary

6 (**) Working conditions and young people

Complete the text with the words below.

educate   labour ✓   conditions
well   paid   wealthy   opportunities
full-time   wages   hours

Support the
ETHICAL CLOTHING COMPANY

Many clothing companies around the world use child [1] *labour* in order to increase their profits. Children have to work long [2] _____ , in very poor working [3] _____ and for very low [4] _____ .
At the Ethical Clothing Company we try to give our workers [5] _____ jobs – between thirty and forty hours a week – and to make sure they are well-[6] _____ and [7] _____ treated by their employers. We use most of our money to help [8] _____ young people and offer them [9] _____ in the future. Because of this, the Ethical Clothing Company isn't [10] _____ like so many other clothes companies.

So help us today!

7 (**) Jobs

Write in the missing letters to complete the definitions.

1 An e **m** p **l o y e** r is the person or company which gives you a job.

2 An a __ vertising e __ __ __ __ t __ __ e makes important decisions in the world of advertising.

3 A c __ __ l – c __ n __ __ __ w __ rker deals with people's problems over the phone.

4 A s __ __ v __ t did jobs like cooking and cleaning in someone's home. *(Old-fashioned)*

5 A f __ __ m l __ __ o __ __ __ r is someone who works in agriculture.

6 A f __ __ __ e __ __ __ n goes out to sea to catch fish.

7 A g __ __ __ r __ __ __ s was a private teacher in someone's home.

8 A m __ n __ r digs underground for coal and metals.

9 A s __ __ t __ __ s a __ __ l __ __ t gives advice about computers and computer software.

10 A p __ b __ __ c r __ __ __ t __ __ __ s c __ __ s __ l __ __ __ t helps people and companies deal with the media.

11 A s __ c __ __ l w __ __ k __ r helps people with personal or family problems.

8 (***) Describing jobs

Complete the sentences with the correct form of the word in bold.

1 Many jobs in the fast-food industry are quite *badly-paid* .   **BAD/PAY**

2 I've done a lot of boring jobs: now I'd like something more _____ . **CHALLENGE**

3 George came from a hard-working, _____ family.   **RESPECT**

4 A lot of the jobs in the factory are very boring and _____ .   **REPEAT**

5 Being a football manager is a very _____ job.   **STRESS**

Give this child hope!

5 mini workbook

* ✱ easy to do
* ✱✱ a bit harder
* ✱✱✱ extra challenge

Grammar

1 ✱ *going to:* predictions

Look at the pictures and write five predictions with *going to* and the verbs below.

> fall asleep   have a baby   play tennis ✓
> rain   take a penalty   win the race

1 They're going to play tennis.

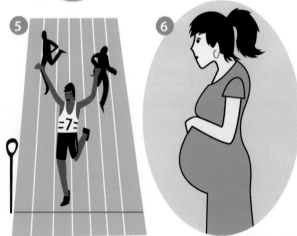

2 ✱ *will:* predictions

Complete the predictions with *will* or *won't*.

1 I think we _'ll_ be there in about an hour.

2 Do you believe people _____ live longer in the future?

3 Tim is so lazy – I'm sure he _____ get into a good university.

4 Do you think Stephanie _____ come to class today?

5 Don't look so worried, I'm sure it _____ hurt at all.

3 ✱✱ *going to* and *will*

Complete the sentences with *going to* or *will*.

1 'Why are you reading a computer magazine?'

  'I _'m going to buy_ (buy) a new computer and I want to find the best price.'

2 Look out! The ice is breaking! You _____ (fall) in the river.

3 I'm sure you _____ (have) a fantastic holiday in Florida.

4 Melanie says she _____ (look) for a job after the summer holiday.

5 Most people believe that the economic situation _____ (get) worse next year.

6 The sun is shining and the weather forecast is good: it _____ (be) another fantastic day!

4 ✱✱ First conditional

Make first conditional sentences using the correct form of the verb in brackets.

1 You _won't pass_ (pass) your English exam unless you _work_ (work) hard.

2 My parents _____ (be) angry if I _____ (arrive) home late again.

3 If you _____ (cook) the dinner, I _____ (do) the washing up.

4 If Jill _____ (not get) here soon, we (have to) _____ go without her.

5 I _____ (not go) to the party unless you _____ (come) with me.

6 If you _____ (not get up) soon _____ (be) late for school.

Ben is flying abroad for the first time. His mother has come to the airport to see him off.

5 (✱✱✱) Future time clauses
Underline the correct answer.

MUM: Now, have you got everything? Passport? Ticket? Money?

BEN: Yes, Mum! Remember I'm going to change my money [1] *before/until/<u>when</u>* I get there. I can use euros on the plane.

MUM: Okay. So, do you want a coffee [2] *before/once/when* the plane leaves?

BEN: It's okay, Mum. I'll get a coffee [3] *after/before/until* I check in.

MUM: All right. Here are some sandwiches. Don't eat them now! Eat them [4] *before/until/when* you're on the plane, and remember to phone me [5] *as soon as/before/until* you arrive. Don't worry about the time, I won't be able to sleep [6] *after/until/when* I hear from you, darling.

BEN: Yes, Mum. I'll send you a text [7] *before/until/when* I get there. I promise.

MUM: Ok. Give me a great big kiss [8] *after/before/when* you go …

BEN: MUM! There are other people here!

6 (✱✱) Read *Grammar Plus*. Then complete the sentences with *in case* and the present simple of the verb in brackets.

Grammar + Plus

in case + present simple

We use *in case* + present simple to say 'because something might happen'.

It usually refers to something we do not want to happen:

*Take a map with you **in case you get lost**.*

1 I'll give you my mobile number *in case there's* (there/be) a problem later.

2 Write down the address _____ (you/forget).

3 I'll take my umbrella with me _____ (it/rain).

4 I'll say goodbye now _____ (I/not see) you tomorrow.

5 Take a photocopy of your passport _____ (you/lose) it.

Vocabulary

7 (✱✱) The environment
Choose the correct answer.

1 Did you know that the USA _____ more carbon dioxide than any other country?
   a produces ✓ b reduces c switches off

2 People can _____ their carbon footprint by making fewer journeys.
   a reduce b save c waste

3 Instead of recycling their old cans, many people just _____ them away.
   a put b take c throw

4 People _____ a lot of energy by leaving the lights on all night.
   a waste b recycle c destroy

5 It's really hot in here. Can someone _____ down the central heating?
   a put b switch c turn

6 From next year, it will be compulsory to use energy- _____ light bulbs.
   a re-cycling b saving c using

8 (✱) Getting around my city
Unscramble the letters to complete the definitions.

1 **s u b s a p s (n)** A card which gives you free travel on buses _____ *bus pass*

2 **t e s t i n a d o n i (n)** The place you are travelling to _____

3 **b e l l e a i r (adj)** Easy to trust or depend on _____

4 **w e d d r o c (adj)** With a lot of people in a small space _____

5 **s p r a g e e n s s (n)** The people travelling on a bus or plane _____

6 **a c c d e n e l l (adj)** Something that was planned but will not happen _____

7 **c k i p p u (vb)** To collect someone in a car _____

8 **i c e s t a n d (n)** The space between two places or things _____

9 **l e c c y n e a l (n)** A special part of the road reserved for cyclists _____

10 **d e e d a l y (adj)** When something begins later than the planned time _____

6 mini workbook

* easy to do
** a bit harder
*** extra challenge

Grammar

1 (**) **Present perfect with *for* and *since***

Rewrite the sentences in two ways with *for* or *since*.

1 It's now ten o'clock. We arrived here four hours ago.

We *'ve been* (be) here since *six o'clock*/for *four hours*.

2 It's now November. He moved here in April.

He _____ (live) here for _____ /since_____ .

3 It's now Friday morning. It started snowing on Wednesday morning. It is still snowing.

It _____ (snow) since _____ / for _____ .

4 It's now 2010. I last saw my cousin in 2007.

I _____ (not see) my cousin for _____/ since _____ .

5 It's now five o'clock. I started waiting at two o'clock. I'm still waiting.

I _____ (wait) since _____/ for _____ .

2 (***) **Questions with *How long* (present perfect and past simple)**

Read the information about the actor Jude Law. Then complete the questions and answers about him.

JUDE LAW
- Born in London – still lives there now
- Married actress Sadie Frost in 1997 – divorced 2003
- Became an actor in 1992
- 2008 – spent two days in Afghanistan working for charity Peace One Day
- Parents moved to France in 1988

Jude Law

1 **Q:** How long *has he lived* (live) in London?

A: He's *lived* in London since *he was born* (be born).

2 **Q:** How long _____ (be) married to Sadie Frost?

A: He _____ to Sadie Frost for _____ .

3 **Q:** How long _____ (be) an actor?

A: He _____ since _____ .

4 **Q:** How long _____ (be) in Afghanistan?

A: He _____ in Afghanistan for _____ .

5 **Q:** How _____ (his parents/live) in France?

A: They _____ in France since _____ .

3 (*) **Present perfect continuous**

Complete the sentences with the present perfect continuous form of the verb in brackets.

1 I *'ve been reading* (read) a really interesting book by John Steinbeck.

2 'How long _____ (wait)?' 'Not long, only about five minutes.'

3 There's my phone! I _____ (look) for it for ages!

4 So what _____ (do) since I last saw you?

5 Marcus _____ (play) computer games all morning!

6 My aunt _____ (not feel) well since she came out of hospital.

4 (***) **Present perfect simple or present perfect continuous**

Complete the sentences with the correct form of the verb in brackets.

1 Paul can't play football because he's *broken* (break) his leg.

2 I _____ (go) to the cinema twice this week.

3 I hope the bus gets here soon. We _____ (wait) for ages.

4 The latest gossip is that Charlie and Lola _____ (split up).

5 I'm afraid Becky's piano playing isn't getting better: she _____ (not practise) enough recently.

6 My brother _____ (act) strangely recently. I wonder what's the matter with him?

7 'How long _____ (learn) English?' 'Since I was eight!'

5 (**) Read *Grammar Plus* and complete the sentences with the correct form of the verb in brackets.

Grammar + Plus

Time expressions for the recent past

Use the following time expressions to talk about the recent past:

lately, recently, in the last few days and *not long ago*

We usually use *in the last few days, lately* and *recently* with the present perfect or present perfect continuous:

The weather's been very good recently.
We've done a lot of work in the last few days.

We use *not long ago* with the past simple:

I saw your friend not long ago.

1 I *'ve been listening* (listen) to a lot of indie music recently.
2 Stephanie and her boyfriend _____ (have) a serious argument not long ago.
3 _____ (you/hear) any news from Matthew lately?
4 A girl called Jody _____ (phone) me several times in the last few days.
5 I'm tired all the time: I _____ (not sleep) well lately.
6 _____ (you/see) any interesting new movies recently?
7 I _____ (apply) for several jobs in the last few days.
8 James _____ (leave) university not long ago and now he's looking for a job.

Vocabulary

6 (***) Complete the texts with the correct form of the verbs below.

> adore   can't stand   go out with ✓
> get to know   have   split up with

Can you be in love with two people at the same time? I've been [1] *going out with* my boyfriend for nearly a year now. He's fantastic and he really [2] _____ me. But recently I've [3] _____ a boy in my street. He's really funny and every time I see him we [4] _____ a really good laugh. I'd love a date with him but I don't want to [5] _____ my boyfriend. Should I tell him? I [6] _____ lies!

> fall out   get on   look after   make fun of

What can I do about my big brother? When we were kids we used to [7] _____ really well, and he even used to [8] _____ me when my parents needed a babysitter, but these days, every time we're together we [9] _____ ! I hate the way he [10] _____ me, too, especially when other people are there! Please help!!

7 (**) Describing emotions

Match the adjectives below to the statements a–f.

> 1 annoyed ☐   2 bored ☐   3 frightened ☐
> 4 depressed ☒   5 embarrassed ☐

a 'I'm so miserable and unhappy.'
b 'I had to close my eyes for most of the film.'
c 'My mother showed my boyfriend photos of me when I was a baby!'
d 'There's nothing to do and nowhere to go!'
e 'Please stop making that stupid noise!'

8 (**) Complete the sentences with the words below.

> excited   scared   guilty   jealous   nervous
> sympathetic   upset ✓   worried

1 Cristina was very *upset* about the unkind things her friends said about her.
2 It's my birthday party on Saturday, and I can't wait! I'm so _____ !
3 It was the most important match of Stephen's life, he felt very _____ as he waited for the game to start.
4 Everybody is very _____ about the latest unemployment figures.
5 I decided to talk to my teacher about my problem, and fortunately she was very _____ .
6 Sophie felt so _____ about taking the money, she decided to give it back.
7 When I was a child, I used to be _____ of ghosts.
8 James felt _____ when he saw his ex-girlfriend on a date with another boy.

7 miniworkbook

✱ easy to do
✱✱ a bit harder
✱✱✱ extra challenge

Grammar

1 ✱✱ **Passive forms**

Complete the sentences with the correct passive form of the verb in brackets.

1 Oliver Twist _was written_ (write) by Charles Dickens in the 1840s.

2 These shoes are really cheap: they _____ (make) of plastic.

3 My bicycle _____ (repair) at the moment.

4 My mobile phone _____ (not steal) so far this year.

5 The winner's name _____ (announce) tomorrow.

6 School uniform must _____ (wear) at all times.

2 ✱✱ **Active to passive**

Change the active sentences into passive ones. Use *by* when necessary.

The world's most valuable coin?

1 People often call 'The Double Eagle' the world's most valuable coin.

The Double Eagle _is often called the world's most valuable coin_ .

2 Did Augustus Saint-Gaudens design the coin?

Was _____ ?

3 Someone bought it for £7.6m at a New York auction in 2002.

It _____ .

4 Have they ever revealed the buyer's identity?

Has _____ .

5 They have discovered ten more Double Eagle coins since 2002.

Ten more Double Eagle coins

_____ .

6 The general public cannot see them at the moment.

They _____ .

7 They keep the coins at Fort Knox in the USA.

The coins _____ .

8 The US Mint should exhibit the coins to the public soon.

The coins _____ .

3 ✱✱✱ **Active or passive?**

Complete the text with the correct form (active or passive) of the verb in brackets.

Is this the world's most famous song?

Is *Happy Birthday to You* the world's most famous song? It is [1] _recognised_ (recognise) by just about everyone, in fact it [2] _____ (probably/sing) somewhere in the world at this moment! But what are the origins of a tune which [3] _____ (become) so famous during the last hundred years? The present song [4] _____ (base) on *Good Morning to You*, which [5] _____ (write) in 1893 by teachers Patty and Mildred J. Hill. The two sisters [6] _____ (teach) the song to their kindergarten students in Kentucky, USA. The children [7] _____ (find) the song easy to learn and sing. The present birthday song has the same tune but the words [8] _____ (change). Since those days the song [9] _____ (sing) by millions of people in many different languages.

In 2008, a special concert for former South African leader Nelson Mandela's 90th birthday [10] _____ (hold) in London. Forty-six thousand people [11] _____ (sing) Happy Birthday, Dear Nelson and the event [12] _____ (see) by millions more people on TV!

4 ✱✱ *have something done*

Complete the sentences with the correct form of *have* and the past participle of the verb in brackets.

1 Are you going _to have_ your hair _cut_ (cut) this afternoon?

2 The doorbell still isn't working: we _____ it _____ (fix) yet.

3 My parents _____ a new kitchen _____ (make) at the moment.

4 My eyes are getting bad … I must _____ them _____ (test) soon.

5 Lucy's parents say she isn't allowed _____ her nose _____ (pierce).

6 If you pay for it, we _____ the window _____ (repair) next week.

5 (✸✸) Read *Grammar Plus*. Then complete the sentences with a suitable phrase with *need(s) + -ing*. Use the verbs below.

Grammar ✚ Plus

need(s) + -ing

Use *need(s) + -ing* to say that it is important or necessary for something to be done (but it's not important who does it).

[cut ✓ mend paint recharge replace wash]

1 The grass in our garden is very long.
   It needs cutting.
2 All those clothes in the basket are dirty.
3 The outside of the house is in very bad condition.
4 There are lots of holes in your jeans.
5 The light bulb in the hall doesn't work.
6 I can't use my phone at the moment.

Vocabulary

6 (✸) Cooking verbs

Match the verbs below to a picture. There are four extra verbs.

[add blend chop grate ✓ grill peel
  pour slice spread serve]

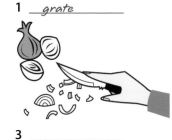

1 _grate_   2 _____

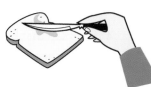

3 _____   4 _____

5 _____   6 _____

7 (✸) Nutrition and health collocations

Choose the correct answer.

1 Regular exercise makes you _____ and healthy.
   a fit ✓   **b** in good shape   **c** strength

2 Lola is on a diet because she wants to _____ weight.
   a decrease   **b** lose   **c** reduce

3 Kieron went to bed early because he _____ a bad headache.
   a felt   **b** took   **c** had

4 My father started to _____ weight after the age of forty.
   a add   **b** increase   **c** put on

5 Mina doesn't have enough _____ to walk to school.
   a energy   **b** fitness   **c** health

6 Long car journeys make some people _____ sick.
   a fall   **b** feel   **c** felt

7 Eczema is a common skin _____ in small children.
   a disease   **b** illness   **c** sickness

8 (✸✸) Adjectives for describing food

1 Which 'B' means 'cooked in steaming water'?
   b _o_ _i_ _l_ _e_ _d_

2 Which 'C' means 'making a crunchy noise when you eat it'?
   c _ _ _ _ _

3 Which 'F' means 'cooked in hot oil'?
   f _ _ _ _

4 Which 'G' means 'cooked with direct heat'?
   g _ _ _ _ _ _

5 Which 'R' describes heavy food which you cannot eat a lot of?
   r _ _ _

6 Which 'S' describes the taste of sugar or honey?
   s _ _ _ _

7 Which 'S' describes the taste of vinegar or lemons?
   s _ _ _

8 Which 'S' means 'with a hot, strong taste'?
   s _ _ _ _

9 Which 'S' is the opposite of 6 – with a sharp, salty taste?
   s _ _ _ _ _ _

10 Which 'T' describes meat which is easy to cut?
   t _ _ _ _ _

8 miniworkbook

* easy to do
** a bit harder
*** extra challenge

Grammar

1 (*) **Second conditional**

<u>Underline</u> the correct answer.

1 If I knew the answer to that question, *I'd tell/I'll tell/I tell* you.

2 Would you be upset if I *cancel/cancelled/ would cancel* our date?

3 If I spoke perfect English, I *don't/won't/ wouldn't* need lessons.

4 I'd come to the concert with you if I *don't have/didn't have/had* a ticket.

5 If you had nowhere to live, where *do/ will/would* you go?

6 You'd do much better at school if you *aren't/wasn't/weren't* so lazy.

2 (**) **Complete the blog with the correct form of the verb in brackets.**

○○○

Back Forward Stop Refresh Home   AutoFill Print Mail

Address: ●

scienceblog

A World without Science?

Call me crazy, but do you ever think the world
[1] *would be* (be) a better place if we [2] _____
(not have) science or scientists?

Think about it. If scientists [3] _____ (not exist),
we [4] _____ (not be able) to build factories:
and if there [5] _____ (be) no factories, we
[6] _____ (not manufacture) weapons – so war
[7] _____ (be) impossible. Also, if all the factories
in the world [8] _____ (stop) working, the
air [9] _____ (become) clean again, no more
pollution! But what about modern medicine? Don't
we depend too much on drugs? Maybe we
[10] _____ (be) healthier if we [11] _____
(not take) a painkiller every time we have a
headache!

As I say, you can call me crazy if you like, but that's
my opinion! What do you think?

3 (***) **First and second conditional**

Complete the conversations with the correct form of the verb in brackets.

A: Have you heard? Tania's expecting a baby.

B: Really? Have they got a name yet?

A: If the baby [1] _is_ (be) a girl they [2] _____ (call) her Clare.

B: What if they [3] _____ (have) a boy?

A: They haven't got a boy's name yet.

B: If I [4] _____ (have) a baby boy, I [5] _____ (call) him Wayne …

A: Wayne??

B: Like Wayne Rooney, he's my favourite footballer!!

C: If you [6] _____ (not have to) learn English, which language [7] _____ (study)?

D: Spanish, probably.

C: Really? But if you [8] _____ (speak) Spanish, who [9] _____ (you/practise) with?

D: Well, there's an Argentinian boy in my school who's really sweet.

C: I see. Well, why don't you speak to him? If you [10] _____ (ask) him nicely, I'm sure he [11] _____ (give) you some Spanish lessons!

D: Okay! Good idea!

4 (**) *wish* + **past simple**

Read sentences 1–6. Write six sentences with *wish* that have the same meaning.

1 I can't speak German but I'd like to.

   I wish _I could speak German_ .

2 I would like to have a bigger bedroom.

   I wish _____ .

3 I'm sorry, I don't know what to do.

   I wish I _____ .

4 She's sad that her friends aren't here.

   She wishes _____ .

5 I don't have enough money to go out tonight.

   I wish _____ .

6 My brother would like to be good at tennis, but he isn't.

   My brother wishes _____ .

5 (✱✱✱) wish + would

Write six sentences with she (wish) + he would(n't).

Sally has an annoying boyfriend!

1 He spends all his time with his friends.

She wishes he wouldn't spend all his time with his friends.

2 He doesn't buy her presents.

3 He talks about football all the time

4 He never takes her to nice places.

5 He always forgets her birthday.

6 He doesn't send her romantic text messages.

6 (✱✱) Read Grammar Plus. Complete the sentences with the correct form of the verb in brackets.

Grammar + Plus

Expressing regret

Use *if only* + past simple to express regret:

If only I had more time. (= I wish I had more time.)

We can also express regret about the past by using *regret + (not) -ing*:

I regret leaving school at 16. (= I'm sorry I left school at 16.)

I regret not listening to my parents' advice. (= I'm sorry I didn't listen.)

1 If only I _could_ (can) speak English perfectly!

2 I regret _____ (leave) the football match before the end.

3 If only you _____ (understand) how sad I feel!

4 Do you regret _____ (not invite) Sam to your party?

5 If only we _____ (not have to) go to school tomorrow!

6 I don't regret _____ (spend) so much time studying.

Vocabulary

7 (✱) Describing buildings

Match the words below to the features 1–9.

> roof   chimney   a four-storey house   attic
> a balcony   the ground floor   the first floor
> a detached house   a semi-detached house

8 (✱✱) Living with other people

Complete the report with the words below.

> asking   borrows   fussy   knocking   lets
> make   nags ✓   noises   sharing
> tidying up   tidy

Teenager wants a divorce

A Broadham teenager wants a divorce – from her family! Lily Spence, seventeen, has written to a lawyer asking for her parents and sister to move out of their house in Acre Lane, Broadham.

'They make my life miserable,' she told us. 'My mother [1] _nags_ me every day about [2] _____ my bedroom. Why does she have to be so [3] _____ ? It's my room, why can't I [4] _____ a mess in there if I want to? I agree I'm not a very [5] _____ person but doesn't she know I have all that schoolwork to do?'

'And my dad is just as bad. He always tells me about [6] _____ the chores but he never does anything himself! He never [7] _____ me use the computer when I need it and he still thinks it's okay to come into my room without [8] _____ on the door. It's just not fair!'

'Then there's my sister, Zoe. She [9] _____ things like make-up and jewellery without [10] _____ ! And she makes really annoying [11] _____ when I'm trying to work. I've had enough!'

Lily has not received an answer from the lawyer yet.

9 mini workbook

* easy to do
** a bit harder
*** extra challenge

Grammar

Nowadays, Ben K. Ballance is a bank manager. But as a teenager in the 1970s, his life was very different …

1 ＊ used to/didn't use to

Write six sentences about Ben with *used to/didn't use to,* using the pictures and the words below.

> be a punk rocker ✓   wear a suit
> have crazy hair   be in a group
> play drums   work in a bank

1 He used to be a punk rocker.

2 ＊＊ Past continuous and past simple

Complete the conversation with the correct form (past simple or past continuous) of the verb in brackets.

ANDREW: I [1] *phoned* (phone) you last night but you [2] _____ (not answer). [3] _____ (leave) your phone at home?

CLAIRE: No, I [4] _____ (not go out) last night. Perhaps I [5] _____ (listen) to some music when you [6] _____ (ring). What time [7] _____ (call) me?

A: About 8 30. What [8] _____ (do) then?

C: Ah yes, I remember [9] _____ (talk) to Jed then. He [10] _____ (come) round at about 8.15.

A: Jed? Who's Jed??

C: Just an old friend from college. He [11] _____ (do) some work near my house and he [12] _____ (decide) to come and see me.

3 ＊＊ Past perfect and past simple

Complete the sentences with the correct form of the verb in brackets.

1 Alan _had known_ (know) Ellen for several months before he _asked_ (ask) her out.

2 I _____ (feel) very nervous because I _____ (not speak) in public before.

3 When we _____ (find) our seats in the cinema, the movie _____ (already/begin).

4 After I _____ (finish) my revision, I _____ (watch) a DVD.

5 Nina _____ (be) hungry because she _____ (not eat) since breakfast.

6 When I finally _____ (get) home, all my family _____ (go) to bed.

4 ＊＊＊ Past tenses

Underline the correct answer.

One day, my sister and I [1] *sat/were sitting* in the kitchen when my dad [2] *arrived/had arrived* home looking very pleased with himself. He [3] *had just bought/bought* a beautiful new Sat Nav system for the car. Up until then, my sister [4] *had always been/was always* the family map reader, but she [5] *had never been/was never being* very good at it and we [6] *had got lost/were getting lost* many times.

The following day, we [7] *had taken/took* our first trip with the new Sat Nav. It [8] *rained/was raining* hard as the voice told us: 'Go straight on for 20 kilometres'. After a while, I could see that my dad [8] *got/was getting* worried. The road [9] *became/had become* nothing more than a narrow track, and the heavy rain [10] *made/was making* it almost impossible to see. Suddenly, we [11] *heard/were hearing* a loud splash and then the engine [12] *had stopped/stopped*.

We [13] *had sat/were sitting* in a metre of water. The Sat Nav [14] *had directed/was directing* us into a lake.

The next day, my sister [15] *became/was becoming* the family map reader again.

5 (✳✳) Read *Grammar Plus*. Then complete the sentences.

Grammar + Plus

Reflexive pronouns and *each other*

We use reflexive pronouns (*himself, herself, themselves,* etc.) when the subject and the object are the same person: **She** fell over and hurt **herself**.

We often use reflexive pronouns with these verbs: *cut, hurt, enjoy, look after*.

We use *each other* when an action or feeling goes in both directions between two people:
Sophie adores Billy, and Billy adores Sophie. They adore each other.

We often use *each other* with verbs like: *(get to) know, love, hate, like*.

1 After fifty years of marriage, my grandparents still love *each other* .

2 Robert needed a bandage after he cut _____ shaving today.

3 Now she's eighteen, Ellie is old enough to look after _____ .

4 Joe and his ex-wife have a terrible relationship: they really hate _____ now.

5 I'd like you all to spend a few minutes chatting so you can get to know _____ better.

6 Maxine and her friends really enjoyed _____ at Jessica's party.

7 I'm surprised that Cheri and Tony are getting married: I didn't even think they liked _____ .

8 Tom had an accident while he was riding his bike but fortunately he didn't hurt _____ .

Vocabulary

6 (✳✳) **First aid**

Unscramble the letters to complete the paragraphs.

1 After Carmen [1](tih) *hit* her head when she was playing volleyball, she (left zyzdi) [2] _____ _____ for a while. We were all worried that she had [3] (nossinucco) _____ , so we took her to hospital immediately.

2 Last week I [4](rapnised) _____ my [5](nekla)_____ playing football. It really [6](thru) _____ !
Our coach put some ice on it to stop the [7](swingell) _____ and he also gave me some [8](rapnikellis) _____ .

3 My mum seems to have lots of accidents when she's cooking. Last month she [9](nurbed relfesh) _____ _____ on a hot pan, then she [10](tuc relfesh) ____ _____ when she was slicing some bread. We had to [11](tup a nadebag) ____ __ _____ on her hand to stop the [12](nedblige) _____ .

4 If you [13](lefe skic) _____ _____ and [14](aveh a dacheeha) ____ __ _____ you could have the [15](spommsty) _____ of a stress-related illness.

7 (✳✳) **Narrative adverbs**

Complete the jokes with the words below.

[a few hours later ✓   eventually   fortunately   unfortunately]

A man went into hospital to have his leg removed. [1] *A few hours later* , he woke up. A doctor was standing by the bed.

'I have good news and bad news,' said the doctor. 'The bad news is [2] _____ we removed the wrong leg.'

There was a very long silence: [3] _____ the man asked the doctor for the good news.

'[4] _____ , the other leg is getting better,' said the doctor with a smile.

[after   first   immediately   in the end   suddenly]

The boss of a firm was working late. [5] _____ he remembered he had to give a thirty minute speech the following day. So he asked his secretary to write the speech for him. But the speech was very long and boring. After he'd finished giving it, he [6] _____ called his secretary.

'That speech was an hour long,' he said angrily. 'At [7] _____ everything was okay: for half an hour everyone seemed happy. But [8] _____ that people started to get bored. [9] _____ everyone fell asleep.'

'It *was* a thirty minute speech,' replied the secretary, 'But I gave you two copies.'

10 mini workbook

* easy to do
** a bit harder
*** extra challenge

Grammar

1 (*) **Reported speech: verb tenses**

Read what Nick told Suzie and then rewrite what he said in reported speech.

Suzie met a young man called Nick on holiday.

Nick: 'I'm a Formula One racing driver.'

1 He said _he was_ a Formula One racing driver.

Nick: 'I won six races last season.'

2 He told Suzie _____ six races last season.

Nick: 'I live in a big house in Monte Carlo.'

3 He said _____ in a big house in Monte Carlo.

Nick: 'I've just bought a holiday home in Florida.'

4 He told Suzie _____ a holiday home in Florida.

Nick: 'I'm flying back to Monte Carlo on Friday.'

5 He said _____ back to Monte Carlo on Friday.

Nick: 'I'll send you tickets for the next race.'

6 He told Suzie _____ tickets for the next race.

Nick: 'You can visit me in Monte Carlo any time.'

7 He said _____ in Monte Carlo any time.

2 (**) **Reported speech to direct speech**

One day Nick phoned Suzie. Complete Nick's original words with the correct pronoun or verb.

> He said he wasn't really a racing driver. He told me he drove a bus and his home wasn't really in Monte Carlo. It was in Manchester, with his mother. He said he thought I really was a special person, and he was sure I'd understand why he hadn't told me the truth when he'd met me.

'¹ I _'m not_ really a racing driver. I ² _____ a bus and ³ _____ home ⁴ _____ really in Monte Carlo. I ⁵ _____ in Manchester with ⁶ _____ mother. I ⁷ _____ you ⁸ _____ a really special person and ⁹ _____ sure you ¹⁰ _____ understand why ¹¹ _____ didn't tell ¹² _____ the truth when I ¹³ _____ you.'

3 (***) **Reported speech: requests and commands**

Gill has entered the London Marathon. Put the messages on her web page into reported speech.

```
000
Back  Forward  Stop  Refresh  Home    AutoFill  Print  Mail
Address

Go for it!!
- Anne

Can you send me a photo?
- Jack

Drink plenty of water!!
- Jade

Run as fast as you can
- Nick

Will you think of me when you finish??
- James x

Please send a sponsor form
- Emily
```

1 Anne (tell) _told her to go for it!_
2 Jack (ask) _____
3 Jade (tell) _____
4 Nick (tell) _____
5 James (ask) _____
6 Emily (ask) _____

4 (**) **Reported questions**

When Hannah brought her new boyfriend home to meet her parents, they asked him lots of questions.

1 How long have you known Hannah?
2 Are you in the same class as Hannah?
3 What are you planning to do when you leave school?
4 Do you think you'll get married one day?
5 What subjects do you study at school?
6 Do you play any sport?
7 Which football team do you support?
8 Are your parents rich?

Hannah told her friend about her parents' questions. Rewrite the questions in reported speech, like this:

1 My mother/father asked him ...

5 (✳✳✳) **Reported speech and direct speech**

Rewrite sentences 1–3 in reported speech and 4–6 in direct speech.

1 'Can you show me some ID, please,' the doorman said to me.

The doorman asked _me to show him some ID_ .

2 'I'm over eighteen, but I left my ID at home,' I said to the doorman.

I told _____ .

3 'I can't let you come in if you don't show me some ID,' the doorman told me.

The doorman said _____ .

4 I said I was a friend of the manager and he'd be very angry with him.

'I'm _____ .'

5 My father asked me where I was and what I was doing.

'Where _____ ?' my father asked me.

6 Jane said she'd come to the party if she was free that weekend.

'I _____ ,' Jane said.

6 (✳✳) **Read** *Grammar Plus* **and complete the sentences, replacing the phrase in brackets.**

Grammar ✚ Plus

More about time expressions in reported speech

Often we change time phrases in reported speech, to put them 'further into the past':

'I met an old friend yesterday'.

*She said that she **had met** an old friend **the previous day**.*

yesterday	⇒ the previous day
this afternoon	⇒ that afternoon
tomorrow	⇒ the next day
in two days' time	⇒ two days later
next week	⇒ the following week

1 Andrea said he'd phoned his grandmother (yesterday) _the previous day_ .

2 Lucy said she'd see her friends (this afternoon) _____ .

3 My friends said they were going to London (tomorrow) _____ .

4 The newsreader said the weather would be better (next week) _____ .

Vocabulary

7 (✳✳) **Newspapers**

Write in the missing letters to complete the definitions.

1 An a _r t i c l e_ is a piece of writing in a newspaper about a particular subject.

2 A r_____w gives the writer's opinion about a new book, a film or TV programme.

3 The h_____e makes predictions based on your star sign.

4 The s_____s n_____s gives information about football and basketball.

5 C_____s are funny drawings in the newspaper.

6 A_____s try to persuade people to buy products and services.

7 A h_____n i_____t story tells you about people and their emotional problems or achievements.

8 A g_____p c_____n tells you about the private lives of celebrities.

9 The e_____r is the person in charge of a newspaper or magazine.

8 (✳✳) **Celebrities and the media**

Complete the text with the words below.

> behave self-centred deserve ✓ desperate
> influenced media pressure privacy print
> publicity

TV Presenter: Today we're talking about celebrities. Do they [1] _deserve_ all the attention they get? Or should we respect their [2] _____ and leave them alone? Here is our showbiz expert, Ken Brogan. Ken, our view of famous people is strongly [3] _____ by TV and newspapers – all the [4] _____ , in fact. Does that mean celebrities [5] _____ badly just to get attention?

Ken Brogan: Well, of course, it's true that some celebrities are extremely [6] _____ : and this makes them [7] _____ for attention, so they do crazy things because they need the [8] _____ . But also editors are under a lot of [9] _____ to sell newspapers, and sometimes they simply [10] _____ lies to get people's attention. Take Jason Dole for example …

Grammar

1 ✱ **Infinitives of purpose**

James went into town on Saturday. Where did he go and why? Complete the sentences.

> look for some new trainers
> get some money ✓   have lunch
> choose some earrings for his girlfriend
> get changed   buy his mum a birthday card

1 He went to the ATM _to get some money_ .

2 He went to the shoe shop _____ .

3 He went to the jeweller's _____ .

4 He went to a burger place _____ .

5 He went to the card shop _____ .

6 Finally, he went home _____ .

2 ✱✱ **Gerunds and infinitives**

Complete the ads, using a gerund or infinitive.

Looking for love ...

Do you hate [1] _being_ (be) alone in the evening? And do you enjoy [2] _____ (watch) romantic movies on the sofa? Do you like [3] _____ (go) for long walks at sunset? If the answer is 'yes', I'd like [4] _____ (meet) you!

sparky brighton

I've finally decided [5] _____ (try) 'Looking for Love'. I don't expect [6] _____ (meet) the right person immediately but I hope [7] _____ (meet) some interesting people, and after that – who knows!

dawn101 leeds

Help! I love [8] _____ (eat) but I can't stand [9] _____ (cook) so if you want [10] _____ (try) some delicious food in expensive restaurants come dine with me!

hungry hippo

If you're looking for fun, I'm the one! Stop [11] _____ (think) about the perfect life, start [12] _____ (live) it! Have a date with me.

Millie.Manchester

I'm planning [13] _____ (travel) around the world next year so I need [14] _____ (practise) my English. Are there any nice English-speaking boys out there?

francesca.italy

3 ✱✱ **Gerunds and infinitives**

Complete the song titles with the correct form of the verb in brackets.

1	_Being_ (be) with you is all I want by CityGirls
2	It's easy _____ (fall) in love – and so hard _____ (forget) by ChattyCat
3	Angry about _____ (lose) you by Mike & The Mob
4	I'm so tired of _____ (wait) here by Tara B
5	I'm so sorry _____ (watch) you go by the Romaines
6	We'll never give up _____ (dance) by Legs Alive
7	It's good _____ (be) back home again by GO4U
8	It was really nice _____ (see) you – now please go away by Sulky Sam

4 ✱✱ Read *Grammar Plus*. Then complete the sentences with the phrases below.

Grammar + Plus

want, would like, expect + infinitive

Use *want/would like/expect* + infinitive to say what we want to do ourselves:

*I **would like to go** home because I **want to go** to bed.*
*I **expect to get** the top marks in class.*

Use *want/would like/expect* + pronoun + infinitive to say what we want other people to do:

*I **want you to do** your homework.*
*I'**d like her to come** home earlier.*
*I **expect her to say** sorry for breaking my phone.*

> to receive to have to study
> us to do ✓ you to do you to tidy up

1 Our teacher expects _us to do_ a lot of work before our exams.

2 My sister wants _____ law at university.

3 I would like _____ what I say, please.

4 Do you want _____ some more tea?

5 I'd like _____ your room before you go out.

6 We expect _____ our test results next week.

5 (✱✱✱) Modals of deduction

Rewrite the sentences replacing the phrase in bold with *must, might, may, could* or *can't*.

1 **It's possible that he's** Canadian because he speaks French and English.

He could be Canadian because he speaks French and English.

2 **I'm sure they're** at home because all the lights are on.

They _____

3 **I'm sure that isn't** Paula's handbag: she always has a red one.

That _____

4 **Perhaps** Ana **knows** the answer: why don't you ask her?

Ana _____

5 **I feel sure** Richard **is very rich**: he drives a very expensive car.

Richard _____

6 **I'm sure you aren't** serious: that's a ridiculous idea!

You _____

Vocabulary

Cultural events

6 (✱) Find words for these things in the grid. Look across and down.

1 two things you could see at an exhibition
paintings, sculpture

2 three things you can listen to

3 four things you see in a theatre

4 the 'feeling' at an event

5 opposite of 'boring'!

6 the person who leads a group of classical musicians

c	o	p	a	i	n	t	i	n	g	s
s	c	o	u	m	c	a	h	o	e	e
c	o	n	d	u	c	t	o	r	x	l
u	s	c	i	s	o	m	k	c	c	i
l	t	b	e	i	s	o	t	h	i	g
p	a	a	n	c	t	s	s	e	t	h
t	g	n	c	i	u	p	h	s	i	t
u	e	d	e	a	m	h	m	t	n	i
r	i	n	i	n	e	e	w	r	g	n
e	o	f	t	s	s	r	w	a	o	g
r	m	c	d	r	d	e	y	k	a	n

7 (✱✱) Street performers

Choose the correct answer.

1 My uncle paid for all our travel expenses – it was very _____ of him.

a expensive **b** generous ✓ **c** sympathetic

2 She's just trying to upset you by saying horrible things. Don't _____ any notice.

a make **b** pay **c** take

3 I can't stand Stacey Emmon's paintings! They look like absolute _____ to me.

a rubbish **b** litter **c** waste

4 It's nice to meet someone who really _____ good music.

a appreciates **b** knows **c** sees

5 Do you object _____ people asking for money in the street?

a against **b** at **c** to

6 People _____ very positively to Adrian's suggestion.

a behaved **b** reacted **c** replied

7 Personally, I found the film very _____ .

a entertained **b** entertaining **c** entertainment

8 The man was so angry he started shouting _____ the customs official.

a with **b** against **c** at

8 (✱✱) Art and money

Complete the sentences with the words below.

> abstract controversial art critic ✓ display
> genius portrait sale support

1 The *art critic* of the *Times* wrote a very good review of the Turner Exhibition at the National Gallery.

2 Zac Feldoni's new film *Z Men* is certainly _____ : some people love it, some hate it.

3 The shop windows in Bond Street _____ all the latest fashions.

4 Do you like pictures of real things and people, or do you prefer _____ art?

5 I bought something at a _____ of paintings by local artists last week.

6 Many people regard the painter Van Gogh as a _____ .

7 One of his most famous paintings is a _____ of his friend, Dr Gachet.

8 Liza's parents are happy to _____ her financially while she looks for a job.

12 mini workbook

✱	easy to do
✱✱	a bit harder
✱✱✱	extra challenge

Grammar

1 ✱ **The third conditional**

Match the sentence halves to make conditional sentences.

1 If I'd woken up on time, … ☐

2 Chelsea would have won the Cup … ☐

3 If we'd bought tickets in advance, … ☐

4 Our holiday would've been a lot better …☐

5 You wouldn't have got so wet … ☐

6 If you'd studied more, … ☐

a if it hadn't rained all time.

b if you'd remembered your umbrella.

c your exam results would have been better.

d I wouldn't have been late for school.

e if their captain hadn't got injured.

f we wouldn't have had to queue up.

2 ✱✱ **Read the story. Complete the sentences with the correct form of the verb in brackets.**

> After losing his job, and desperate for money, a Chicago man decided to rob a bank. Too nervous to speak, he wrote down his instructions on the back of an envelope he had in his pocket. He left the bank with £10,000. He was in a hurry, so he didn't notice he'd dropped the envelope as he left the bank.
>
> When the police arrived, they looked at the envelope. The robber's name and address was on the other side.
>
> The police arrested him soon after.

1 If the man _had kept_ (keep) his job, he _wouldn't have tried_ (not try) to rob the bank.

2 If he _____ (feel) so nervous, he _____ (not write) down his instructions.

3 If _____ (think) about it, he _____ (use) a different piece of paper.

4 If he _____ (not be) in a hurry, he _____ (not drop) the envelope.

5 If he _____ (not drop) the envelope, the police _____ (not know) his name and address.

6 If the police _____ (not know) his address, they _____ (find) him so quickly.

3 ✱✱ **Quantifiers: *both, either, all* or *none***

Read the information about *Girls-R-Us*. Complete the sentences with *both, neither, all,* or *none*.

	Nationality	Home city	Pets?	Smoke/ Drink?
Topaz	British	Brighton, UK	Yes – two cats	No
Kayla	British	London, UK	No	No
Nadia	British	London, UK	Yes – my cat, Mr. J	No
Suzi	American	London, UK	No	No

1 Topaz, Kayla and Nadia are __all__ British.

2 Kayla and Suzi _____ live in London but _____ of them has a pet.

3 _____ of the girls live in the USA.

4 _____ the girls live in England.

5 _____ of the girls smoke or drink.

4 ✱✱ **Quantifiers**

Complete the dialogues with the quantifiers.

[a little bit of ✓   a lot of   no   plenty]

A: How about ¹ _a little bit of_ food before we go? We've got ² _____ of time before the train leaves.

B: Hmm. There are ³ _____ people in the queue and there are ⁴ _____ free seats in the cafeteria. Let's eat on the train.

[a lot of   all   every   several   a few]

A: You've got ⁵ _____ tango CDs. Do you like Argentinian music?

B: Yes, but they're not mine, unfortunately. They ⁶ _____ belong to my brother. He's been to Argentina ⁷ _____ times and ⁸ _____ time he goes, he brings back ⁹ _____ more CDs!

5 (✱✱) Read *Grammar Plus*. Then rewrite the sentences with *might have* or *could have*.

Modal verbs in conditional sentences

In conditional sentences, we can use the modal verb *could* or *might* for possible consequences in the past:

*If he had worked harder, **he might have passed** the exam.* (= perhaps he would have passed, but he didn't)

*If our best player hadn't been injured, **we could've won the game**.* (= it would have been possible for us to win, but we didn't)

1 Perhaps I would have come to the game if you'd invited me. (might)

I might have come to the game if you'd invited me.

2 It would have been possible for the firemen to stop the fire if they'd arrived earlier. (could)

The firemen _____ .

3 If we'd left the house earlier, perhaps we would have caught the bus. (might)

If we'd left the house earlier _____

_____ .

4 If you'd told me, it would have been possible for me to help you. (could)

If you'd told me, I _____ .

5 Perhaps they would have died if the ambulance hadn't arrived. (might)

They _____ .

Vocabulary

6 (✱✱) Word families

Complete the sentences with the correct form of the word in bold.

1 Antibiotics are one of the most important _inventions_ in history. **invent**

2 If you see anything suspicious, you should _____ the police immediately. **information**

3 Archaeologists have made an important _____ near York. **discover**

4 Modern means of _____ help us stay in touch with friends all over the world. **communicate**

5 When I was a child, my parents encouraged me to watch _____ TV programmes. **education**

6 It was a very _____ film and the audience enjoyed it. **entertain**

7 The _____ of micro chips made it possible to produce smaller computers. **develop**

8 Five hundred years ago, our _____ of the universe was much more limited than today. **know**

9 The _____ of new jobs has been one of the government's main objectives. **create**

7 (✱✱✱) Describing objects

Read the clues and complete the crossword.

ACROSS

3 Furniture is usually made of this.
6 The shape of a tube.
7 They connect one electrical device to another.
8 Iron, gold and silver are all types of …
9 It's used for curtains, clothes, bags.
11 You can hear music through these.
13 The opposite of *fat*.
14 It's used to turn on an electrical device.

DOWN

1 You use this to hold things (e.g. suitcase, cup).
2 A ball is this.
4 The shape of a basketball court.
5 A man-made substance, used in many ways.
9 A table or a floor is usually this!
10 Animal skin used for shoes, bags.
12 You can keep money in these, or put your hands in them!

Quiz answers and activities

Unit 1, page 9, exercise 5

Quiz key

Questions 1, 4, 5, 8: T = 2; PT = 1; NT =0
Questions 2, 3, 6, 7: T = 0; PT= 1; NT = 2

14–16 points: Your concentration is very good – well done!

6–13 points: Your concentration isn't bad but read the tips on page 9 for ways of improving.

0–5 points: Oh dear! You really need to do something about your concentration. Read the tips on page 9 carefully and try one each week until your concentration span improves.

Unit 2, page 12, exercise 3

Quiz key

If most of your answers were a:
You are an ambitious sportsman/woman but are you a good team player?

If most of your answers were b:
You are average at sport but you are a good team player.

If most of your answers were c:
Oh dear … perhaps you're very musical?

Unit 2, page 17, exercise 10

Andy Murray: **Tennis player**

- Born 15 May 1987; from Dunblane, Scotland.
- He has won many tennis tournaments, and has reached number three in the world.
- He played in the final of the US Open in 2008 and the Australian Open in 2010, and has beaten the top players in the world a number of times.
- He first started playing tennis when he was two years old. His mother was a tennis player and his older brother is also a successful professional tennis player.
- When he was fifteen he moved to Barcelona in Spain to get better training. He says it was very difficult to live away from his family when he was so young.
- He has had several injuries, and has missed important competitions because of them.
- He hopes to win 'Grand Slam' tournaments, and become world number one.

Unit 4, page 33, exercise 7

Florence
- Very smart and polite but not very friendly. Seems reliable.
- Wants to work at least 20 hours a week because she needs the money.
- No experience of working in a shop or restaurant

Yara
- Smart, friendly, polite, seems reliable.
- No experience in a shop or restaurant but very interested in fashion.
- Studying hard so doesn't want to work too many hours.

Jack
- Polite and friendly but a bit shy. Seems reliable.
- A bit scruffy.
- A few weeks' experience of working in a sandwich bar.
- Happy to work evenings and weekends but doesn't want to work every Saturday night.

Real Time, Unit 5, page 42, exercise 4

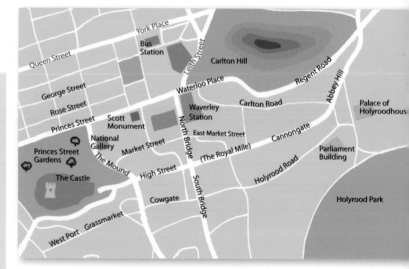

Unit 8, page 60, exercise 5 (student A)

House A

Word List

Unit 1
Pages 4–5

act (v)	/ækt/
compulsory (adj)	/kəmˈpʌlsəri/
dance (n)	/dɑːns/
democratic (adj)	/ˌdeməˈkrætɪk/
discipline (n)	/ˈdɪsəplɪn/
drama (n)	/ˈdrɑːmə/
head teacher (n)	/ˌhed ˈtiːtʃə/
mixed school (n)	/ˌmɪkst ˈskuːl/
optional (adj)	/ˈɒpʃənəl/
performing arts (n)	/pəˌfɔːmɪŋ ˈɑːts/
private school (n)	/ˈpraɪvət skuːl/
pupils (n)	/ˈpjuːpəlz/
responsibilities (n)	/rɪˌspɒnsəˈbɪlətiz/
rules (n)	/ruːlz/
secondary school (n)	/ˈsekəndəri ˌskuːl/
single-sex school (n)	/ˌsɪŋgəl seks ˈskuːl/
specialise (v)	/ˈspeʃəlaɪz/
staff (n)	/stɑːf/
state school (n)	/ˈsteɪt ˌskuːl/
subjects (n)	/ˈsʌbdʒɪkts/
sweep (v)	/swiːp/
vote (v)	/vəʊt/
wear a uniform (v)	/ˌweər ə ˈjuːnɪfɔːm/

Pages 6-7

apprenticeship (n)	/əˈprentɪsʃɪp/
career (n)	/kəˈrɪə/
competition (= rivalry) (n)	/ˌkɒmpəˈtɪʃən/
coursework (n)	/ˈkɔːswɜːk/
do well in something (v)	/ˌduː ˈwel ɪn ˌsʌmθɪŋ/
earn (v)	/ɜːn/
fail an exam (v)	/ˌfeɪl ən ɪgˈzæm/
get good marks (v)	/ˌget ˌgʊd ˈmɑːks/
get the sack (v)	/ˌget ðə ˈsæk/
job satisfaction (n)	/ˌdʒɒb sætɪsˈfækʃən/
mate (n)	/meɪt/
pass an exam (v)	/ˌpɑːs ən ɪgˈzæm/
pay rise (n)	/ˈpeɪ raɪz/
promotion (n)	/prəˈməʊʃən/
qualifications (n)	/ˌkwɒlɪfɪˈkeɪʃənz/
revise (v)	/rɪˈvaɪz/
salary (n)	/ˈsæləri/
start school (v)	/ˌstɑːt ˈskuːl/
successful (adj)	/səkˈsesfəl/
unemployed (adj)	/ˌʌnɪmˈplɔɪd/

Pages 8-9

amazing (adj)	/əˈmeɪzɪŋ/
ambition (n)	/æmˈbɪʃən/
attention span (n)	/əˈtenʃən ˌspæn/
concentrate (v)	/ˈkɒnsəntreɪt/
concentration (n)	/ˌkɒnsənˈtreɪʃən/
decision (n)	/dɪˈsɪʒən/
distraction (n)	/dɪˈstrækʃən/
goldfish (n)	/ˈgəʊldˌfɪʃ/
ignore (v)	/ɪgˈnɔː/
improve (v)	/ɪmˈpruːv/
improvement (n)	/ɪmˈpruːvmənt/
information (n)	/ˌɪnfəˈmeɪʃən/
learn (v)	/lɜːn/
make sense of (v)	/ˌmeɪk ˈsens əv/
problem (n)	/ˈprɒbləm/
set goals (v)	/ˌset ˈgəʊlz/
skills (n)	/skɪlz/
solution (n)	/səˈluːʃən/
solve (v)	/sɒlv/
useless (adj)	/ˈjuːsləs/
workspace (n)	/ˈwɜːkspeɪs/
worth reading (prep)	/ˌwɜːθ ˈriːdɪŋ/

Pages 10-11

accurately (adv)	/ˈækjʊrətli/
background (n)	/ˈbækgraʊnd/
bat (n)	/bæt/
clarification (n)	/ˌklærəfɪˈkeɪʃən/
concert (n)	/ˈkɒnsət/
conclusion (n)	/kənˈkluːʒən/
conversation (n)	/ˌkɒnvəˈseɪʃən/
cool (adj)	/kuːl/
dream (n)	/driːm/
impress (v)	/ɪmˈpres/
instrument (n)	/ˈɪnstrəmənt/
introduce yourself (v)	/ˌɪntrəˈdjuːs jəˌself/
meet (v)	/miːt/
musician (n)	/mjuːˈzɪʃən/
reputation (n)	/ˌrepjʊˈteɪʃən/
stranger (n)	/ˈstreɪndʒə/

Unit 2
Pages 12-13

be into something (v)	/bi ˈɪntə ˌsʌmθɪŋ/
beat (v)	/biːt/
black belt (n)	/ˈblæk belt/
blow (v)	/bləʊ/
clue (n)	/kluː/
coach (n)	/kəʊtʃ/
competition (=tournament) (n)	/ˌkɒmpəˈtɪʃən/
decide (v)	/dɪˈsaɪd/
defender (n)	/dɪˈfendə/
device (n)	/dɪˈvaɪs/
do your best (v)	/ˌduː jə ˈbest/
dressing room (n)	/ˈdresɪŋ ruːm/
electronic (adj)	/ˌelɪkˈtrɒnɪk/
enter (v)	/ˈentə/
get changed (v)	/ˌget ˈtʃeɪndʒd/
get fit (adj)	/ˌget ˈfɪt/
go running (v)	/ˌgəʊ ˈrʌnɪŋ/
goal (n)	/gəʊl/
goggles (n)	/ˈgɒgəlz/
gym (n)	/dʒɪm/
injured (adj)	/ˈɪndʒəd/
join (v)	/dʒɔɪn/
lose (v)	/luːz/
match (n)	/mætʃ/
nervous (adj)	/ˈnɜːvəs/
notice board (n)	/ˈnəʊtɪs bɔːd/
opponent (n)	/əˈpəʊnənt/
persuade (v)	/pəˈsweɪd/
race (v)	/reɪs/
racquet (n)	/ˈrækɪt/
referee (n)	/ˌrefəˈriː/
saddle (n)	/ˈsædl/
score (v)	/skɔː/
scoreboard (n)	/ˈskɔːbɔːd/
sick (adj)	/sɪk/
sign (n)	/saɪn/
sofa (n)	/ˈsəʊfə/
sporty (adj)	/ˈspɔːti/
stadium (n)	/ˈsteɪdiəm/
stopwatch (n)	/ˈstɒpwɒtʃ/
striker (n)	/ˈstraɪkə/
support (v)	/səˈpɔːt/
table tennis (n)	/ˈteɪbəl ˌtenɪs/
team (n)	/tiːm/
waiting room (n)	/ˈweɪtɪŋ ruːm/
whistle (n)	/ˈwɪsəl/
win a match (v)	/ˌwɪn ə ˈmætʃ/

Word List

Pages 14-15

achievement (n)	/əˈtʃiːvmənt/
break a record (v)	/ˌbreɪk ə ˈrekɔːd/
camping (v/n)	/ˈkæmpɪŋ/
can't stand (v)	/ˌkɑːnt ˈstænd/
club (n)	/klʌb/
coast (n)	/kəʊst/
don't mind (v)	/ˌdəʊnt ˈmaɪnd/
find boring (v)	/ˌfaɪnd ˈbɔːrɪŋ/
instructor (n)	/ɪnˈstrʌktə/
kick (n)	/kɪk/
local (adj)	/ˈləʊkəl/
love doing something (v)	/ˌlʌv ˈduːɪŋ ˌsʌmθɪŋ/
martial arts (n)	/ˌmɑːʃəl ˈɑːts/
movement (n)	/ˈmuːvmənt/
not bad for a (adj)	/ˌnɒt ˈbæd fər ə/
passionate (adj)	/ˈpæʃənət/
perfect (adj)	/ˈpɜːfekt/
proud (adj)	/praʊd/
quite enjoy (v)	/ˌkwaɪt ɪnˈdʒɔɪ/
respect (n)	/rɪˈspekt/
sailing (n)	/ˈseɪlɪŋ/
see the point of something (v)	/ˌsiː ðə ˈpɔɪnt əv ˌsʌmθɪŋ/
surf board (n)	/ˈsɜːf bɔːd/
Taekwondo (n)	/taɪˈkwɒndəʊ/
wave (n)	/weɪv/
world record (n)	/ˌwɜːld ˈrekɔːd/

Pages 16-17

champion (n)	/ˈtʃæmpiən/
develop (v)	/dɪˈveləp/
dive (v)	/daɪv/
exist (v)	/ɪgˈzɪst/
fans (n)	/fænz/
form (n)	/fɔːm/
found (v)	/faʊnd/
hold (= organise) (v)	/həʊld/
hopes (n)	/həʊps/
injuries (n)	/ˈɪndʒəriz/
invent (v)	/ɪnˈvent/
leather (n)	/ˈleðə/
legend (n)	/ˈledʒənd/
medal (n)	/ˈmedl/
origin (n)	/ˈɒrɪdʒɪn/
point out (v)	/ˌpɔɪnt ˈaʊt/
port (n)	/pɔːt/
record (n)	/ˈrekɔːd/
routine (n)	/ruːˈtiːn/
rubber (n)	/ˈrʌbə/
rules (n)	/ruːlz/
similar (adj)	/ˈsɪmələ, ˈsɪmɪlə/
spread (v)	/spred/
teenager (n)	/ˈtiːneɪdʒə/
title (n)	/ˈtaɪtl/
training (v/n)	/ˈtreɪnɪŋ/
trophy (n)	/ˈtrəʊfi/
variation (n)	/ˌveəriˈeɪʃən/

Unit 3
Pages 20-21

argumentative (adj)	/ˌɑːgjʊˈmentətɪv/
bald (adj)	/bɔːld/
basketball (n)	/ˈbɑːskɪtbɔːl/
bright blue (adj)	/ˌbraɪt ˈbluː/
celebrity (n)	/səˈlebrəti/
confident (adj)	/ˈkɒnfɪdənt/
dark (adj)	/dɑːk/
elegant (adj)	/ˈeləgənt/
fair (adj)	/feə/
famous (adj)	/ˈfeɪməs/

glamorous (adj)	/ˈglæmərəs/
in her teens (adj)	/ɪn ə ˈtiːnz/
in his twenties/thirties etc. (adj)	/ɪn ɪz ˈtwentiz, ˈθɜːtiz/
intelligent (adj)	/ɪnˈtelɪdʒənt/
medium-length (adj)	/ˌmiːdiəm ˈleŋθ/
middle-aged (adj)	/ˌmɪdl ˈeɪdʒd/
physically (adj)	/ˈfɪzɪkli/
plump (adj)	/plʌmp/
quiet (adj)	/ˈkwaɪət/
round (adj)	/raʊnd/
scruffy (adj)	/ˈskrʌfi/
shy (adj)	/ʃaɪ/
slim (adj)	/slɪm/
straight hair (adj)	/ˌstreɪt ˈheə/
talkative (adj)	/ˈtɔːkətɪv/
tidy (adj)	/ˈtaɪdi/
untidy (adj)	/ʌnˈtaɪdi/
wavy (adj)	/ˈweɪvi/

Pages 22-23

angry (adj)	/ˈæŋgri/
argumentative (adj)	/ˌɑːgjʊˈmentətɪv/
beautiful (adj)	/ˈbjuːtəfəl/
cope (v)	/kəʊp/
dominant (adj)	/ˈdɒmɪnənt/
earring (n)	/ˈɪərɪŋ/
freckles (n)	/ˈfrekəlz/
girly (adj)	/ˈgɜːli/
gymnastics (n)	/dʒɪmˈnæstɪks/
heavy metal (adj)	/ˌhevi ˈmetl/
horror (adj)	/ˈhɒrə/
identical (adj)	/aɪˈdentɪkəl/
kind (adj)	/kaɪnd/
leader (n)	/ˈliːdə/
light (brown) (adj)	/ˌlaɪt ˈbraʊn/
make-up (n)	/ˈmeɪk ʌp/
nice (adj)	/naɪs/
popular (adj)	/ˈpɒpjʊlə/
quadruplets (n)	/ˈkwɒdrʊpləts/
quads (n)	/kwɒdz/
rare (adj)	/reə/
sensitive (adj)	/ˈsensətɪv/
sets (n)	/sets/
sociable (adj)	/ˈsəʊʃəbəl/
strict (adj)	/strɪkt/
strong personality (n)	/ˌstrɒŋ ˌpɜːsəˈnæləti/
tall (adj)	/tɔːl/
tomboy (adj)	/ˈtɒmbɔɪ/

Pages 24-25

admire (v)	/ədˈmaɪə/
ambitious (adj)	/æmˈbɪʃəs/
arguments (n)	/ˈɑːgjʊmənts/
attitude (n)	/ˈætɪtjuːd/
bossy (adj)	/ˈbɒsi/
careful (adj)	/ˈkeəfəl/
complain (v)	/kəmˈpleɪn/
concentrating (v)	/ˈkɒnsəntreɪtɪŋ/
conscientious (adj)	/ˌkɒnʃiˈenʃəs/
criticism (n)	/ˈkrɪtɪsɪzəm/
decision (n)	/dɪˈsɪʒən/
dynamic (adj)	/daɪˈnæmɪk/
easy-going (adj)	/ˌiːzi ˈgəʊɪŋ/
effect (n)	/ɪˈfekt/
grow up (v)	/ˌgrəʊ ˈʌp/
hard-working (adj)	/ˌhɑːd ˈwɜːkɪŋ/
indecisive (adj)	/ˌɪndɪˈsaɪsɪv/
insensitive (adj)	/ɪnˈsensətɪv/
jealous (adj)	/ˈdʒeləs/
mature (v)	/məˈtʃʊə/

middle child (n)	/ˌmɪdl ˈtʃaɪld/
only child (n)	/ˌəʊnli ˈtʃaɪld/
organised (adj)	/ˈɔːgənaɪzd/
pro-active (adj)	/prəʊ ˈæktɪv/
psychologist (n)	/saɪˈkɒlədʒɪst/
punctual (adj)	/ˈpʌŋktʃuəl/
reflects (v)	/rɪˈflekts/
resentment (n)	/rɪˈzentmənt/
self-centred (adj)	/ˌself ˈsentəd/
sibling (n)	/ˈsɪblɪŋ/
take control (v)	/ˌteɪk kənˈtrəʊl/
treatment (n)	/ˈtriːtmənt/
typical (adj)	/ˈtɪpɪkəl/
upset (adj)	/ˌʌpˈset/

Pages 26-27
appear (v)	/əˈpɪə/
attract (attention) (v)	/əˌtrækt əˈtenʃən/
audience (n)	/ˈɔːdiəns/
bass guitarist (n)	/ˌbeɪs gɪˈtɑːrɪst/
beer (n)	/bɪə/
brave (adj)	/breɪv/
break (n)	/breɪk/
ceremony (n)	/ˈserəməni/
classmate (n)	/ˈklɑːsmeɪt/
determined (adj)	/dɪˈtɜːmɪnd/
drummer (n)	/ˈdrʌmə/
form (a band) (v)	/ˌfɔːm ə ˈbænd/
inspiration (n)	/ˌɪnspəˈreɪʃən/
original (adj)	/əˈrɪdʒənəl/
personality (n)	/ˌpɜːsəˈnæləti/
recording (n)	/rɪˈkɔːdɪŋ/
relative (n)	/ˈrelətɪv/
speak your mind (v)	/ˌspiːk jə ˈmaɪnd/
talent show (n)	/ˈtælənt ʃəʊ/
talented (adj)	/ˈtæləntɪd/
title (n)	/ˈtaɪtl/
vegetarianism (n)	/ˌvedʒəˈteəriənɪzəm/

Unit 4
Pages 28-29
career opportunities (n)	/kəˈrɪər ɒpəˌtjuːnətiz/
carry (v)	/ˈkæri/
child labour (n)	/ˌtʃaɪld ˈleɪbə/
climb (v)	/klaɪm/
coal mine (n)	/ˈkəʊl maɪn/
common (adj)	/ˈkɒmən/
developed country (n)	/dɪˌveləpt ˈkʌntri/
disgusting (adj)	/dɪsˈgʌstɪŋ/
earn one's living (v)	/ˌɜːn wʌnz ˈlɪvɪŋ/
educate (v)	/ˈedjʊkeɪt/
employer (n)	/ɪmˈplɔɪə/
factory (n)	/ˈfæktəri/
full-time (adj)	/ˌfʊl ˈtaɪm/
graduate (n)	/ˈgrædʒuət/
long hours (n)	/ˌlɒŋ ˈaʊəz/
minimum wage (n)	/ˌmɪnəməm ˈweɪdʒ/
navy (n)	/ˈneɪvi/
part-time (adj)	/ˌpɑːt ˈtaɪm/
rope (n)	/rəʊp/
rum (n)	/rʌm/
sailor (n)	/ˈseɪlə/
servant (n)	/ˈsɜːvənt/
shocked (adj)	/ʃɒkt/
smart (adj)	/smɑːt/
wages (n)	/ˈweɪdʒɪz/
wealthy (adj)	/ˈwelθi/
well-paid (adj)	/ˌwel ˈpeɪd/
well-treated (adj)	/ˌwel ˈtriːtɪd/
work permit (n)	/ˈwɜːk ˌpɜːmɪt/

working conditions (n)	/ˈwɜːkɪŋ kənˌdɪʃənz/

Pages 30-31
advertising executive (n)	/ˈædvətaɪzɪŋ ɪgˌzekjʊtɪv/
artistic (adj)	/ɑːˈtɪstɪk/
aspect (n)	/ˈæspekt/
badly paid (adj)	/ˌbædli ˈpeɪd/
call centre (n)	/ˈkɔːl ˌsentə/
challenging (adj)	/ˈtʃæləndʒɪŋ/
chat (v)	/tʃæt/
consultant (n)	/kənˈsʌltənt/
escape (v)	/ɪˈskeɪp/
farm labourer (n)	/ˌfɑːm ˈleɪbərə/
fisherman (n)	/ˈfɪʃəmən/
fun (adj)	/fʌn/
governess (n)	/ˈgʌvənəs/
heroine (n)	/ˈherəʊɪn/
loo (n)	/luː/
lucky (adj)	/ˈlʌki/
miner (n)	/ˈmaɪnə/
pocket money (n)	/ˈpɒkɪt ˌmʌni/
public relations (n)	/ˌpʌblɪk rɪˈleɪʃənz/
repetitive (adj)	/rɪˈpetətɪv/
respectable (adj)	/rɪˈspektəbəl/
rude (adj)	/ruːd/
servant (n)	/ˈsɜːvənt/
script (n)	/skrɪpt/
social worker (n)	/ˈsəʊʃəl ˌwɜːkə/
stressful (adj)	/ˈstresfəl/
supervisor (n)	/ˈsuːpəvaɪzə/
systems analyst (n)	/ˌsɪstəms ˈænəlɪst/

Pages 32-33
can (n)	/kæn/
candidate (n)	/ˈkændɪdət/
clothes catalogue (n)	/ˈkləʊðz ˌkætəlɒg/
design (v)	/dɪˈzaɪn/
essential (adj)	/ɪˈsenʃəl/
exotic (adj)	/ɪgˈzɒtɪk/
experience (n)	/ɪkˈspɪəriəns/
fortune (n)	/ˈfɔːtʃən/
game tester (n)	/ˈgeɪm ˌtestə/
graphics (n)	/ˈgræfɪks/
human statue (n)	/ˌhjuːmən ˈstætʃuː/
job agency (n)	/ˈdʒɒb ˌeɪdʒənsi/
key (to success) (n)	/ˌkiː tə səkˈses/
level (n)	/ˈlevəl/
make your fortune (v)	/ˌmeɪk jə ˈfɔːtʃən/
model (n)	/ˈmɒdl/
mosquito (n)	/məˈskiːtəʊ/
outdoor (adj)	/ˌaʊtˈdɔː/
pastime (n)	/ˈpɑːstaɪm/
patient (adj)	/ˈpeɪʃənt/
photo shoot (n)	/ˈfəʊtəʊ ˌʃuːt/
placard (n)	/ˈplækɑːd/
polite (adj)	/pəˈlaɪt/
publication (n)	/ˌpʌblɪˈkeɪʃən/
reaction (n)	/riˈækʃən/
reliable (adj)	/rɪˈlaɪəbəl/
rewarding (adj)	/rɪˈwɔːdɪŋ/
shiny (adj)	/ˈʃaɪni/
stand still (v)	/ˌstænd ˈstɪl/
suitable (adj)	/ˈsuːtəbəl/
tiring (adj)	/ˈtaɪərɪŋ/
useful (adj)	/ˈjuːsfəl/

Unit 5
Pages 36-37
alone (adj)	/əˈləʊn/
bus pass (n)	/ˈbʌs pɑːs/

Word List

carbon dioxide (n)	/ˌkɑːbən daɪˈɒksaɪd/
carbon footprint (n)	/ˌkɑːbən ˈfʊtˌprɪnt/
central heating (n)	/ˌsentrəl ˈhiːtɪŋ/
conference (n)	/ˈkɒnfərəns/
considerably (adv)	/kənˈsɪdərəbli/
create (v)	/kriˈeɪt/
cycling (v)	/ˈsaɪklɪŋ/
damage (v)	/ˈdæmɪdʒ/
destroy (v)	/dɪˈstrɔɪ/
energy-saving (adj)	/ˈenədʒi ˌseɪvɪŋ/
environment (n)	/ɪnˈvaɪrənmənt/
fuel (n)	/ˈfjuːəl/
get hurt (v)	/get ˈhɜːt/
global warming (n)	/ˌgləʊbəl ˈwɔːmɪŋ/
government (n)	/ˈgʌvəmənt/
healthier (adj)	/ˈhelθiə/
kilos (n)	/ˈkiːləʊz/
lifestyle (n)	/ˈlaɪfstaɪl/
light bulb (n)	/ˈlaɪt bʌlb/
mild (adj)	/maɪld/
motorway (n)	/ˈməʊtəweɪ/
noisy (adj)	/ˈnɔɪzi/
pollution (n)	/pəˈluːʃən/
produce (v)	/prəˈdjuːs/
protect (v)	/prəˈtekt/
protestor (n)	/prəˈtestə/
public transport (n)	/ˌpʌblɪk ˈtrænspɔːt/
recycle (v)	/ˌriːˈsaɪkəl/
reduce (v)	/rɪˈdjuːs/
remove (v)	/rɪˈmuːv/
reporter (n)	/rɪˈpɔːtə/
riot police (n)	/ˈraɪət pəˌliːs/
save (v)	/seɪv/
switch off/on (v)	/ˌswɪtʃ ˈɒf, ˈɒn/
tense (adj)	/tens/
throw away (v)	/ˌθrəʊ əˈweɪ/
traffic (n)	/ˈtræfɪk/
turn down/up (v)	/ˌtɜːn ˈdaʊn, ˈʌp/
vegan (n)	/ˈviːgən/
waste (v)	/weɪst/
wildlife (n)	/ˈwaɪldlaɪf/

Pages 38-39

affect (v)	/əˈfekt/
airship (n)	/ˈeəˌʃɪp/
Californian (adj)	/ˌkæləˈfɔːniən/
cancelled (adj)	/ˈkænsəld/
crowded (adj)	/ˈkraʊdɪd/
cycle (v)	/ˈsaɪkəl/
cycle lane (n)	/ˈsaɪkəl leɪn/
delayed (adj)	/dɪˈleɪd/
destination (n)	/ˌdestɪˈneɪʃən/
distance (n)	/ˈdɪstəns/
driver's licence (n)	/ˈdraɪvəz ˌlaɪsəns/
encourage (v)	/ɪnˈkʌrɪdʒ/
form (v)	/fɔːm/
get into trouble (v)	/ˌget ɪntə ˈtrʌbəl/
green (adj)	/griːn/
journey (n)	/ˈdʒɜːni/
passenger (n)	/ˈpæsəndʒə/
pick someone up (v)	/ˌpɪk sʌmwʌn ˈʌp/
relax (v)	/rɪˈlæks/
reliable (adj)	/rɪˈlaɪəbəl/
rollerblade (v)	/ˈrəʊləbleɪd/
skate (v)	/skeɪt/
sleep over (v)	/ˌsliːp ˈəʊvə/
strike (n)	/straɪk/
traffic jam (n)	/ˈtræfɪk dʒæm/
unreliable (adj)	/ˌʌnrɪˈlaɪəbəl/

Pages 40-41

advice (n)	/ədˈvaɪs/
alternative (n)	/ɔːlˈtɜːnətɪv/
altitude (n)	/ˈæltɪtjuːd/
appeal (v)	/əˈpiːl/
assemble (v)	/əˈsembəl/
awesome (adj)	/ˈɔːsəm/
bond (n)	/bɒnd/
coast (n)	/kəʊst/
collect (v)	/kəˈlekt/
combine (v)	/kəmˈbaɪn/
correspondent (n)	/ˌkɒrɪˈspɒndənt/
cruise ship (n)	/ˈkruːz ʃɪp/
disturb (v)	/dɪˈstɜːb/
eco-friendly (adj)	/ˌiːkəʊ ˈfrendli/
endangered (adj)	/ɪnˈdeɪndʒəd/
environmentally-friendly (adj)	/ɪnˌvaɪrənmentl-i ˈfrendli/
extinct (adj)	/ɪkˈstɪŋkt/
flatmates (n)	/ˈflætmeɪts/
green (adj)	/griːn/
howl (v)	/haʊl/
luxury (adj)	/ˈlʌkʃəri/
opportunity (n)	/ˌɒpəˈtjuːnəti/
pack up (v)	/ˌpæk ˈʌp/
permanently (adv)	/ˈpɜːmənəntli/
pod (n)	/pɒd/
remain (v)	/rɪˈmeɪn/
remote (adj)	/rɪˈməʊt/
replace (v)	/rɪˈpleɪs/
requires (v)	/rɪˈkwaɪəz/
revolutionary (adj)	/ˌrevəˈluːʃənəri/
runway (n)	/ˈrʌnweɪ/
sanctuary (n)	/ˈsæŋktʃəri/
scenery (n)	/ˈsiːnəri/
sightseeing (n)	/ˈsaɪtˌsiːɪŋ/
trend (n)	/trend/
tropical (adj)	/ˈtrɒpɪkəl/
voluntary work (n)	/ˈvɒləntəri wɜːk/
volunteer (n)	/ˌvɒlənˈtɪə/
waste (n)	/weɪst/
wild (adj)	/waɪld/
without (adv)	/wɪðˈaʊt/
wolf (n)	/wʊlf/

Pages 42-43

acquaintances (n)	/əˈkweɪntənsɪz/
adore (v)	/əˈdɔː/
crafts (n)	/krɑːfts/
culture (n)	/ˈkʌltʃə/
directions (n)	/dɪˈrekʃənz/
guided tour (n)	/ˌgaɪdɪd ˈtʊə/
gun (n)	/gʌn/
historic (adj)	/hɪˈstɒrɪk/
industrial (adj)	/ɪnˈdʌstriəl/
leads to (v)	/ˈliːdz tə/
location (n)	/ləʊˈkeɪʃən/
messenger (n)	/ˈmesəndʒə/
monument (n)	/ˈmɒnjʊmənt/
narrow (adj)	/ˈnærəʊ/
novel (n)	/ˈnɒvəl/
political (adj)	/pəˈlɪtɪkəl/
politician (n)	/ˌpɒləˈtɪʃən/
population (n)	/ˌpɒpjʊˈleɪʃən/
silly (adj)	/ˈsɪli/
steps (n)	/steps/

Unit 6
Pages 44-45
adore (v)	/əˈdɔː/
annoyed (adj)	/əˈnɔɪd/
area (n)	/ˈeəriə/
argument (n)	/ˈɑːgjʊmənt/
bored (adj)	/bɔːd/
can't stand (n)	/ˌkɑːnt ˈstænd/
close (friend) (adj)	/ˌkləʊs ˈfrend/
colleague (n)	/ˈkɒliːg/
cousin (n)	/ˈkʌzən/
distant (adj)	/ˈdɪstənt/
end a relationship (v)	/ˌend ə rɪˈleɪʃənʃɪp/
ex-boy/girlfriend (n)	/ˌeks ˈbɔɪfrend, -ˈgɜːlfrend/
fall out (v)	/ˌfɔːl ˈaʊt/
gardener (n)	/ˈgɑːdnə/
get on with (v)	/get ˈɒn wɪð/
get to know (v)	/get təˈnəʊ/
go out with (v)	/gəʊ ˈaʊt wɪð/
great aunt/uncle (n)	/ˌgreɪt ˈɑːnt, -ˈʌŋkəl/
hate (v)	/heɪt/
have a good relationship (v)	/hæv ə ˌgʊd rɪˈleɪʃənʃɪp/
have a laugh (v)	/hæv ə ˈlɑːf/
keep in touch (v)	/ˌkiːp ɪn ˈtʌtʃ/
look after (v)	/lʊk ˈɑːftə/
make fun of (v)	/meɪk ˈfʌn əv/
make jokes about (v)	/ˌmeɪk ˈdʒəʊks əˌbaʊt/
next-door neighbour (n)	/ˌnekst dɔː ˈneɪbə/
old school friend (n)	/ˌəʊld ˈskuːl frend/
pet (n)	/pet/
retired (adj)	/rɪˈtaɪəd/
school bag (n)	/ˈskuːl bæg/
split up (v)	/ˌsplɪt ˈʌp/
stay in contact (v)	/ˌsteɪ ɪn ˈkɒntækt/
step-brother/sister (n)	/ˈstep ˌbrʌðə, -ˌsɪstə/
take care of (v)	/teɪk ˈkeər əv/
team mate (n)	/ˈtiːm meɪt/
trip (n)	/trɪp/

Pages 46-47
annoyed (adj)	/əˈnɔɪd/
accidentally (adv)	/ˌæksɪˈdentl-i/
amusement park (n)	/əˈmjuːzmənt pɑːk/
bored (adj)	/bɔːd/
bully (n)	/ˈbʊli/
chat room (n)	/ˈtʃæt ruːm/
chatting (v)	/ˈtʃætɪŋ/
crazy (adj)	/ˈkreɪzi/
delete (v)	/dɪˈliːt/
depressed (adj)	/dɪˈprest/
disappointed (adj)	/ˌdɪsəˈpɔɪntɪd/
drive (v)	/draɪv/
embarrassed (adj)	/ɪmˈbærəst/
excited (adj)	/ɪkˈsaɪtɪd/
Facebook (n)	/ˈfeɪsbʊk/
fine (adj)	/faɪn/
frightened (adj)	/ˈfraɪtnd/
guilty (adj)	/ˈgɪlti/
interested (adj)	/ˈɪntrəstɪd/
jealous (adj)	/ˈdʒeləs/
melodramatic (adj)	/ˌmelədrəˈmætɪk/
nasty (adj)	/ˈnɑːsti/
nervous (adj)	/ˈnɜːvəs/
online (adj)	/ˈɒnlaɪn/
public (adj)	/ˈpʌblɪk/
realised (v)	/ˈrɪəlaɪzd/
social networking site (n)	/ˌsəʊʃəl ˈnetwɜːkɪŋ ˌsaɪt/
socialise (v)	/ˈsəʊʃəl-aɪz/
stuff (n)	/stʌf/
sympathetic (adj)	/ˌsɪmpəˈθetɪk/
text (sms) (n)	/tekst/

unfit (adj)	/ʌnˈfɪt/
upset (adj)	/ʌpˈset/
victim (n)	/ˈvɪktɪm/
worried (adj)	/ˈwʌrid/

Pages 48-49
add (v)	/æd/
architect (n)	/ˈɑːkɪtekt/
average (adj)	/ˈævərɪdʒ/
bother (v)	/ˈbɒðə/
briefly (adv)	/ˈbriːfli/
build (v)	/bɪld/
business (n)	/ˈbɪznəs/
catch (what you said) (v)	/ˌkætʃ wɒt jʊ ˈsed/
comfortable (adj)	/ˈkʌmfətəbəl/
compartment (n)	/kəmˈpɑːtmənt/
crime (n)	/kraɪm/
crime thriller (n)	/ˈkraɪm ˌθrɪlə/
deaf (adj)	/def/
director (n)	/dəˈrektə/
drunk (adj)	/drʌŋk/
entirely (adv)	/ɪnˈtaɪəli/
era (n)	/ˈɪərə/
extract (n)	/ˈekstrækt/
get involved (v)	/get ɪnˈvɒlvd/
impression (n)	/ɪmˈpreʃən/
island (n)	/ˈaɪlənd/
lake (n)	/leɪk/
lie (n)	/laɪ/
main character (n)	/ˌmeɪn ˈkærəktə/
marry (v)	/ˈmæri/
murder (v)	/ˈmɜːdə/
murmur (v)	/ˈmɜːmə/
nosy (adj)	/ˈnəʊzi/
novelist (n)	/ˈnɒvəlɪst/
part (n)	/pɑːt/
pocket (n)	/ˈpɒkɪt/
profession (n)	/prəˈfeʃən/
published (v)	/ˈpʌblɪʃt/
relationship (n)	/rɪˈleɪʃənʃɪp/
reluctantly (adv)	/rɪˈlʌktəntli/
ride (n)	/raɪd/
separated (adj)	/ˈsepəreɪtɪd/
set (v)	/set/
shake hands (v)	/ˌʃeɪk ˈhændz/
sit up (v)	/ˌsɪt ˈʌp/
smooth (adj)	/smuːð/
staying (in the USA) (v)	/ˈsteɪ-ɪŋ/
suggest (v)	/səˈdʒest/
throat (n)	/θrəʊt/
unusual (adj)	/ʌnˈjuːʒʊəl/
vacation (n)	/vəˈkeɪʃən/
wander (v)	/ˈwɒndə/

Unit 7
Pages 52-53
alcohol (n)	/ˈælkəhɒl/
baked (adj)	/beɪkt/
beans (n)	/biːnz/
billion (n)	/ˈbɪljən/
blend (v)	/blend/
bowl (n)	/bəʊl/
burger (n)	/ˈbɜːgə/
cacao farms (n)	/kəˈkaʊ fɑːmz/
campaigner (n)	/kæmˈpeɪnə/
chocolate (n)	/ˈtʃɒklət/
chop (v)	/tʃɒp/
cook (v)	/kʊk/
cookbook (n)	/ˈkʊkbʊk/
crisps (n)	/krɪsps/
customers (n)	/ˈkʌstəməz/

developing world (n) /dɪˌveləpɪŋ ˈwɜːld/
dish (n) /dɪʃ/
electric blender (n) /ɪˌlektrɪk ˈblendə/
fairtrade (adj) /ˈfeətreɪd/
fast food (n) /ˌfɑːst ˈfuːd/
fizzy drink (n) /ˌfɪzi ˈdrɪŋk/
gram (n) /græm/
grated (cheese) (adj) /ˌgreɪtɪd ˈtʃiːz/
grill (v) /grɪl/
hot dog (n) /ˈhɒt dɒg/
ingredient (n) /ɪnˈgriːdiənt/
instructions (n) /ɪnˈstrʌkʃənz/
juice (n) /dʒuːs/
kilo (n) /ˈkiːləʊ/
locally (adv) /ˈləʊkəli/
melt (v) /melt/
mix (v) /mɪks/
modern (adj) /ˈmɒdn/
originally (adv) /əˈrɪdʒnəli/
packaging (n) /ˈpækɪdʒɪŋ/
peel (v) /piːl/
pizza (n) /ˈpiːtsə/
plastic (n) /ˈplæstɪk/
pour (v) /pɔː/
prepare (v) /prɪˈpeə/
recipe (n) /ˈresəpi/
rubbish (n) /ˈrʌbɪʃ/
serve (v) /sɜːv/
slave (n) /sleɪv/
slice (v) /slaɪs/
smoothie (n) /ˈsmuːði/
snack (n) /snæk/
spread (= cover) (v) /spred/

Pages 54-55
abroad (n) /əˈbrɔːd/
balanced diet (n) /ˌbælənst ˈdaɪət/
beautician (n) /bjuːˈtɪʃən/
bench (n) /bentʃ/
blood pressure (n) /ˈblʌd ˌpreʃə/
caffeine (n) /ˈkæfiːn/
cobbler (n) /ˈkɒblə/
diet (n) /ˈdaɪət/
dry cleaner (n) /ˌdraɪ ˈkliːnə/
dye (v) /daɪ/
Elizabethan (adj) /ɪˌlɪzəˈbiːθən/
energy (n) /ˈenədʒi/
experience (v) /ɪkˈspɪəriəns/
expert (n) /ˈekspɜːt/
fat (n) /fæt/
feel sick (v) /ˌfiːl ˈsɪk/
fibre (n) /ˈfaɪbə/
fit (n) /fɪt/
frog (n) /frɒg/
headache (n) /ˈhedeɪk/
health (n) /helθ/
healthily (adv) /ˈhelθəli/
healthy (adj) /ˈhelθi/
heart (n) /hɑːt/
jeweller (n) /ˈdʒuːələ/
liver (n) /ˈlɪvə/
lose weight (v) /ˌluːz ˈweɪt/
mention (v) /ˈmenʃən/
nails (n) /neɪlz/
optician (n) /ɒpˈtɪʃən/
peacock (n) /ˈpiːkɒk/
period (n) /ˈpɪəriəd/
pierce (v) /pɪəs/
protein (n) /ˈprəʊtiːn/
put on weight (v) /ˌpʊt ɒn ˈweɪt/

repair (v) /rɪˈpeə/
roasted (adj) /ˈrəʊstɪd/
skin (n) /skɪn/
skin disease (n) /ˈskɪn dɪˌziːz/
style (v) /staɪl/
tattoo (n) /təˈtuː, tæˈtuː/
vitamins (n) /ˈvɪtəmɪnz/
wax (v) /wæks/
weighed (v) /weɪd/
whiten (v) /ˈwaɪtn/

Pages 56-57
advert(isement) (n) /ˈædvɜːt, ədˈvɜːtɪsmənt/
arrange (v) /əˈreɪndʒ/
boiled (adj) /bɔɪld/
chain (n) /tʃeɪn/
charcoal (n) /ˈtʃɑːkəʊl/
cone (n) /kəʊn/
covered (v) /ˈkʌvəd/
crispy (adj) /ˈkrɪspi/
delicious (adj) /dɪˈlɪʃəs/
export (v) /ɪkˈspɔːt/
extraordinary (adj) /ɪkˈstrɔːdənəri/
filling (n) /ˈfɪlɪŋ/
float (v) /fləʊt/
folded (adj) /ˈfəʊldɪd/
food stall (n) /ˈfuːd stɔːl/
french fries (n) /ˈfrentʃ fraɪz/
fried (adj) /fraɪd/
grilled (adj) /grɪld/
interesting (adj) /ˈɪntrəstɪŋ/
kiosk (n) /ˈkiːɒsk/
lettuce (n) /ˈletɪs/
mayonnaise (n) /ˌmeɪəˈneɪz/
noodle (n) /ˈnuːdl/
oil (n) /ɔɪl/
pancake (n) /ˈpænkeɪk/
passer-by (n) /ˌpɑːsə ˈbaɪ/
pie (n) /paɪ/
queue up (v) /ˌkjuː ˈʌp/
rich (adj) /rɪtʃ/
roadside (adj) /ˈrəʊdsaɪd/
salt (n) /sɔːlt/
savoury (adj) /ˈseɪvəri/
soup (n) /suːp/
sour (adj) /saʊə/
sour cream (n) /ˌsaʊə ˈkriːm/
speciality (n) /ˌspeʃiˈæləti/
spicy (adj) /ˈspaɪsi/
sweet (adj) /swiːt/
taste (n) /teɪst/
tasty (adj) /ˈteɪsti/
tender (adj) /ˈtendə/
toothpick (n) /ˈtuːθˌpɪk/
treat (n) /triːt/
tried (v) /traɪd/
visitor (n) /ˈvɪzətə/

Pages 58-59
arrive (v) /əˈraɪv/
enquire (v) /ɪnˈkwaɪə/
enthusiastic (adj) /ɪnˌθjuːziˈæstɪk/
equipment (n) /ɪˈkwɪpmənt/
guitarist (n) /gɪˈtɑːrɪst/
microphone (n) /ˈmaɪkrəfəʊn/
minimum (adj) /ˈmɪnəməm/
recording facilities (n) /rɪˈkɔːdɪŋ fəˌsɪlətiz/
refreshment area (n) /rɪˈfreʃmənt ˌeəriə/
rehearsal room (n) /rɪˈhɜːsəl ruːm/
space (n) /speɪs/

studio (n)	/ˈstjuːdiəʊ/
tidy up (v)	/ˌtaɪdi ˈʌp/
trouble (n)	/ˈtrʌbəl/

Unit 8
Pages 60-61

apartment block (n)	/əˈpɑːtmənt ˌblɒk/
attic (n)	/ˈætɪk/
balcony (n)	/ˈbælkəni/
basement (n)	/ˈbeɪsmənt/
bus fare (n)	/ˈbʌs feə/
cheap (adj)	/tʃiːp/
chimney (n)	/ˈtʃɪmni/
curve (n)	/kɜːv/
detached (adj)	/dɪˈtætʃt/
first floor (n)	/ˌfɜːst ˈflɔː/
ground floor (n)	/ˌɡraʊnd ˈflɔː/
incredibly (adv)	/ɪnˈkredəbli/
inherit (v)	/ɪnˈherɪt/
overlooks (v)	/ˌəʊvəˈlʊks/
roof (n)	/ruːf/
semi-detached (adj)	/ˌsemi dɪˈtætʃt/
storey (n)	/ˈstɔːri/
strange (adj)	/streɪndʒ/
style (n)	/staɪl/
terrace (n)	/ˈterəs/
traditional (adj)	/trəˈdɪʃənəl/
weird (adj)	/wɪəd/

Pages 62-63

annoying (adj)	/əˈnɔɪ-ɪŋ/
approve (v)	/əˈpruːv/
argue (v)	/ˈɑːɡjuː/
borrow (v)	/ˈbɒrəʊ/
cause (v)	/kɔːz/
chores (n)	/tʃɔːz/
complaint (n)	/kəmˈpleɪnt/
criticise (v)	/ˈkrɪtɪsaɪz/
drive someone mad (v)	/ˌdraɪv sʌmwʌn ˈmæd/
elder brother (n)	/ˌeldə ˈbrʌðə/
flatmate (n)	/ˈflætmeɪt/
fussy (adj)	/ˈfʌsi/
habit (n)	/ˈhæbɪt/
heartbroken (adj)	/ˈhɑːtˌbrəʊkən/
knock (v)	/nɒk/
leave (v)	/liːv/
let (v)	/let/
little (sister) (adj)	/ˌlɪtl ˈsɪstə/
lonely (adj)	/ˈləʊnli/
loud (adj)	/laʊd/
mess (n)	/mes/
miserable (adj)	/ˈmɪzərəbəl/
moan (v)	/məʊn/
nag (v)	/næɡ/
noise (n)	/nɔɪz/
share (v)	/ʃeə/
snore (v)	/snɔː/
spend (v)	/spend/
spoilt (adj)	/spɔɪlt/
sympathise (v)	/ˈsɪmpəθaɪz/
tidy (adj)	/ˈtaɪdi/
van (n)	/væn/

Pages 64-65

addictive (adj)	/əˈdɪktɪv/
attempt (n)	/əˈtempt/
compromise (v)	/ˈkɒmprəmaɪz/
conflict (n)	/ˈkɒnflɪkt/
contestants (n)	/kənˈtestənts/
controversial (adj)	/ˌkɒntrəˈvɜːʃəl/

convince (v)	/kənˈvɪns/
copied (v)	/ˈkɒpid/
desert island (n)	/ˌdezət ˈaɪlənd/
dictator (n)	/dɪkˈteɪtə/
educational (adj)	/ˌedjuˈkeɪʃənəl/
format (n)	/ˈfɔːmæt/
game show (n)	/ˈɡeɪm ʃəʊ/
harmful (adj)	/ˈhɑːmfəl/
inevitably (adv)	/ɪˈnevətəbli/
influence (n)	/ˈɪnfluəns/
jungle (n)	/ˈdʒʌŋɡəl/
loft (n)	/lɒft/
mindless (adj)	/ˈmaɪndləs/
outgoing (adj)	/ˌaʊtˈɡəʊɪŋ/
phenomenon (n)	/fɪˈnɒmənən/
pleasant (adj)	/ˈplezənt/
presentation (n)	/ˌprezənˈteɪʃən/
private lives (n)	/ˌpraɪvət ˈlaɪvz/
reality TV (n)	/riˈæləti tiː ˈviː/
reflect (v)	/rɪˈflekt/
relationships (n)	/rɪˈleɪʃənʃɪps/
relax (v)	/rɪˈlæks/
seek (v)	/siːk/
selfish (adj)	/ˈselfɪʃ/
soap opera (n)	/ˈsəʊp ˌɒpərə/
strangers (n)	/ˈstreɪndʒəz/
take part (v)	/teɪk ˈpɑːt/
task (n)	/tɑːsk/
variety (n)	/vəˈraɪəti/
viewer (n)	/ˈvjuːə/

Unit 9
Pages 68-69

accident (n)	/ˈæksɪdənt/
ankle (n)	/ˈæŋkəl/
bandage (n)	/ˈbændɪdʒ/
bleed (v)	/bliːd/
burn (v)	/bɜːn/
concussion (n)	/kənˈkʌʃən/
cream (n)	/kriːm/
cut (n)	/kʌt/
cut yourself (v)	/ˈkʌt jəˌself/
dizzy (adj)	/ˈdɪzi/
downstairs (n)	/ˌdaʊnˈsteəz/
exercise (n)	/ˈeksəsaɪz/
experiment (n)	/ɪkˈsperɪmənt/
first aid (n)	/ˌfɜːst ˈeɪd/
hit (v)	/hɪt/
hurt (v)	/hɜːt/
ice (n)	/aɪs/
knife (n)	/naɪf/
lecture (n)	/ˈlektʃə/
loose (adj)	/luːs/
painkillers (n)	/ˈpeɪnˌkɪləz/
pan (n)	/pæn/
patient (n)	/ˈpeɪʃənt/
plaster (n)	/ˈplɑːstə/
proud (adj)	/praʊd/
radiator (n)	/ˈreɪdieɪtə/
rest (v)	/rest/
shave (v)	/ʃeɪv/
sick (n)	/sɪk/
situation (n)	/ˌsɪtʃuˈeɪʃən/
skateboard (n)	/ˈskeɪtbɔːd/
sprain (v)	/spreɪn/
stitches (n)	/ˈstɪtʃɪz/
swell (v)	/swel/
symptom (n)	/ˈsɪmptəm/

Word List

Pages 78-79

adopt (v)	/əˈdɒpt/
arrest (v)	/əˈrest/
attention (n)	/əˈtenʃən/
ban (v)	/bæn/
behave badly (v)	/bɪˈheɪv ˈbædli/
billionaire (n)	/ˌbɪljəˈneə/
cell (n)	/sel/
charity work (n)	/ˈtʃærɪti wɜːk/
comment (n)	/ˈkɒment/
court (n)	/kɔːt/
deserve (v)	/dɪˈzɜːv/
desperate (adj)	/ˈdesprət/
freeway (n)	/ˈfriːweɪ/
glad (adj)	/glæd/
heiress (n)	/ˈeəres/
incident (n)	/ˈɪnsɪdənt/
influence (n)	/ˈɪnfluəns/
journalist (n)	/ˈdʒɜːnəl-ɪst/
kindness (n)	/ˈkaɪndnəs/
lies (n)	/laɪz/
limousine (n)	/ˌlɪməˈziːn/
media (n)	/ˈmiːdiə/
miracle (n)	/ˈmɪrəkəl/
move into (v)	/ˈmuːv ˌɪntə/
personal assistant (n)	/ˌpɜːsənəl əˈsɪstənt/
print (v)	/prɪnt/
prison (n)	/ˈprɪzən/
privacy (n)	/ˈprɪvəsi, ˈpraɪ-/
publicity (n)	/pʌˈblɪsəti/
regret (v)	/rɪˈgret/
release (v)	/rɪˈliːs/
self-centred (adj)	/ˈself-ˌsentəd/
sharply (adv)	/ˈʃɑːpli/
split up (v)	/ˈsplɪt ʌp/
statement (n)	/ˈsteɪtmənt/
under pressure (n)	/ˌʌndə ˈpreʃə/
witnesses (n)	/ˈwɪtnəsɪz/

Pages 80-81

allegedly (adv)	/əˈledʒɪdli/
appropriate (adj)	/əˈprəupri-ət/
bite (v)	/baɪt/
break in (v)	/ˌbreɪk ˈɪn/
defence lawyer (n)	/dɪˈfens ˌlɔːjə/
excitement (n)	/ɪkˈsaɪtmənt/
feel sorry (for) (v)	/ˌfiːl ˈsɒri fə/
fine (n)	/faɪn/
gap year (n)	/ˈgæp jɜː/
get out of control (v)	/get ˌaut əv kənˈtrəul/
get-together (n)	/ˈget təˌgeðə/
grades (n)	/greɪdz/
hack into (v)	/ˈhæk ˌɪntə/
headline (n)	/ˈhedlaɪn/
horrified (adj)	/ˈhɒrɪfaɪd/
law (n)	/lɔː/
massive (adj)	/ˈmæsɪv/
millionaire (n)	/ˌmɪljəˈneə/
network (n)	/ˈnetwɜːk/
prison sentence (n)	/ˈprɪzən ˌsentəns/
prize money (n)	/ˈpraɪz ˌmʌni/
prosecutor (n)	/ˈprɒsɪkjuːtə/
punishment (n)	/ˈpʌnɪʃmənt/
scream (v)	/skriːm/
serious (adj)	/ˈsɪəriəs/
several (adj)	/ˈsevərəl/
squad (n)	/skwɒd/
steal (v)	/stiːl/
sympathy (n)	/ˈsɪmpəθi/
threaten (v)	/ˈθretn/
trivial (adj)	/ˈtrɪviəl/

Unit 11
Pages 84-85

atmosphere (n)	/ˈætməsfɪə/
audience (n)	/ˈɔːdɪəns/
backing muscian (n)	/ˈbækɪŋ mjuːˌzɪʃən/
band (n)	/bænd/
classical (adj)	/ˈklæsɪkəl/
conductor (n)	/kənˈdʌktə/
costume (n)	/ˈkɒstjum/
council (n)	/ˈkaunsəl/
cultural event (n)	/ˌkʌltʃərəl ɪˈvent/
exciting (adj)	/ekˈsaɪtɪŋ/
exhibition (n)	/ˌeksəˈbɪʃən/
expensive (adj)	/ɪkˈspensɪv/
fashion show (n)	/ˈfæʃən ʃəu/
keen (adj)	/kiːn/
lighting (n)	/ˈlaɪtɪŋ/
litter (n)	/ˈlɪtə/
major (adj)	/ˈmeɪdʒə/
modern art (n)	/ˌmɒdn ˈɑːt/
musical (n)	/ˈmjuːzɪkəl/
opera (n)	/ˈɒpərə/
orchestra (n)	/ˈɔːkəstrə/
painting (n)	/ˈpeɪntɪŋ/
performance (n)	/pəˈfɔːməns/
performers (n)	/pəˈfɔːməz/
play (n)	/pleɪ/
queueing (v)	/ˈkjuːɪŋ/
residents (n)	/ˈrezɪdənts/
rock festival (n)	/ˈrɒk ˌfestɪvəl/
sculpture (n)	/ˈskʌlptʃə/
set (n)	/set/
stage (n)	/steɪdʒ/
ticket (n)	/ˈtɪkɪt/

Pages 86-87

appreciate (v)	/əˈpriːʃieɪt/
banana (n)	/bəˈnɑːnə/
busker (n)	/ˈbʌskə/
chalk (n)	/tʃɔːk/
comment (n)	/ˌdekəˈreɪʃənz/
decorations (n)	/ˈkɒment/
drawing (n)	/ˈdrɔːɪŋ/
entertaining (adj)	/ˌentəˈteɪnɪŋ/
flag (n)	/flæg/
generous (adj)	/ˈdʒenərəs/
lamb (n)	/læm/
make (money) (v)	/ˌmeɪk ˈmʌni/
motorbike (n)	/ˈməutəbaɪk/
object to (v)	/əbˈdʒekt tə/
often (adv)	/ˈɒfən/
optical illusion (n)	/ˌɒptɪkəl ɪˈluːʒən/
piece (n)	/piːs/
react (positively) (v)	/riˌækt ˈpɒzətɪvli/
react (negatively) (v)	/riˌækt ˈnegətɪvli/
rubbish (adj)	/ˈrʌbɪʃ/
rude (adj)	/ruːd/
rush hour (n)	/ˈrʌʃ auə/
shout (v)	/ʃaut/
street lamps (n)	/ˈstriːt læmps/
street performer (n)	/ˈstriːt pəˌfɔːmə/
take notice (v)	/teɪk ˈnəutɪs/
various (adj)	/ˈveəriəs/

Pages 88-89

abstract (adj)	/ˈæbstrækt/
auction (n)	/ˈɔːkʃən/
be worth (v)	/bi ˈwɜːθ/
canvas (n)	/ˈkænvəs/
compare (v)	/kəmˈpeə/
conceptual artist (n)	/kənˌseptʃuəl ˈɑːtɪst/

Word List

contemporary (adj)	/kənˈtempəri/
controversy (n)	/kənˈtrɒvəsi/
critic (n)	/ˈkrɪtɪk/
drip (v)	/drɪp/
genius (n)	/ˈdʒiːniəs/
graffiti (n)	/græˈfiːti/
have the last laugh (v)	/hæv ðə ˌlɑːst ˈlɑːf/
looter (n)	/ˈluːtə/
masterpiece (n)	/ˈmɑːstəpiːs/
portrait (n)	/ˈpɔːtrɪt/
poverty (n)	/ˈpɒvəti/
remind (me of) (v)	/rɪˈmaɪnd mi əv/
shark (n)	/ʃɑːk/
sheet (n)	/ʃiːt/
shopping trolley (n)	/ˈʃɒpɪŋ ˌtrɒli/
soldier (n)	/ˈsəʊldʒə/
swirl (n)	/swɜːl/
ugly (adj)	/ˈʌgli/
underwear (n)	/ˈʌndəweə/
valuable (adj)	/ˈvæluəbəl/
wallpaper (n)	/ˈwɔːlˌpeɪpə/
well-known (adj)	/ˌwel ˈnəʊn/

Pages 90-91

brilliant (adj)	/ˈbrɪljənt/
ceiling (n)	/ˈsiːlɪŋ/
duet (n)	/djuˈet/
great sound (n)	/ˌgreɪt ˈsaʊnd/
highlight (n)	/ˈhaɪlaɪt/
hit (n)	/hɪt/
imagine (v)	/ɪˈmædʒɪn/
keyboard player (n)	/ˈkiːbɔːd ˌpleɪə/
lyrics (n)	/ˈlɪrɪks/
manager (n)	/ˈmænɪdʒə/
opinion (n)	/əˈpɪnjən/
recommend (v)	/ˌrekəˈmend/
respond (v)	/rɪˈspɒnd/
soul (n)	/səʊl/
star (n)	/stɑː/
venue (n)	/ˈvenjuː/

Unit 12
Pages 92-93

antibiotics (n)	/ˌæntɪbaɪˈɒtɪks/
authorities (n)	/əˈθɒrətiz/
copper (n)	/ˈkɒpə/
creation (n)	/kriˈeɪʃən/
cure (v)	/kjʊə/
demonstrate (v)	/ˈdemənstreɪt/
develop (v)	/dɪˈveləp/
development (n)	/dɪˈveləpmənt/
discovery (n)	/dɪsˈkʌvəri/
diseases (n)	/dɪˈziːzɪz/
drug (n)	/drʌg/
empire (n)	/ˈempaɪə/
gunpowder (n)	/ˈgʌnˌpaʊdə/
information (n)	/ˌɪnfəˈmeɪʃən/
invention (n)	/ɪnˈvenʃən/
knowledge (n)	/ˈnɒlɪdʒ/
millions (n)	/ˈmɪljənz/
mobile phone (n)	/ˌməʊbaɪl ˈfəʊn/
painkiller (n)	/ˈpeɪnˌkɪlə/
penicillin (n)	/ˌpenəˈsɪlɪn/
political views (n)	/pəˌlɪtɪkəl ˈvjuːz/
poverty (n)	/ˈpɒvəti/
primitive (adj)	/ˈprɪmətɪv/
printing press (n)	/ˈprɪntɪŋ ˌpres/
rocket (n)	/ˈrɒkɪt/
telephone (n)	/ˈteləfəʊn/

time zone (n)	/ˈtaɪm zəʊn/
vaccine (n)	/ˈvæksiːn/
wheel (n)	/wiːl/
wire (n)	/waɪə/
world wide web (n)	/ˌwɜːld waɪd ˈweb/

Pages 94-95

catch on (v)	/ˌkætʃ ˈɒn/
cushion (n)	/ˈkʊʃən/
cutting (n)	/ˈkʌtɪŋ/
cylindrical (adj)	/sɪˈlɪndrɪkəl/
drawers (n)	/drɔːz/
fabric (n)	/ˈfæbrɪk/
features (n)	/ˈfiːtʃəz/
flat (adj)	/flæt/
handle (n)	/ˈhændl/
have a clear out (v)	/hæv ə ˈklɪər aʊt/
high (adj)	/haɪ/
holding (n)	/ˈhəʊldɪŋ/
leather (n)	/ˈleðə/
long (adj)	/lɒŋ/
measuring (v)	/ˈmeʒərɪŋ/
metal (n)	/ˈmetl/
purse (n)	/pɜːs/
rectangular (adj)	/rekˈtæŋgjʊlə/
round (adj)	/raʊnd/
scissors (n)	/ˈsɪzəz/
speaker (n)	/ˈspiːkə/
spreading (n)	/ˈspredɪŋ/
stairs (n)	/steəz/
storing (n)	/ˈstɔːrɪŋ/
switch (n)	/swɪtʃ/
thin (adj)	/θɪn/
wallet (n)	/ˈwɒlɪt/
weird (adj)	/wɪəd/
wood (n)	/wʊd/

Pages 96-97

car manufacturing (n)	/ˈkɑː mænjəˌfæktʃərɪŋ/
compassion (n)	/kəmˈpæʃən/
computer-generated (adj)	/kəmˌpjuːtə ˈdʒenəreɪtɪd/
dispose of (v)	/dɪˈspəʊz əv/
estimate (v)	/ˈestəmeɪt/
facial expression (n)	/ˈfeɪʃəl ɪkˌspreʃən/
fashionable (adj)	/ˈfæʃənəbəl/
fight (v)	/faɪt/
generation (n)	/ˌdʒenəˈreɪʃən/
greetings (n)	/ˈgriːtɪŋz/
indestructible (adj)	/ˌɪndɪˈstrʌktəbəl/
mankind (n)	/ˌmænˈkaɪnd/
medicine (n)	/ˈmedsən/
mention (v)	/ˈmenʃən/
pity (n)	/ˈpɪti/
real-life (adj)	/ˈrɪəl laɪf/
receptionist (n)	/rɪˈsepʃənɪst/
resemble (v)	/rɪˈzembəl/
serve (drinks) (v)	/ˌsɜːv ˈdrɪŋks/
show emotion (v)	/ˌʃəʊ ɪˈməʊʃən/
sit around (v)	/ˌsɪt əˈraʊnd/
take over (v)	/ˌteɪk ˈəʊvə/
concern (n)	/kənˈsɜːn/
deprive (v)	/dɪˈpraɪv/
design (v)	/dɪˈzaɪn/
frontline soldier (n)	/ˌfrʌntlaɪn ˈsəʊldʒə/
gossip (n)	/ˈgɒsɪp/
make up (v)	/ˌmeɪk ˈʌp/
mood (n)	/muːd/
obey (v)	/əˈbeɪ/
old people's home (n)	/ˌəʊld piːpəlz ˈhəʊm/
retail sales (n)	/ˌriːteɪl ˈseɪlz/

Quiz answers and activities

Unit 6, page 49, exercise 7

The real plot of STRANGERS ON A TRAIN

THE BOOK

Bruno told Guy that he would tell the police that Guy had paid him to murder Miriam, unless Guy murdered his father for him. Guy didn't know what to do and decided that he only had one choice – to murder Bruno's father so that Bruno would leave him alone. So he went to his apartment and shot him while he was asleep. A private detective eventually caught him.

THE FILM

Guy is horrified by what Bruno has done and refused to murder Bruno's father. Bruno then tried to make the police believe that Guy was Miriam's murderer. However, Guy managed to prove that he was innocent and had not made any agreement with Bruno.

Unit 8, page 60, exercise 5 (student B)

House B

Unit 11, page 86, exercise 6

Titles: Lambanana,
   The Little Brothers,
   untitled

Unit 11, page 87, exercise 9

- late at night   - in a big city
- contemporary   - husband and wife/friends
- all know each other - drunk

Real Time, Unit 11, page 91, exercise 8

Notes for concert review:
Dakota — new pop group from Brighton
— four members — Singer Tanya Bryant
and guitarist Richard Horton write
songs.
Hove Sports Hall February 19th —
audience of 250 people — first song 'Don't
Let It Rain On Me' — audience quiet at
the beginning but everyone singing at the
end — last song 'One More Time'.
Good gig — recommend anyone who
likes classic pop with intelligent lyrics.

Student B

Real Time, Unit 9, page 74, exercise 6

- Greet A and ask how (s)he is. You are busy. Ask if A is doing anything one day next week.
- Respond. Agree.
- Respond and end the conversation.

Real Time, Unit 11, page 91, exercise 5

- Ask if it's okay to ask your friend's opinion about something.
- Explain the problem.
- Agree with A. End the conversation.